The Imagination of Edward Thomas

For Angela and Natasha
and for John Brown

Contents

Preface

Edward Thomas (1878–1917) was a professional man of letters for over fifteen years, a poet for barely two; he was known in his lifetime as a literary reviewer, a critic, and a writer of 'nature books'. But as the prose went out of print and faded from most readers' memories, appreciation of his poetry grew; new editions and impressions of his *Collected Poems*, first published in 1920, appeared with increasing frequency. As a nature writer[1] Thomas at his best is unsurpassed, and, given time and a congenial subject, he was a perceptive and original critic; yet his posthumous reputation rests entirely on the poems he wrote at the end of his life. Between December 1914 and January 1917, astonishingly, he wrote 142 poems, a very large proportion of them good poems; a collection of such quality might plausibly represent the siftings of a much longer poetic career, and since dates of composition for almost all the poems are known (both Edna Longley's edition of *Poems and Last Poems*, 1973, and R. George Thomas's edition of *The Collected Poems*, 1978, present them in chronological order), a chronological study, as for a longer-lived poet, would be conceivable. Even in such a short span of time there are formal developments to be noted, and one could trace sequences of thought in certain groups of poems, but by and large these possibilities do not warrant a strictly historical approach. The course I have followed, on the whole ignoring chronology, is, I think, a more profitable one. The first seven chapters explore and chart the domain of Thomas's imagination, identifying characteristic ways of thinking and feeling, plotting the configuration of concerns, attitudes and values that constitutes his mental and moral outlook. The experience of the poems cannot, of course, be divorced from the rendering of that experience, and my discussion of poems in these chapters is guided by recognition of that fact, but a detailed examination of Thomas's poetic craft is reserved for the last three chapters.

This way of studying Thomas's work, this particular ordering of commentary, has one consequence that perhaps needs a word of explanation. Certain poems, inevitably, are called upon several times for illustration, to focus different facets of the same poem; sometimes, too, characteristics of a poem already discussed are re-examined and displayed in a different light, and of course stylistic qualities that perhaps received passing mention earlier in the book are given closer attention in the last two chapters. The recall of poems for further elucidation is not merely a convenience: it has the advantage of demonstrating, simply and directly, the manifold character of poems. A poem is the meeting-place of word and reader and contexts that change, and in different circumstances of consideration it has different significances. Charles Tomlinson, in a recent poem, finds an illuminating analogy in the ambiguities of sense experience. 'Nature Poem' is about nature and about poetry and about the 'nature' of a poem. It reflects, first, upon the power of nature to fuse and confuse – blending contraries, 'August heat' and 'momentary breeze' for instance, 'until you feel the two as one', persuading our senses that resemblances are identities, 'This sound/Of water that is sound of leaves'; it then likens these effects to the living inconclusion and inconclusiveness of a poem:

> So many shades,
> So many filled recesses, stones unseen
> And daylight darknesses beneath the trees,
> No single reading renders up complete
> Their shifting text – a poem, too, in this,
> They bring the mind half way to its defeat,
> Eluding and exceeding the place it guesses,
> Among these overlappings, half-lights, depths,
> The currents of this air, these hiddennesses.

A poem will not stay still: it cannot be pinned down to a single formulation of its significance and qualities, however finely adjusted to the particulars of the poetic experience. Criticism is persuasion: it tries so to set out quotation and exposition, so to organize total presentation, as to persuade a reader, or to invite him to consider the claim, that a writer is of such and such a kind and calibre. One aim of my own 'shifting text' is to be persuasive.

Readers of Edward Thomas have been fortunate in his recent editors. Rarely overlapping in the annotation they provide, *Poems and Last Poems* (1973), edited by Edna Longley, and *The Collected Poems of Edward Thomas* (1978), edited by R. George Thomas, complement each other. Not only are they scrupulous in matters of strictly editorial concern, they are also exceptionally sensitive to the poetry. Mrs Longley's commentary, which I have been consulting for over a decade, learning from it and testing my readings against hers, besides being informative, is a work of critical perspicacity. Inevitably, when I cite her remarks I do so to register some measure of disagreement. Mostly, however, both differences and coincidences of opinion have gone unrecorded and I would therefore recommend a comparison between what she and I have to say about any poem discussed in the following pages. Quotations, with a few indicated exceptions, adhere to the text of R. George Thomas's edition, based on a re-examination of the poet's manuscripts, typescripts and notebooks. I should add here that my remarks on biographies of Edward Thomas in Chapter 8 do not apply to R. George Thomas's *Edward Thomas: A Portrait* (1985), which was published after this book went to press. Drawing on material not investigated by, or not available to, previous biographers, Thomas's biography provides the psychologically perceptive, balanced, and credible portrait that has been notably lacking for so long.

I would like to record my gratitude to friends who have helped at different stages in the preparation and writing of this book. With some comments on an early essay Walter Stein opened my eyes to an aspect of Thomas's sensibility that I had scarcely noticed before; these few comments have had more influence on the direction of my thinking since than he or I could have anticipated. W. J. Keith has given support and encouragement and cast a shrewd eye over more than one version of the text. D. W. Harding has allowed me to take issue with remarks on Thomas that appeared in an early essay, 'A Note on Nostalgia' (*Scrutiny* I); they had some influence on later criticism, but express a view of Thomas that he no longer holds. All the more reason, therefore, to thank him for his generous comments on those parts of the book that he has seen. With their help I reached a conclusion and delivered the book into the hands of the publisher. At this stage no author looks forward to yet more revisions, but I must thank Michael Black for his detailed, unignorable criticism and his encouragement to rethink and recast some of the chapters. I am also grateful to Hilary Gaskin for an instructive dialogue about the text, and her many improvements to it. My thanks finally to Carol Robb and Doreen Morton who deciphered an atrocious script with relative ease and typed and retyped this book in the midst of many other pressing duties.

Acknowledgments are due to the editors of *Ariel, Four Decades* and *University of Toronto Quarterly* for kind permission to reprint material which first appeared in their pages. I am also indebted to the University of Toronto for the leisure to write this book provided by a sabbatical leave, and to the Canada Council (as it then was) for the award of a Leave Fellowship.

1 The imaginative prose

I

Although this is a book about the poet, the chronology of Thomas's career is in itself peculiar enough to invest his earlier, prose writings with a special interest for the student of his poetry. Individual and perceptive though some of his criticism is, it does not merit separate consideration in a study of the poems. But there are good reasons for looking more closely at the imaginative prose; for his work in this field constituted his literary apprenticeship and had a deeper and more direct influence on his poetry than the work of any other poet. It is no longer necessary to substantiate the textual relationship. Some of the close parallels between particular passages and the poems have been examined by William Cooke,[1] and many more have been pointed out by Edna Longley in the annotations to her edition of *Poems and Last Poems*. H. Coombes[2] and W. J. Keith[3] have, besides, each given a chapter to the nature writing, providing balanced estimates of Thomas's achievement in that genre; Edna Longley in her Introduction to *A Language Not to be Betrayed*, a selection of Thomas's critical and imaginative prose, though concentrating on the former, writes briefly but judiciously about the latter. In a book principally concerned with Thomas's poetic achievement, the interest of the prose is that in its best parts it expresses the same structure of consciousness, the same 'inscape', to use Hopkins's term, as is revealed more finely in the poetry. It would be tedious to demonstrate the similarities in outlook between them by methodical comparison – the connections will, I trust, emerge of themselves during the later chapters – but the aim of this chapter in charting the central themes, attitudes and emphases of the imaginative prose is, none the less, to present them as a prototype of the imaginative world embodied in the poetry.

The nature books would not repay this attention if they had no interest other than as preparations for the poetry. The best of them are indeed distinctly individual contributions to the genre and rank Thomas with its ablest practitioners – Richard Jefferies, W. H. Hudson, Henry Williamson, and on occasions H. J. Massingham. Yet Thomas's descriptive and reflective writings about the natural world in general and the English countryside in particular were long out of print, and not until the widening of interest in his work that accompanied the centenary of his birth in 1978 were any of them reissued. The obvious explanation for their neglect is that their reputation was overshadowed by the acknowledged excellence of the poetry. It is also true that none of the nature books can be unreservedly recommended. The very early essays and sketches are marred by sentimentality and a Paterian self-consciousness of style; very little written by him in this mode before about 1906 is worth considering. In that year, starting with *The Heart of England*, he set about pruning his style. We come upon passages in that book, and long stretches of writing in the later books, that impress us as sensitive and thoughtful renderings of original experience; we begin, too, to catch glimpses in the writer's voice and habits of expression, in images and attitudes, of the future poet. But we find still that he is most successful when he works on a small scale; some of his best pieces are very late, of the same date and inspiration as the poetry, and are mostly contained in the posthumous gathering, *The Last Sheaf*. None of the more ambitious volumes, not even *The South Country* and *In Pursuit of Spring*, the most impressive of them, makes a satisfactory whole. Knowing the superior achievement of the poetry suggests a possible, if perhaps no more than partial, explanation for the discomfort or embarrassment we sometimes feel when reading even his finest prose: that the material of thought and feeling does not go easily into the box provided for it.

Yet some of it does have a lasting interest. The effect of the more remarkable short pieces and of the books mentioned is cumulatively impressive, and this is because a pattern of concerns, not sharply visible in the individual piece or volume, begins to emerge when we look at them together; then it is possible to see that at least the best parts of his imaginative prose belong to one sustained endeavour. Rather than try to define what this is, let me start with a suggestive quotation from a little book called *The Country*: '*There is nothing left for us to rest upon, great, venerable, or mysterious, which can take us out of ourselves, and give us that more than human tranquillity now to be seen in a few old faces of a disappearing generation*' (p. 6).

This is spoken not by the author but by an unnamed character. Since he appears also, as Mr. Torrance, in the semi-autobiographical *The Happy-Go-Lucky Morgans*, it is clear that he speaks for at least an aspect of Thomas; though the fact that he is first introduced as a man of a certain temperament and history allows us to discount an element of excess and flamboyant gesture in the utterance. The theme of the book, as the quoted sentence indicates – and it is the underlying preoccupation in most of the other nature books – is not so much the country-lover's nature as something the soul needs to complete itself. The ultimate source for such sentiments is, of course, in Wordsworth.[4] But something in the mood of the sentence reminds us more directly of Matthew Arnold, inheritor and transmitter of Wordsworthian attitudes to nature; the phrase 'nothing left for us to rest upon' may indeed echo a statement in 'The Study of Poetry'. Having identified as 'high seriousness' the quality that distinguishes the loftiest poetry, the 'criticism of life' offered, for example, by Homer, Dante and Shakespeare, Arnold proposes that (in an age which transfers to poetry some of the authority of religion) it is this which 'gives to our spirits what they can rest upon'.[5] The difference is that what Arnold claims for the great classics Thomas looks for in nature.

Thomas's prose contains a bewildering variety of responses to experience, affirming in one paragraph what is denied in the next, spanning in the same essay or book the gulf between Romantic affirmation and a peculiarly modern scepticism, centred on a self-distrust that has more in common with Conrad's nihilism than Hardy's 'pessimism'.[6] The nearest he comes to unqualified Romanticism is when in *The Country* he speaks of 'the destiny which binds us to infinity and eternity' (p. 12). Thomas's sensibility was composed of scepticism, agnosticism, and aspirations to a certainty beyond both, in about the same proportions as was E. M. Forster's. He never claimed, as both Yeats and Lawrence did, that he was a religious man; nor was he one to the degree that they were. Yet all three were inheritors of Romantic traditions, and one way of seeing that whole movement is as an attempt to accommodate displaced religious impulses (an interpretation assumed by T. E. Hulme, for example, when he sourly dismissed Romanticism as 'spilt religion'). Religion binds man to a life that transcends self and time. The problem for the religious man deprived of a deity is to find the infinite in the finite and the eternal in the temporal. It is not surprising therefore that in *Howards End* and *The Rainbow* conceptions of infinity and eternity should play an important part.

Thomas found his absolutes, on those occasions when he could convince himself of their existence, where Wordsworth found his, in nature; certainly, as far as he was concerned, there was nowhere else to look. In *The Happy-Go-Lucky Morgans* he quotes (or rather, misquotes) from *The Prelude* the statement that earth is 'where we have our happiness or not at all' (p. 221).[7] He was hostile to Christianity and all forms of supernaturalist belief. Earth is the most permanent thing we know: of this he was always certain. On Salisbury Plain he enjoyed feeling that it had existed long 'before man or God had been invented',[8] and on another occasion he notes with approval of W. H. Hudson that the earth 'he reverences and loves . . . is, humanly speaking, everlasting'.[9] In the life of a landscape, moulding and moulded by man, we feel 'our oneness with the past and the future':[10] it is our only image of the unchangeably human. It is also the prime thing which is not man and not made by him. Nature is not only human nature; we derive from it, too, 'a sense of oneness with all forms of life'.[11] Although Thomas received his degree in history, as a writer he showed little interest in the short perspectives of the historian; for him the essential history of mankind belongs with natural history, meaning both the history of other 'forms of life' and, in an extension of the ordinary sense, the history of nature. The perspectives he favoured were those of the archaeologist, the geologist and the geographer. This is not to say that his writing reveals any detailed intellectual or practical knowledge of these subjects; rather, that one could imagine him, thirty years later, responding with intimate recognition to Jacquetta Hawkes's imaginative use of her archaeological and geological knowledge in *A Land*. He once expressed the wish that historians were habitually as much geographers as Belloc was.[12] Two searches, then, are in question: the search for a timeless reality, or as near to it as one can get, and the search for a life embracing more than human life. Both pursuits – their quarry forms of the eternal and the infinite – are manifestations of the same urge, to be at home in the universe. Man wants a life that does not end, and, if his philosophical assumptions are, roughly speaking, naturalistic, that is a life co-eval with the life of the universe. He wants, too, to belong to a reality co-extensive with the universe, which for Thomas means a community with all its creatures. In his most sanguine moments he was of Meredith's opinion that Earth, conceived not merely as a source of sensuous pleasure nor as the 'inhuman enchantress' who seduces man from his humanity, provides 'sanity and true perspective'.[13]

'The literary and philosophical movement imperfectly described as the romantic revival and return to Nature,' he writes in *The South Country*, 'shows man in something like his true position in an infinite universe' (pp. 141–2). Though here he associates himself with the Romantic viewpoint, he was not usually so sanguine, and even in his essay on Meredith in *The Literary Pilgrim in England*, sympathetic though it is, there are signs that Thomas could not wholly subscribe to the naturalist faith. Only that power called Earth, which is more than what most people mean by God, he writes, 'could fulfil the desire of a man to make himself, not a transitory member of a parochial species, but a citizen of the Earth' (p. 54). The careful phrasing betrays Thomas's ultimate reservations. 'Citizen of the Earth' is a grand concept, and the reference to the human animal as 'a parochial species' declares his discontent with any reality that falls short of such an ideal; but man's life *is* 'transitory', and only the 'desire' exists to make it otherwise. The God-like power called Earth '*could* fulfil' his desire if it existed, but no guarantee is given that it does. The sentence testifies more to a felt discrepancy between aspiration and actuality than to any positive belief.

Convinced that eternity and infinity are only to be found in nature, Thomas seeks in human settlements, and is most moved by, signs of a 'harmony of man and his work with nature'.[14] He is unimpressed by a monumental magnificence, which implies defiance of the environment; for him the grandest achievements are the least ostentatious, the subtly unobtrusive, for they express a desire to be *at home* in the universe. His highest praise for Jefferies is that, as the countryside of Wiltshire and Gloucestershire and its people was the subject of half his work, so he 'was the genius, the human expression of this country, emerging from it, not to be detached from it any more than the curves of some statues from their *maternal* stone'.[15] The most enviable condition is to feel that you both possess and are possessed by the land you live in. Houses in Thomas's work are frequently images of such a home. In *The South Country* he describes one in a wood, whose thatch was 'impregnated with free air and light' and was companioned by trees that 'communed with the heavens' (p. 200). As a symbol of home its attractiveness is even 'enhanced by a touch of primaeval gloom', because it suggests connections with a pre-human age. So pictured, it seems to promise what man wants most of all; if it does not defeat, it fends off, night, proclaiming life to be stronger than death.

This house, it will be noticed, strikes a balance between separation from and identity with the universe, between the human and the natural. It would not deserve the charge that Raymond Williams, with some justification, levels against Thomas's frequently fanciful and idealized portraits of countrymen, that they are reduced to nature.[16] The same impulse, however, lies behind these character studies as informs the descriptions of houses in harmonious relation with earth and sky: they are images of man at home in nature, and are all variations of one type. Always man's main life is out of doors,[17] often he is primitive or wild – an Indian,[18] say, or an early man for whom trees were a religion,[19] a tramp or a gipsy; he may be represented, like Lob (in the poem named after him), as the archetypal Englishman.[20] If the creature to whom we are introduced in *The South Country*, seemingly almost an outgrowth of earth itself, is compared with the old countryman Bettesworth, whose conversation is recorded so faithfully for us by George Sturt, an author whom Thomas admired, it becomes plain that he is more fabulous invention than ordinary human being. Yet there is at least some realism in the portrait of him. 'It is barely credible,' Thomas writes, 'that he grew out of a child, the son of a woman, and not out of earth itself. . . . Doubtless he did, but like many a ruined castle, like his own house, he has been worn to part of earth itself' (p. 202): reduced to nature, indeed, but it was partly due to the wearing action of time.

Nor does Williams take into account in his criticism the fact that Thomas clearly knew what he was doing when he transferred the half-human characters of folklore to the pages of his travel books. 'If I may say so,' he writes elsewhere in *The South Country*, with a touch of amusement at his own fancifulness, the gamekeeper, whom he likens to 'the stump of a tree', is 'the fit emanation of the brown woodland man' (p. 179). He is not trying to picture the real countryman but to imagine the sort of man whose powers would give him 'equality with the conditions of life' as Thomas conceives them. These are roughly as Hardy conceived them: conscious man is a misfit in, because he has outgrown, unconscious nature; therefore men such as these, being only half-human, 'jarred least on the music of the spheres' (p. 171). They are pre-civilized, like Norgett in *In Pursuit of Spring*, who 'hardly talked at all . . . Speech was an interruption of his thoughts, and never sprang from them'; walking with him was 'to sleep as we walked'. Thomas, the real Thomas, always stresses his separation from these characters. Norgett's positive, active silence did him good, he says, but he had to *learn* to share it; 'it was unpleasant to wake up' from the sleep of walking with him, but he always did, feeling compelled to leave 'that cold, calm presence'. We note too that, not belonging fully to the (however imperfect) world of men, Norgett's presence was felt to be repellently cold as well as seductively calm.[21] Thomas consistently honoured his friend W. H. Hudson as one of the very 'few who could speak of "earth which is our home" without rhodomontade',[22] whose kinship was with the life that existed before towns came into being, who felt a stranger amongst 'pale civilized faces'.[23] But one of those pale civilized faces undoubtedly was Thomas's, and it is as though Hudson's apparent immunity from the sort of unease in nature that he himself frequently felt struck him as very nearly superhuman. Hudson's one prayer and aim in life, he says, is 'to be still, somewhere in the sun or under trees where birds are':[24] He was a settler not a traveller; and for Thomas (who went 'in pursuit of Spring', traced the Icknield Way and wrote of the charms and seductions of never-ending roads), however much he yearned for stillness, travelling, in restless quest for something, is the human condition.

Auden, in deliberate repudiation of Romantic attitudes, was in the habit of contrasting life in nature with life in historical time. For him, as a Christian, history – time and change – holding out the hope of improvement, was the realm in which man's spirit dwelt, in which the soul discovered and proved itself; and in saying so he was returning to the main line of Western thought from which Romanticism was a deviation. Thomas was not, in the end, a Romantic, but that movement was more responsible for the direction in which his mind naturally travelled than any other single source of influence. He had his doubts about the sanctity of nature, but, not hoping for a personal immortality, he had no belief at all in man's spiritual development through time and beyond time. In history, man's fear of death, his 'batlike fear about immortality',[25] drives him to assert himself against what he conceives as the enmity of nature, to build, when he builds 'for eternity', as in his churches, monuments to himself and his restless desires. Animals, he points out, are free of such restlessness.[26] Man's grandest edifices are 'too permanent an expression of the passing things'.[27] In the perspective of nature, history can be seen as an attempt to endow what is transitory and insignificant with permanence. We may contrast the 'majestic quiet' of nature, as he describes it in *The Country* (pp. 11–12), with the 'somewhat foreign tranquillity' he senses in the cathedral close at Wells, where the 'discreet, decent, quiet houses' raise the spectre of a noise and disorder diplomatically excluded: a man-made quiet out of tune with nature, interrupted as it is by 'the typical cathedral music, that of the mowing-machine, destroying grass and daises innumerable'.[28] At the centre of this religious silence is the undisclosed turbulence of man's self-concern, and so Thomas prefers the anonymous buildings and the trees to the sight of a cathedral thrusting itself into history.[29] This central disquiet even has its social analogues: there is a hinted discord in the juxtaposition of the 'many rich tombs' in the choir chapels and 'the rich towered west front' of Wells cathedral on one side of the square with the 'homely houses' on the other three sides. Thomas considers religious architecture a 'majestic but dead language', and he means not merely that Christianity is no longer a living faith but that it always was at variance with nature, and, rather than growing into acceptance, was imposed like church Latin by one class upon another. He insists that it 'never was a popular language',[30] and an order that excluded the many is evidently a smaller affair than one that includes everyone and everything. Thomas is expressing a democratic sentiment – not a narrowly political but a naturalistic faith – when he speaks of a 'commonwealth' of creatures.[31] Hence the interest, to which Hudson drew attention in his foreword to *Cloud Castle and Other Papers*, and which is evinced in many prose passages and book reviews, in the 'natural mystics' like Traherne and Blake, who, as he says in *The South Country*, 'see the patterns which all living things are weaving', and are 'concerned in all the world' (p. 133). Nature alone 'takes us out of ourselves' by giving us a 'more than human tranquillity'.[32] It makes possible the only kind of self-transcendence open to us.

As for Jefferies and Wordsworth before him, nature was for Thomas a source, perhaps the only source, of 'joy', a restorative for the mind as for the body. He concludes his excellent study of Jefferies on this distinctly Wordsworthian note: 'for he allied himself to Nature, and still plays his part in her office of granting health, and hearty pleasure, and consolation, and the delights of the senses and of the spirit, to men' (p. 337). Nature invigorates, and develops in men a buoyancy and a resilience against hardship. In some fine pages that describe George Sturt's Bettesworth, Thomas gives us a man whose virtues and strengths were engendered from intimate life-long connection with the country and its tasks. Everything he does and says shows 'his physical strength, his robust and gross enjoyment, his isolation, his breeding and independence, his tenderness without pity, his courage, his determination to endure'.[33] Thomas admires, even envies, the man who, in the middle of 'laying turf under continuous rain and in an uncomfortable attitude', could make 'the unexpected comment: "Pleasant work this. I could very well spend my time at it, with good turfs."'[34] But 'unexpected' tells us how far from Bettesworth's condition Thomas knows himself to be; this is a joy he has not experienced. Nor does he idealize the life of this 'unlettered peasant'.[35] 'Pain and sorrow are not absent, and afar off we see a gray glimpse of the workhouse; but the whole is joyful. Even when Bettesworth "felt a bit Christmassy" there is no melancholy; his head seems "all mops and brooms."'[36] 'Melancholy', too, reminds the reader what, by contrast, the proportion of dejection to happiness was in Thomas's own experience of nature. His evidence for a pervasive joyousness in Bettesworth's life is the buoyancy of his 'peasant' speech; it lacks, for example, the self-engrossment that the word 'melancholy' implies, an implication that Thomas was certainly conscious of when he made it the title of one of his poems.

As with so many late Victorian and Edwardian writers, with Thomas a personally felt sense of loss attached itself to a larger conviction that the rapid and drastic changes witnessed towards the end of the nineteenth century represented a process not of natural transition but of the present's total if perhaps unwitting and involuntary abandonment of the past. Writers have varied in their interpretation and dating of the crisis, and Thomas himself held no consistent point of view; but most writers, and Thomas usually, connected it with industrialism and the growth of urbanism, and saw the gulf between old and modern England as beginning to widen alarmingly in the late eighteenth century. Thus, for Thomas, Gilbert White, who was 'so happy and remote from our time that he thought the dying fall of the true willow-wren "a joyous easy laughing note" ',[37] belongs securely in the old world, though, historically, on the brink of the new. This will seem sentimental only to someone who misses the wry humour in this observation and the delicacy of perception that finds a psychological significance in the totally changed appearance that the same world wears for different generations. On other occasions he moves the dividing line further back in time – for instance, to the transitional period between the Middle Ages and the Renaissance, when, he says, 'Villon . . . inaugurated modern literature with the cry – "Mais où sont les neiges d'antan?" ' (*The South Country*, p. 109) – but the method of differentiation is the same. Chaucer wrote before Villon, out of a way of feeling and viewing his experience that we cannot share though we can yearn to possess it; for Chaucer, as not for us,

> there is something hearty in his tears that hints of laughter before and after . . . Sorrow never changes him more than shadow changes a merry brook . . . he seems to speak of a day when men had not only not so far outstripped the lark and nightingale as we have done, but had moments when their joy was equal to the lark's above the grey dew of May dawns. (p. 110)

This is hardly our image of Chaucer; moreover the writing is impressionistic and fanciful in ways that Eliot has persuaded us to distrust, but no more so than Eliot's own useful phrase 'dissociation of sensibility', the fancifulness of which is, however, disguised from us by the pseudo-scientific language of psychology. This passage from *The South Country*, it is true, sounds dangerously like 'reducing man to nature'; certainly Thomas's point is that Chaucer was closer to nature than we are. But again his evidence is the language used – the kind of consciousness it discloses and its difference from ours; the test employs the data of literary criticism. He quotes to illustrate what he detects as a quality of laughter in sorrow,

> Allas, Fortune! it was great crueltee
> Swich briddes for to putte in swich a cage![38]

We notice how the lines brim with a compassion that does not overflow, how the poet and his subject remain distinct; the words have, as it were, clear outlines, and imply the existence beyond the present world of sorrow, evoked with all the tenderness of an unflawed humanity, of another world – a world of birds and a world of freedom; and this world, we are made to feel, is the 'real' one. Thomas implies that it is the world of nature, and that 'joy' prevails in Chaucer's as in White's and Bettesworth's experience because, to invoke again Thomas's spokesman in *The Country*, they have *something to rest upon*. The principal distinction between the traditional and the modern world, for Thomas, is that in one perception is objective and in the other it is subjective: joy depends on belonging to something outside ourselves, melancholy ensues from incarceration within the self.

He argues that joy even prevails in Hardy, and quotes in support of his claim,

> Let me enjoy the earth no less
> Because the all-enacting Might
> That fashioned forth its loveliness
> Had other aims than my delight.

The poem is a light-hearted affair 'but by no means repudiates or makes little of Joy, and is at least as likely as, "Lord, with what care has thou begirt us round," to make a marching song'.[39] The line of verse quoted is, pointedly, from Herbert's poem 'Sin', for Thomas is comparing the resources of a naturalist and a Christian faith; as he remarks earlier, quoting the whole poem, it follows one on Nature in *The Temple*. Indeed, throughout *In Pursuit of Spring* runs a thread of anti-Christian comment. At several stages on his journey westward the author stops to examine the epitaphs in the churchyards (possibly Thomas is parodying, as *Three Men in a Boat* parodies, a feature of late Victorian and Edwardian topographical literature), usually as an occasion for some acid observation on the righteous or gloomy or tyrannical or life-denying character of the sentiments commonly expressed in them. He quotes the epitaph of Benjamin Rogers in Mickleham churchyard:

> Here peaceful sleep the aged and the young,
> The rich and poor, an undistinguished throng.
> Time was these ashes lived; a time must be
> When others thus shall stand and look at thee.

Slyly mistaking 'lived' for 'loved' – 'Time was these ashes lov'd', he had at first written – he then copies out the epitaph of his wife, Mary:

> How lov'd, how valu'd once avails thee not:
> To whom related, or by whom begot.
> A heap of dust alone remains of thee.
> 'Tis all thou art, and all the proud shall be.

The utterance of a 'desperate Christian', 'the lines were composed in a drab ecstasy of conventional humility'. To this comment he adds: 'I even doubt if she really thought that love was of as little importance as having a lord in the family.'[40]

Love is seen here as man's identifying characteristic – but man as part of nature; it is the antithesis of, indeed the opposing principle to, the no less characteristic dissatisfaction with life that subordinates every human impulse to the restless pursuit of an immortal state. 'Pagan', as in the description of Bettesworth as an 'unlettered pagan English peasant', is used therefore as a word of praise throughout this book. Contentment with natural life, we are to take it, is the hallmark of paganism and not of Christianity. Yet, as his own melancholy denies Thomas full participation in the – so to speak – prelapsarian state enjoyed by Chaucer and Gilbert White, as his 'pursuit of spring' is no less a quest for immortality than a lover's celebration of nature, so his praise of paganism is equivocal. Every so often on his journey he encounters a man he calls the Other Man. Like Thomas the Other Man has escaped from London and is in search of some kind of freedom; he is an alter-ego but an eccentric and often ludicrous one, Thomas's mocking picture of the hypochondriacal literary drudge, who 'rambled on and on about himself, his past, his writing, his digestion'. Cycling down to Shepton Mallet 'he sang, as if it had been a hymn of the new Paganism, a ribald song beginning, – "As I was going to Salisbury upon a Summer's day". When he had done he shouted across at me, "I would rather have written that song than take Quebec." ' He wouldn't stay with the writer at Shepton because, he said, it was 'a godless place'. Thomas 'laughed, supposing he lamented the lack of Apollo or Dionysus or Aphrodite' (p. 231). Apparently he was wrong, but his amused, affectionate but condescending attitude to the man is unmistakable. He has considerably more respect for Meredith, the apostle of the new paganism, but in his shrewd chapter on him in *A Literary Pilgrim in England* it is clear that he is aware of the same wilfully challenging quality in Meredith's worship of 'Mother Earth' as in the Other Man's. He says that in Meredith's writing the 'joy of the limbs, the senses, and the brain . . . are expressed . . . with a kind of braced hedonistic Puritanism';[41] and this is because he is 'a Londoner's poet', who leads a double life, his social and intellectual life in the metropolis, his 'religious' life in the Home Counties. 'The beauty of his country has something almost hectic, violent, excessive, about it, caused, perhaps, by contrast with the city.'[42]

II

It comes as no surprise to hear that Jefferies's books were a 'gospel'[43] to the young Thomas. Nature was for him more than the country-lover's nature. He was deeply read in all the naturalist writers, but it was through Jefferies principally that he entered into a close and deep relationship with the Wordsworthian tradition. Yet even where his declaration of the Romantic faith seems most confident and challenging, a note of uncertainty is frequently to be heard. It may sound as no more than a caution or hesitancy in the phrasing, intimating something less than total conviction, but at times Thomas betrays a deep distrust of his own assertions. The implication may be merely that the writer doubts his ability to live according to his avowed creed. Beyond that, however, may be the darker suspicion that no faith exists that could allay his chronic discontent, and that his Romantic naturalism begs questions that must at last be faced; at this point self-criticism shades into a more general scepticism, as it does in his ironic treatment of the new paganism. When scepticism and Romantic yearning achieve simultaneous expression, then we have a rendering of Thomas's experience as complete and as painfully honest as in the poems. At its best the prose is of the same order as the poetry: thought and perception are related and organized in the same way and with very nearly the same allusive delicacy. Prose of course is slower, and needs a larger canvas on which to display its significances; only by examining a passage of some length is it possible to discover the same complex awareness at work as in the poetry. In the later books there are many such stretches of writing. Perhaps the best for my purpose – which is, at this stage in my argument, to show Thomas working to express the full range of his sensibility – is the description, in *In Pursuit of Spring*, of his bicycle ride through Semington, Melksham and Staverton and his arrival in Trowbridge.

Here, in the last six pages (pp. 210–15) of Chapter 6, as in the poetry, the focus is on the details of the external scene, and the strategy of description is similar: to make us conscious, as Leavis says, 'of the inner life which the sensory impressions are notations for'.[44] The scene and the experience associated with it are immediately recognizable to the reader of the poems. There is the writer's arrival in a village, and, though a stranger, the feeling he has of belonging there. But first he describes the bicycle ride that brings him to the place. The extraordinary ease of progress, experienced as an ecstasy of motion, tempts him to compose from the passing sights an earthly image of Elysium.

Motion was extraordinarily easy that afternoon, and I had no doubts that I did well to bicycle instead of walking. It was as easy as riding in a cart, and more satisfying to a restless man. At the same time I was a great deal nearer to being a disembodied spirit than I can often be. I was not at all tired, so far as I knew. No people or thoughts embarrassed me. I fed through the senses directly, but very

12

temperately, through the eyes chiefly and was happier than is explicable or seems reasonable. This pleasure of my disembodied spirit (so to call it) was an inhuman and diffused one, such as may be attained by whatever dregs of this our life survive after death. In fact, had I to describe the adventure of this remnant of a man I should express it somewhat thus, with no need of help from Dante, Mr. A. C. Benson, or any other visitors to the afterworld. In a different mood I might have been encouraged to believe the experience a foretaste of a sort of imprisonment in the viewless winds, or of a spiritual share in the task of keeping the cloudy winds 'fresh for the opening of the morning's eye'. Supposing I were persuaded to provide this afterworld with some of the usual furniture, I could borrow several visible things from that ride through Semington, Melksham, and Staverton.

And he proceeds to borrow for his picture of Elysium, amongst others, the following items: the 'many-windowed naked mass' of a factory as large as a cathedral, called the Phoenix Swiss Milk, indeed 'surmounted by a stone phoenix' to commemorate its restoration after being destroyed by fire; facing it across the river, a small church whose windows 'flamed in the last sunbeams' while 'the tombstones were clear white'; alongside the river, the level three furlongs of perfectly green meadow.

It would be a suitable model for the meadow of heavenly sheen where Aeneas saw the blessed souls of Ilus and Assaracus and Dardanus and the bard Musaeus, heroes and wise men, and the beautiful horses of the heroes, in that diviner air lighted by another sun and other stars than ours.

Essentially this is a natural–mystical experience of the sort in which, as W. H. Hudson testified, Thomas frequently expressed interest. However, the ingredients of this vision of an afterworld, a 'diviner' world than ours, compose a strange mixture of Christian and Classical imagery, of the sacred and the profane; and the tone is consistently ironic and unbelieving. The (as it were) resurrected milk factory parodies the Christian resurrection of the dead; equally, an amused scepticism plays over his description of the bicycle ride as a quasi-spiritual experience, when he 'was happier than is explicable or seems reasonable'. Though prepared to enjoy the experience for what it is, he will not claim that the intensity of his happiness is 'reasonable'. He compares the sensation of riding effortlessly to that of 'a disembodied spirit', at the same time lightly mocking the idea *and himself for being attracted to it*. The pleasure is judged, self-deprecatingly, to be 'an inhuman and diffused one', not one to enhance and concentrate a man's humanity. A man who was chronically tired and constantly reproached by his thoughts and 'embarrassed' by people, Thomas is tempted by, but cannot condone in himself the satisfaction he receives from, such moments of respite from tiredness and social discomfort, of seeming release from the body. Urbane self-amusement turns to amiable contempt when he reduces 'a disembodied spirit' to 'this remnant of a man', vessel of 'whatever dregs of this our life survive after death', and goes on to ridicule Shelleyan pantheism, the naturalist theology, for anticipating 'a sort of imprisonment in the viewless winds'. If, in the words of Thomas's spokesman in *The Country*, nature 'can take us out of ourselves', we must not mistake being taken out of ourselves for this seeming transport of the spirit out of the body, an illusion of the senses. The product of the same restlessness that distinguishes his passion for country life from W. H. Hudson's ('It was easy as riding in a cart, and more satisfying to a restless man'), a restlessness that has driven all men to dream of immortality, it is an enchantment of the senses especially welcome to one for whom, though not 'a desperate Christian' (like Mary Rogers of the epitaph) but a lover of earth, Hudson's untroubled contentment with the conditions of natural life is a rare experience.

After this exaltation of the spirit his entry into the village of Trowbridge is like a coming down to earth. By contrast with 'the diviner air lighted by another sun and other stars than ours', this land was lighted by the ordinary sun that rises and sets daily; and before he had reached his destination this ordinary 'sun was fading over Challimead'. Yet coming down to earth is not in these circumstances a *dis*enchantment: while different from the ecstasy of the journey, it has its own blessedness. In Trowbridge, though spring was due, 'the pewits cried as if it were winter', and the signs were that 'there would be another frost to-night'; but 'at corners and crossways figures were standing talking, or bidding farewell', and there was a warmth of *people*. Being there had the mixed, uncertain (between winter and spring) character of mundane reality; but something of the afternoon's mood remained as he 'rode on easily through the chill, friendly land'. Later in the evening, having walked out of the village, his feelings on returning to it echo feelings he had had while riding, when, unwontedly, 'no people or thoughts embarrassed' him: now, too, 'though a stranger, I believed that no one wished harm to me'. It was not his own village, but briefly he enjoyed the illusion of belonging; 'here and there a yellow window square gave out a feeling of home, tranquillity, security.' A man slightly drunk, swaying towards him and then away again, posed a momentary threat to 'the quiet and the safety' of the place; but a gate shut, he was 'absorbed' back into the darkness, and peace was restored.

The difference between the intense happiness of the bicycle ride and the sheltered peace here in the village is that the former is the experience of a solitary, and the latter the experience of a solitary in touch, however tenuously, with other people. The solitary, a man alone with his thoughts, needs the silence of the inanimate world; the social being needs the security of company and the feeling of home. A tranquil but apparently unremarkable end to a day's travel, what makes the ordinary extraordinary is that the two experiences here complement and harmonize with each other: 'clear hoofs hammering and men or girls talking in traps were but an *added music* to the *quiet* throughout the evening' (my italics, here and in subsequent discussion). It was a 'chill' evening, with a night frost likely, but Thomas now 'began to feel some confidence in the Spring'.

The equal satisfaction of solitary and social needs, a fragile equilibrium, does not last beyond twilight. On his evening walk, as it gets darker, the appeal of solitude grows stronger and once more takes a firm hold. The 'light' ecstasy of the day finds its counterpart in a 'dark' ecstasy of the night. Gradually, as he drew away from the village, 'the quiet and the safety' deepened into something qualitatively different. First, '*ordinary* speech was not to be heard', only the sounds of a harmonium, a voice singing, and in the distance a dog barking, and after an interval the sound of a gate falling to; then '*nobody* was in the road', and on the green 'all was still and silent'. As twilight merged into night the cottages became 'merely blacker stains on the darkness'. At the last house a 'dog growled, but in a subdued tone, as if only to condemn [his] footsteps on the deserted road'.

Rows of elm trees on both sides of the road succeeded. I walked more slowly, and at a gateway stopped. While I leaned looking over it at nothing, there was a long silence that could be felt, so that a train whistling two miles away seemed as remote as the stars. The noise could not overleap the boundaries of that silence. And yet I presently moved away, back towards the village, with slow steps.

The dog had growled as if to deprecate a taste for 'silence' and the 'nothing' of blackness, and to condemn a man's preference for solitude to human company. Thomas's movement away from the world of people, as it were slowly expunging it from his mind, corresponds to and keeps pace with the growing stillness and the gradual extinguishment of light by advancing darkness. 'Ordinary speech' had given way to the silence and otherness of 'pollard willows fringing the green', which in the dusk seemed 'like a procession of men, strange *primaeval* beings pausing [like the narrator] to meditate in the darkness'. Now, safe in that impregnable, 'dark, soft, and tranquil' world, 'I felt,' he confesses, 'that I could walk on thus, sipping the evening silence and solitude, *endlessly.*' Like the intoxication of the day's riding, when he felt near being 'a disembodied spirit', this night-world of 'silence and solitude' – holding enticements no less 'inhuman and diffused' – induces an illusion of immortality. Both experiences speak seductively of an unassailable peace, a solace endlessly available to whoever seeks it.

And yet Thomas, seeking it and having it in his possession, lets it go, turning his footsteps 'back towards the village', to the lights and sounds of common life. The danger in these privileged moments, which appeal to the natural mystic in Thomas, is that addiction to them confirms and extends the gap that separates the solitary from his neighbour. While still entranced in his night-world, the light from the inn door seemed 'a bright cave in the middle of the darkness: the illumination had a kind of blessedness such as it might have had to a cow, not without *foreign-ness*'. The charm of Trowbridge was its power to suggest, if only a mitigation of that foreignness, the possibility of a more familiar rela-tionship: 'though a stranger, I believed that no one wished harm to me'; the noise of horses' hoofs and the talk of men or girls were 'but an added music to the quiet'. The deliciously humorous comparison of the ecsta-tic's view to the consciousness of a cow discloses a hitherto concealed critical detachment in the author and prepares us for his final readjust-ment to the demands of social life. He had felt that he 'could walk on thus . . . endlessly'.

But at the house where I was staying I stopped as usual. I entered, blinked at the light, and by laughing at something, said with the intention of being laughed at, I swiftly again naturalized myself.

These are the last words of the chapter and bring the episode to an end. The very last sentence adds touches that refine to a delicate precision a tremulous balance between the competing claims of solitary and social pleasures. Adjustment to the demands of social life is not capitulation. These 'moments of everlastingness', as Thomas will call them in his poem 'The Other', are indeed *short*-lasting, and too much enjoyment of them is likely to unbalance our humanity. This is true, but at the same time the narrator's return to normal (social) consciousness, which is likened to the process of *naturalization*, a foreigner's admission to the position and rights of citizenship, by that comparison ironically calls into question the root word 'natural'; for, bringing into play a complex set of learned responses to tiny social signals ('laughing at something, said with the intention of being laughed at'), it is, though necessary, hardly natural at all, or natural in a highly sophisticated sense of the word. Naturalization is, in fact, for Thomas, as it largely is for anyone, the adoption of elaborate conventions for maintaining a state of community between individuals who have little in common and only a superficial knowledge of each other. The word indeed assumes that social intercourse is not his 'real' element. We have to set this against his willingness none the less to conform to a nominally *common* life.

In these pages Thomas is at once the romantic and the sceptic. The romantic craves both the equanimity and the exaltations of solitude, and an impossible freedom from the artifice and compromise incident to the conduct of social relations. The position of the sceptic is less easily defined; it does not lie simply in the refutation of these cravings. The implications of his irony are elusive because they do not *rest upon* the firm foundations of countering beliefs or principles: the narrator is poised precariously between opposing scepticisms. On the one hand, he derides immortal longings, whether they are embodied in the after-worlds of pagan and Christian imagination or concealed in the language of natural mysticism; on the other, he observes himself with little more than an amused tolerance practising the arts of social appeasement: he mocks the solitary for desiring the extraordinary and the home-seeker for submitting to the ordinary.

Throughout the narrative Thomas's scepticism is never more than playful; the mockery is cool rather than mordant. It takes quick note in passing of something 'inhuman' in the happiness of the bicycle ride, which is there also, unnamed but more apparent, in the night scene; in his confession, just before re-entering the house, that he felt he could enjoy 'the evening silence and solitude endlessly', we glimpse too the illusion along with the rareness and brevity of such moments – the short-lasting posing as the everlasting: these are side-glances, which note the facts but do not pause to weigh them. The dominant emphasis is on the *satisfaction* of these solitary experiences. Yet the cool quizzical tone, that keeps an arm's length distance between the narrator and his subject, and the bearing of certain observations, not stressed but leaving questions in the reader's mind, clearly distinguish Thomas's naturalism from the grander, and grandly cadenced, assertions of the Romantics. There are passages in Thomas's prose writing which probe and question the psychological implications of that word 'inhuman' when used to describe the pleasure of being a 'disembodied spirit', and are less reticent about what draws him to the silence and darkness that lie in wait for him just outside the village. He does not say, but a little reflection tells us that beyond the gateway where he stopped and looked at *nothing*, which marked the boundary of the *silence* calling to him, is death. That self-transcendence may be separated by a hair's breadth from self-extinction is the burden of Mr. Torrance's cautionary remark in *The Happy-Go-Lucky Morgans* concerning a desire for union with nature: 'To unite yourself with the universe you may be tempted to destroy the boundary of self and universe, and die' (p. 222). The temptation is frequently dramatized in the prose and the poetry, associated invariably with dusk and coming darkness, or scenes of rain, or both. *The South Country* ends with a hymn to rain going about its 'eternal business' of scouring, stripping and quenching life.

At all times I love rain . . . I like to see it possessing the whole earth at evening, smothering civilization, taking away from me myself everything except the power to walk under the dark trees and to enjoy as humbly as the hissing grass, while some twinkling house-light or song sung by a lonely man gives a foil to the immense dark force. (p. 275)

The 'nothing' that blacked out vision and the 'long silence that could be felt' hint facts about natural life that are left alone here but are the theme of several passages in Thomas's prose about the alienness or otherness of nature. On many occasions, it is true, he *celebrates* that otherness, as he does when he describes the song of a bird in *The South Country*: 'Beautiful as the notes are for their quality and order, it is their inhumanity that gives them their utmost fascination, the mysterious sense which they bear to us that earth is something more than a human estate, that there are things not human yet of great honour and power in the world' (p. 34). The mind is halted briefly none the less by 'inhumanity', as it is by 'inhuman and diffused' in *In Pursuit of Spring*; although, challenging customary usage, it is made to mean 'not human' rather than 'not humane', it is a provocatively uncompromising word for 'things of great *honour* . . . in the world'. I can think of few passages of prose more evocative of the rich life of the senses than, in the next chapter, the description of a rain-freshened landscape, that ends with a mention of 'all the joys of life that come through the nostrils from the dark, not understood world which is unbolted for us by the delicate and savage fragrances of leaf and flower and grass and clod, of the plumage of birds and fur of animals and breath and hair of women and children' (pp. 54–5). Yet the mind's incomprehension of that world leads immediately to this uneasy question: 'How can our thoughts, the movement of our bodies, our human kindnesses, ever fit themselves with this blithe world?' And some such question moves at the back of Thomas's description of a winter scene in *The Icknield Way* (pp. 239–41). But in this piece one feels the question to be a more uncomfortable presence in the writer's mind. In intention – and largely this is how it reads – it is a celebration of the independent life of nature. A brilliant day of sun on snow is re-created:

The black brook, full of the white reflections of its snowy banks and beginning to steam in the sun, was hourly growing and coiling all its long loops joyously through the land. The dabchick was laughing its long shrill titter under the alder roots. Faint, soft shadows fell on to the snow from the oaks, whose grey skeletons were outlined in snow against the clear deep blue of the now dazzling sky. Thrushes were beginning to sing, as if it had always been warm and bright.

18

But in the fields at the foot of the hills

no birds sang and no stream gurgled. The air was full of the pitiful cries of young lambs at their staggering play in the shallow snow. One ewe stood with her new-born lamb in a stamped, muddy circle tinged with blood amidst the pure white.

The blood that stains the white brilliance of the day is, it is true, the blood of the afterbirth, and, to set against the lamb's 'pitiful cries', our final view of the mother is of her 'with her head down, her eyes upon me, her whole nature upon the lamb buried in her wool, part of her'. Yet the intimations of pain in the scene are inescapable and are reinforced immediately:

A kestrel had killed a gold-crest upon the bank, and as I approached it sailed away from the crimson-centred circle of feathers on the snow.

Creation and destruction in nature manifest themselves in indiscriminately similar ways. The summary of the scene's meaning, which follows immediately, returns us, however, to the joyousness of the brook and the laughter of the dabchick:

But the wind had been the chief inhabitant of the slopes, and unseen of mortal eyes it had been luxuriously, playfully carving the snow which submerged the hedge. The curved wind-work in the drift, deeply ploughed or deliberately chiselled, remained in the stillness as a record of the pure joy of free, active life contented with itself.

The picture expresses unequivocally Thomas's admiring appreciation; yet following and seeming to ignore the account of the gold-crest's death, words like 'luxuriously' and 'playfully' also give us, without comment, the Olympian indifference to human feeling in the creation of such beauty. The writer has described this scene because it is the setting of a story he has culled from a newspaper, of a man driven by poverty and illness to move his family into the derelict barn of an abandoned farmhouse, where his seventh child is born; charged with neglect of his children, he has been given a prison sentence and his family sent to the workhouse. Thomas is now visiting the barn, and the paragraph depicting the wind's playful carving of the snow ends with this sentence: 'It was the same blithe hand which had shaped the infant born in this black barn.' The shock of confrontation between 'pure joy', the joy of self-delighting life, and human misery, is given rhetorical bite by the alliterative contrast of 'blithe' and 'black'. The human associations of the place further accentuate the disparity between the hopes of man and the ways of nature. He notes that in its dilapidation open on both sides to the snow-light and the air the barn looked the work rather of nature than of man. The old thatch was grooved, riddled, and gapped, and resembled a grassy bank that has been under a flood the winter through; covered now in snow it had the outlines in miniature of the hill on which it was built.

The apparently satisfying return of man's work to nature thus accomplished conceals, however, a deeper pathos: the lofty porches, still upright, suggested a church and consequently

a pathetic, undermined dignity: without them it would have seemed wholly restored to nature, amiably and submissively ruinous, with a silence in which not the most perverse mind could have detected melancholy.

Man cannot, as nature can, play with death: the barn is not a willing partner to its ruin, however picturesque the result, nor is man reconciled to his mortality. A late essay, 'The Moon', printed in the posthumous *Cloud Castles and Other Papers*, puts it plainly. Watching moonlight 'playing alone among the trees' ('the kind of play that makes the frost flowers on dead sticks in the woods on winter nights'), Thomas comes to the point of imagining a deity, the god in nature, 'with as little anthropomorphism as possible, certainly without personification'; what it reveals to him is that he, the human observer, is 'a pure accident' (p. 196).

Thomas disliked the Christian religion, especially in its Victorian dress, for reasons that would have made any religion unacceptable to him – for its spirituality and moralism. He suspected, without going into the matter, that elevation of the spirit means debasement of the body, that perfection of the spirit entails depletion and devaluation of the life of the senses. He was sceptical of any belief, religious or otherwise, that is tinged with idealism in this sense of the word. In the attitudes of Romantic naturalism – a religious or, to remove the paradox, a religiose naturalism – and the experiences of the natural mystic, attitudes and experiences for which he felt considerable sympathy, at times, as we have seen, he detected idealism in disguise. The fullest treatment of this theme is in 'The Friend of the Blackbird', a fable included in *The Last Sheaf* (pp. 205–15), the second of the two collections of essays and sketches to be published posthumously. In setting out to distinguish the excesses of the nature-worshipper from what is 'reasonable' in a naturalistic view, Thomas was clearly trying to define a form of naturalism to which with a good conscience he could give his assent. The fable tells how a man was converted from the austerities of a chapel faith – the man a minister widely known for 'his furious pieties in the pulpit' and his misanthropy out of it – to a belief in the God of

Nature; how the confidence of his naturalist religion was shaken on his death-bed but reaffirmed in his last moments. So summarized, the issue seems plain and the antithesis between supernatural and natural deity sharply drawn; but this is not so. Thomas presents the man in his nature-worshipping phase as a blend of Norgett – one of those wild men who live on terms of 'equality with the conditions of life'[45] – and a natural visionary. He felt himself to be in 'community' with birds, animals and trees and in a mystical communion with nature: 'They are me,' he said, and 'I am them. We are one. We are organs and instruments of one another.' When the narrator first met him he saw in his eyes a 'blissfulness . . . so intense as to be unearthly'. The terms of this description, however, call to mind Thomas's bicycle ride through Semington, Melksham and Staverton, and his sensation of being like a 'disembodied spirit', feeling 'happier than is explicable or seems reasonable'; they warn us of some excess or partiality in this mystical experience. Our suspicion grows when a certain insecurity in the man's mood is brought to our attention. He found disquieting 'the laughing, discordant notes' that in late spring often conclude the blackbird's song; 'the bird seemed to be laughing at himself', and it reminded the man of the cynical phrases at the end of Byron's stanzas: 'he could not enjoy this in bird or poet'. The blackbird's meaning is not pursued; the doubt raised is allowed to subside and almost to disappear from view during the ensuing description of the man's last illness. The two Gods, ranged on opposite sides, are seen to do battle for the man's soul, and his last words are: 'the little God torments me . . . But I go to the Great One. It is well.' But something is still unclear to the narrator. 'It was a fantastic whim for Whatever overpowered him in that friendless death-chamber, amid snow and silence, to wrest such blasting *discords* out of an *instrument* that had seemed in the lane to know only natural joy and tranquillity' (my italics). Hinting at an analogy with 'the laughing, discordant notes' that *conclude* the blackbird's song, the narrator, unable to share the dying man's simple belief but speaking for him and personally involved in his dilemma, here remarks the contradiction at the heart of the naturalistic faith. His uncertainty forms itself into a question, one with which he confronts the dying man's final assertion, and with which the fable ends: 'Friend of the blackbird, is it well?' Since Thomas was not a Christian, the doctrines of 'the little God' have no claims on his attention; his interest in the tale is in the counterclaims of naturalism. His instinctive sympathies lie with the power that can bring to a bitter, morose man 'natural joy and tranquillity'; nevertheless his final question concerns the adequacy to man's desires not of the Christian God but of the God of Nature. The root of the problem, the prompter of unanswerable questions, is our mortal condition, which sets a natural limit to natural joy. The deaths of the man's father and his sweetheart having first made a recluse of him and then turned him to the fierce, bitter religion of the chapel, it was appropriate that on his own death-bed he should once again feel the power of the Christian God. The narrator's concluding words, sadly but unequivocally, question the basis of the dying man's restored faith in the Great One of Nature. For death is the harsh, seemingly cynical note that spoils what the simple believer hears as 'the pure melody' of nature. 'Whatever had overpowered him' at the end and left him 'friendless' was the very deity to whom, in the assurance of his benevolence, he had dedicated his life. The power of the supernatural God, then, is the power of man's discontent with the time-limits and the decay of natural joy. But it is even clearer here than in the pages of *In Pursuit of Spring* that the same discontent, the same immortal longings, feed the ecstasy of the natural mystic; they are as responsible for his wilful blindness to the fact of death and his (betraying word) 'unearthly' vision as for the Christian's repudiation of natural joy. In this the faiths are equal and equally delusive.

III

At times Thomas's mind settles, not on what he believed or disbelieved, but on the curious nature of man himself, whose dissatisfaction with things as they are makes so compelling his need to imagine something better. He meditates on this aspect of man's character frequently and with varying degrees of indulgence and disapproval. In *The South Country* it is usually with indulgence. Speaking of the ultimately inexplicable response that many landscapes provoke in the human mind, he yet tries to explain the appeal for him that a certain coombe has (pp. 152–4). It is 'a huge, flat-bottomed, grassy coombe, smooth as a racecourse, that winds out of the cornland into the heart of the Downs ... At length the windings shut out the plain, and the coombe is a green hall roofed by the hot blue sky.' In its utter solitude, void of all human trace, we can imagine the elements of life, 'pure earth and wind and sunlight', that might bring us to a 'region out of space and out of time in which life and thought and physical health are in harmony with sun and earth'. Out of such intimations, we might assume, the complementary vision has taken shape of 'a man whom human infelicity, discontented with the past, has placed in a golden age', a vision, Thomas insists, to which it has been the peculiar task of 'prophet and poet' to restore us.

On the whole, in *The South Country* this sentimental account of the poetic impulse is allowed to go unqualified. Thus of two lovers gathering nuts glimpsed through a gateway, a moment of beauty given by memory a quality of timelessness, he assures us that 'to rescue such scenes from time is one of the most blessed offices of books' (pp. 221–2). Five years later his own poems, though visions of a golden age sometimes and idyllic moments frequently have a part in them, will demonstrate the insufficiency of these simple-minded critical attitudes. The sensibility disclosed in this book is, however, rarely as simple as this. He ponders, for example, with great delicacy and a trace of puzzlement the tendency of memory to select from scenes of mixed joy and pain only the elements of joy, and to make childhood Edens out of them (pp. 126–8). It is a perceptive piece of introspective writing, conveying very attractively the 'drowsy pleasure in the mere act of memory' while at the same time registering in the lightest of touches certain reservations concerning such experiences. 'Why, as we whirled past them in a train, does the sight of a man and child walking quietly beside a reedy pond, the child stooping for a flower and its gossip unheard – why should we tremble to reflect that we have never tasted just that cloistered balm?' 'Cloistered', without breaking the spell by insisting on itself, suggests where the answer to his question lies. Yet in his final explicit comment, the fine apprehension rendered in the previous paragraphs slips from him as he concludes that, perhaps, memory sifts out the painful elements from a remembered scene because 'only an inmost *true self* that desires and is in harmony with joy can perform these long journeys' (pp. 127–8; my italics). And, whatever complications of awareness are present in some of the writing, such a conclusion accords with the general tenor of the book. In the first chapter, trying to account for something that eludes analysis in his feeling for the land he calls the South Country, he decides that the term refers less to the southern counties known to the topographical writer than to a country of the mind in which 'the spirit [can] disport itself' (p. 11). So, 'when the lark is high he seems to be singing in some keyless chamber of the brain' (p. 13).

With more of a critical detachment he records how the perfection of sight and smell that is achieved at several stages in the pageant of autumn's dying 'awakens the never more than lightly sleeping human desire of permanence'. But 'the motion of the autumn is a fall, a surrender, requiring no effort', and therefore 'the mind cannot long be blind to the cycle of things as in the spring it can' (p. 272). Romantic desire and realistic check combine in a way that anticipates the more complicated, wry, paradoxical spirit in which, later, Thomas undertakes his 'pursuit of spring'. There, in the later book, he has the use of a wider range of tones and manages a subtler poise in attitudes. One characteristic episode leads to a meditation on man's romantic nature. It begins with the serene, tranquil mood of cycling on the Winchester road towards Dunbridge, a milder version of the 'light' ecstasy he is to describe in another chapter. It does not, however, outlast the onset of rain. Moreover, the fact that this is the Easter holiday co-operates with the natural disobligingness of people to ensure his failure to *find room at the inns* of Dunbridge (that this is a Christian festival is, I think, no accident). Brought down from his tranquil state, in a sourer mood he takes the train to Salisbury, where he finds 'a bed and a place to sit and eat in', and where, listening to the rain and the creaking signboard, he reflects 'on the imperfection of inns and life, and on the spirit's readiness to grasp at all kinds of unearthly perfection such, for instance, as that which had encompassed me this evening before the rain' (p. 119). The hinted analogy with the plight of Mary at Bethlehem, which I have accentuated in my own relation of the incident, is in Thomas's casual, unemphasized, not exact – it works in the oblique way of images in his poems – but it is close enough to explain the reference to 'the imperfection of inns and life'. Inns are the unsuitable accommodation for the spirit provided by the world. But the body gets tired and needs bodily comfort; reluctantly he has to admit this at the end of yet another day's riding. For a moment he lets his eyes follow the hill-slopes upwards, remembering from a former occasion and imagining again 'the glory and the peace of the Plain' above, 'of the unbounded Plain and the unbounded sky, and the marriage of sun and wind that was being celebrated upon them'. But one cannot always be experiencing hill-top exaltations: 'I had to go down, not up, to find a bed that I knew of seven or eight miles from Tinhead and Edington' (p. 172). The shape of the book, being that of a journey out of London towards the west of England which is at the same time a flight from winter and a 'pursuit of Spring', mirrors the search for a blend of earthly and unearthly perfection. So, nearing his destination in the west and finding spring finally established there, once more the writer looks longingly at the 'half-earthly and half-aerial heights' of Exmoor before him, and in the sunset over a nearby hill is again able to imagine – but the figure delivers its meaning more directly – 'the marriage of heaven and earth'. Characteristically this mood is followed, too, by an ironic 'descent' to the mundane, accompanied this time by a quick parody of the whole idealizing bent of the author's mind. 'Here, though, it was six, and notwithstanding the marriage of heaven and earth, I had tea, and furthermore ate cream with a spoon, until I had had almost as much as I desired' (pp. 287–8). This is not the only example of self-parody. The whole design of the book, indeed, is parodied in the narrator's long, relentlessly specific account, which sends the Other Man to sleep, of his search for the perfect clay-pipe (pp. 119–26).

Some paragraphs in *The South Country*, reflecting on the feeling of near-reverence wakened in him by the prospect of a great country house and its estate, run the full gamut of responses to the romantic disposition (pp. 116–19). It is not the real house, 'not feudalism, or the old nobility and gentility, that we are bowing down to, but only to Nature without us and the dream within us'. 'It is the alien remote appearance of the house and land serene in the May evening light which creates this reverence in the mind.' Such houses are 'castles in Spain. They are fantastic architecture. We have made them out of our spirit stuff and have set our souls to roam their corridors and look out of their casements upon the sea or the mountains or the clouds. It is because they are accessible only to the everywhere wandering irresistible and immortal part of us that they are beautiful.' Though conscious of the dream status of such feelings, here Thomas is letting himself submit to their enchantment. But it is of a piece with the perfection of the parkland surrounding the house that 'the cattle graze as on a *painted* lawn' and that 'the scene *appears* to have its own sun, mellow and serene, that knows not moorland or craggy coast or city' (my italics). The delicate disclosure of the illusion in all this loveliness leads immediately to this: 'Only a thousand years of settled continuous government of far-reaching laws, of armies and police, of roadmaking, of bloody tyranny that poisons quietly without blows, could have wrought earth and sky into such a harmony.' Hard recognitions such as this are part of the complex organization of attitudes in this meditation; they are there not to debunk romantic feeling but to discriminate among its objects. Yearning 'for something undivined, imperfectly known, guessed at, or hoped for, in ourselves; for a wider and less tainted beauty, for a greater grace' may be the reason why we endow a flawed reality with an inappropriate mystery, but the yearning itself is not entirely repudiated; the impulse obviously has something fine and worthy in it. The poise achieved in this passage is best represented by the sentence that concludes it. Desire to tread the 'holy ground' of a hill-top transfigured into a 'glowing and insubstantial thing' by the evening light gives rise to this reflection: 'It is an odd world where everything is fleeting yet the soul desires permanence even for fancies so unprofitable as this.'

IV

The discontent and restlessness pondered in these pages of *The South Country* and *In Pursuit of Spring* are, of course, specifically Thomas's own. They are emotions plausibly represented as universal responses to the human condition, experienced in some degree by everyone, but any reader of his poems will know that they were felt by Thomas with a peculiar, unrelieved urgency. I have already noted the frequent appearance in his writings of semi-mythological figures; wild, pre-civilized, only half-human, they are expressions of Thomas's need to imagine *antitheses* of himself, contented beings living on terms of 'equality with the conditions of life'. One aspect of their nature, however, I did not emphasize, but I must now draw attention to it – their nomadism. Most of them, unlike Norgett, are wanderers and travellers; in this respect, therefore, they share something with their creator. His name for the type in *The Happy-Go-Lucky Morgans* is the 'superfluous man', and he applies the same phrase to himself in *The South Country*.[46] In Turgenev's story 'The Diary of a Superfluous Man' it labels for the first time a character of which there are many variants in nineteenth century Russian literature. For Thomas he is both a perennial type, a sport of creation whose animal wildness is incompatible with some of the basic requirements of the human condition (the need to labour, for example), and a person specifically ill-adapted to the materialism and commercialism of the modern world; his likeness to the Russian type consists in his having no use or function in the society available to him.

There are numerous characters of this kind in Thomas's work; in *The South Country* alone we have the umbrella man, the watercress man, the two casual labourers who are discovered reaping oats but 'are not men of the farm, but rovers who take their chance and have done other things than reaping in their time' (p. 230); one of them, a Hampshire man, he describes as 'a citizen of the world, without wife or home or any tie' (p. 231), and in this he is like a fourth character, an 'outcast' who was not even an irregular worker but 'employed only such labour as was needed to make his bread and occasionally clothes and a pipe' (p. 253). The watercress man, who turns into a folk character called Jackalone (re-appearing as Jack Noman in the poem 'May the Twenty-third'), who 'laid no plans as a youth' and has had no 'thought of the day after tomorrow', was for years 'the irresponsible jester to a smug townlet', and since then has lived by 'the sale of a chance rabbit or two' and 'by casual shelter in barns, in roofless cottages, or under hedges' (p. 25). The umbrella man, who has had other occupations too, 'had always wandered, and knew the South Country between Fordingbridge and Dover as a man knows his garden . . . I never met a man who knew England as he did' (p. 192). Evidently he has a fair slice of Thomas's own disposition, and is admired for it – admired, however, because his wanderlust has untrammelled expression, and does not have to accommodate itself to adverse conditions (such as having to support a wife and three children), or co-exist with competing instincts and compulsions (for instance, a homing instinct in Thomas as powerful as the rootlessness here idealized as wanderlust, and a compulsion to maintain a regular middle-class standard of living on the irregular earnings of a free-lance writer). The umbrella man's face 'moved with free and broad expressions as he thought and remembered, like an animal's face. Living alone and never having to fit himself into human society, he had not learnt to keep his face in a vice' (pp. 192–3).

No man felt himself to be less 'free' than Thomas, or desired more to be released from the economic and social constrictions of his life. Yet he was as much a prisoner of his own personality as of external circumstances. He condemned himself, by a tyrannous conscience and by the profession he chose, to a life of appalling labour, and was constitutionally incapable of being either irresponsible or improvident. These characters, then, are not plain *anti-selves* like Norgett, but conceivable *alter egos*. In creating them, Thomas has tried to imagine extensions of himself or of an aspect of himself: that is, a form of his own restlessness that would express, not the discontent of a rootless, homeless man, but a vitality liberated from the stifling conventions of human society. A deep self-disgust on Thomas's part has given them the ability to thrive in the exiled state that symbolizes the emotional impoverishment of his own existence. The mind of the 'outcast', for example, 'shy and suspicious of men' (p. 254), like Thomas though he is, is none the less a *tabula rasa* on which the world perceived by the senses imprints itself with a purity and a clarity inaccessible to the well-stocked mind. 'Of history and science he knew nothing, of literature nothing; he had to make out the earth with his own eyes and heart.' To a man who repeatedly lamented the derivative bookishness of his prose style, and came to see his early exposure to literature and a precocious literary ambition as the corrupting agents, this kind of 'outcast' was a living reproach. 'He drew no philosophy from Nature, no opinions, ideas, proposals for reforms, but only the wisdom to live, happily and healthily and simply, himself. I dare say modernity was in his blood, but no man seemed to belong less to his time' (p. 253). Juxtaposing a description of one of these characters with the self-revelation of the poem 'Old Man' affords the most remarkable demonstration of the relation in which they stand to their author. For the same rhetoric and very nearly the same words are used to suggest a mythical, almost superhuman confidence of life in the watercress man – 'He has never had father or mother or brother or sister or wife or child' (p. 25) – as are used to conclude, in 'Old Man', a chilling evocation of lost meaning and lost connections:

> Neither father nor mother, nor any playmate;
> Only an avenue, dark, nameless, without end.

Wanderers, tramps, outcasts of society, they belong to no human community, not even a rural community, but to nature itself. In this the Hampshire man stands for them all: 'In his walk and attitude and talk – except in his accent – there is little of the countryman' (p. 231). Conceivably, Thomas saw them as counterweights to an imbalance in the evolved nature of man. For he expressed the view that man is essentially 'a more or less harmonious combination of the peasant and the adventurer';[47] or, alternatively, of the 'husbandman' and the 'hunter';[48] perhaps they are meant to embody possibilities of life lost in the long process of man's settlement and domestication. But it is clear that Thomas is half deluding himself. Though civilization is often identified with the growth of towns and complex social organization, the seeds of civilization, the conditions that made these possible, are certainly to be found in the change from the semi-nomadic life of the hunters to the settled state of the neolithic farming communities. Human life as we know it owes its essential characteristics to the neolithic revolution that produced that change, and in harking back to a rootless pre-civilized state, trying to find a justifying analogy with his own modern rootlessness, Thomas is guilty of the primitivism that he himself diagnosed in the Georgian poets.[49] Pre-civilized is pre-human: the more his characters belong to nature the less human they become.

Yet, productions of some kind of self-deception though they are, these wanderers are not – any more than the settled countrymen like Norgett – simply creatures of fantasy, providing an easy dream-satisfaction for their author. He keeps his distance from them. Both types are set before us chiefly to dramatize Thomas's sense of his own *comparative* unreality. Against, for example, the farmer, who leads an isolated life in a wooded part of Hampshire and whose eyes have 'that look of harmony with day and night', he feels himself to be 'but a wraith': 'three-quarters of [the farmer's] living is done for him by the dead; merely to look at him is to see a man five generations thick, so to speak'.[50] This is what it means to have roots; having none, Thomas lacks this 'density' of life. Yet equally he lacks something that the gipsy whom he saw at Goodwood race-track had. One of a tribe of 'nomads working and idling' there, his difference from the crowd of onlookers, of which Thomas was one, that 'had nothing in common but internal solitude and external pursuit of pleasure', was his 'strange content' disturbed by 'no fear of tomorrow, death, or anything else'. The same image is used to mark the distinction between Thomas's life and the gipsy's as between his life and the farmer's: 'He was no ghost. But the crowd was ghostly.'[51]

Sometimes his nomadic characters are there only to point a self-mocking remark, as when in *In Pursuit of Spring*, describing two tramps asleep, one 'with clear outstanding pale profile, hands clasped over the fifth rib, and feet stuck up, like a carved effigy', he adds: 'I was as glad to see them sleeping in the sun as to hear the larks singing', and 'I would have done the same if I had been somebody else' (p. 98). That he is not somebody else, however, is as clearly the message of the description as of the comment. The marmoreal composure of the tramp is a parody image of an unconscious harmony with nature only playfully wished for. It is no more part of the tramp's experience than it is of Thomas's, but is attributed to him by way of wry acknowledgement and amused acceptance of a romanticism in himself that he cannot disown but finds slightly absurd. The effect is a lighter, more overtly mocking version of that obtained by these lines in 'October':

> and now I might
> As happy be as earth is beautiful,
> Were I some other or with earth could turn
> In alternation of violet and rose . . .

The tramps are *ironic* projections of Thomas's yearnings. They are not contradictions but counterparts of another type – we might call him the town-bred nature-lover – frequently depicted in his prose work; for the type is usually a diagnostic, often ironic self-portrait, so modified as to make his feelings for the country characteristically indicative of urban man's false relationship to nature. A chapter in *The South Country* entitled 'A Return to Nature' is given over to the self-presentation of one such character. Born in a Welsh village, he was brought to London at the age of seven, and, like Thomas, lived in Wandsworth and went to a middle-class school close by. From childhood excursions with his father, a city clerk, he learned to love the country but never felt at home in it. 'My people have not built,' he explains to the narrator, 'they were oil or grit in a great machine' (p. 87). And so he could belong nowhere. He describes a childhood experience that, recurring occasionally, has more than any other experience shaped his sense of himself. Left alone for a while on one of these country excursions, 'there was suddenly opened before me – like a yawning pit, yet not only beneath me but on every side – infinity, endless time, endless space' (p. 75). What might have been 'to a more blessed child' a mystical vision of oneness with 'earth and stars and sea and remote time', was for a person without secure roots 'a terror that enrolled me as one of the helpless, superfluous ones of the earth' (p. 75). And for the 'town-bred Englishman', his self-deprecating label for himself in *The Icknield Way*, there are only lost possibilities. No matter how much he loves the country, since it is not in his blood 'he must meditate upon what might have been, and be content to make five shillings out of his meditation, if he is a journalist' (p. 147).

The almost casual self-contempt of this remark perhaps obscures a well-considered position. In his study of Walter Pater, Thomas bases his criticism of Pater's style and sensibility upon the diagnosis of one radical deficiency in the man. He is 'one who continually writes of all things as a "spectacle"' (p. 185). Earlier in the book he gives a moral significance to this deficiency. 'He is the spectator still: he sees, not life, but pictures of life, fantastic, changeful, dreamlike' (p. 84). He uses the same distinction in *The Country* to divide the aesthete's appreciation of nature, 'seeing it as the site for a house or a picnic, or the subject of a picture' (p. 49), from that of the countryman, whose sensations, feelings and knowledge are all bound up with the sights, sounds and smells of the country; it is not a spectacle to him, but, as it were, flows in his veins. The townsman belongs with the aesthete and the writer of nature books among the spectators of, rather than participants in, life; together they make a picture of modern, essentially urban man. He lives at a conscious remove from what he experiences, and he feels more an imaginative sympathy with the natural world than a direct relationship with it. Thomas takes the word 'impulse' from Wordsworth's 'One impulse from a vernal wood', and contrasts the closeness of man to nature expressed by the word, with the conscious emotion felt by, say, the London commuter when he reads of the passion of Gunnar the outlaw for the fair cornfields of his homeland. Gunnar defied the death penalty and returned. 'Men read this and thrill, but on the morrow take the same train to Waterloo, coming faithfully home at night to the dwelling which never seemed to them fair at all. That is the merit of the town life, to produce myriads of sympathies, few impulses.'[52] 'Merit' is a studiously impartial, even generous word for what it describes; following a description of the thinness of the townsman's experience, it is perhaps to be read ironically. Certainly, where imaginative sympathy seduces men to the worship of a distorted image of natural life, Thomas is coolly dismissive: 'the freedom and simplicity connected by them with some forms of country life foster that cultivation of the instinctive and primitive which is the fine flower of a self-conscious civilization, turning in disgust upon itself'.[53] There is an element of self-accusation in this too.

Roving outcast and superfluous man – the semi-mythic immunity of the former from the real privations of exile, no less than the direct revelation of unease and ambivalence in the latter – bear witness, in their complementary ways, to Thomas's own chronic discontent, and suggest a common interpretation of that discontent. For the most part he sees himself as a peculiarly sensitive and unhappy representative of a generation that has come to recognize its separation from the whole life of nature. But seeking the meaning of the 'unreality' he feels in his own life and in the life of the modern types he portrays, in his latest works he arrives at a less simple explanation. Grounded in self-knowledge still, his speculations lead him finally to a theory concerning the social changes that have taken place in England since the Middle Ages but especially in the previous one or two hundred years. Our sense of unreality is, according to this, a sign of a lack of wholeness in modern man's experience; the consequence not of a disconnection from outer nature but of a split in the inner nature of man, paralleling the division between town and country that began to appear shortly after the death of Chaucer but did not become a visible rift until the later eighteenth century. Thomas was interested in William Morris partly as a key figure in this reading of English history. Mackail's life of Morris reveals him as at once a 'hearty countryman' and 'a conscious and satisfied Cockney', but for Thomas the significant fact is that

the union was an imperfect one. For most of his life he was a somewhat dismayed countryman, but an imperfect Londoner. Probably he was one of those survivors who cannot accept the distinction and division between town and country which has been sharpening ever since

> 'London was a grey-walled town,
> And slow the pack-horse made his way
> Across the curlew-haunted down.'[54]

He contrasts 'the modern sad passion for Nature' – a phrase that captures his sense of a relationship lost – with the matter-of-fact attitude of the eighteenth century. For Smollett 'the country was neither a bore nor a religion, but an unexacting neighbour'.[55] Town and country living were part of a whole life, taken for granted, unsentimentalized. 'The town was not yet a symbol of bondage, a scapegoat of civilization.'[56] The modern nature lover's experience of nature is coloured with the lurid hues of his intense desire to possess what he cannot possess. Thomas even dares to suggest that Meredith, apostle of paganism and open air life, is in fact 'a Londoner's poet', for whom the countryside exists to release the city-dweller from his bondage.[57] The city is the scapegoat for him as it is for Arnold, and for Thomas as he frequently presents himself. He quotes some lines from 'Thyrsis', the feeling of which, he says, 'helps to give the country a kind of allegorical thinness, as if it were chiefly a symbol of escape from the world of "men and towns" '.[58] And on the boyhood explorations of nature undertaken by the narrator of *The Happy-Go-Lucky Morgans* with a friend, he makes this judgment: 'No wonder Our Country was supernaturally beautiful. It had London for a foil and background' (p. 68). Another consequence in Arnold's work of this artificial relationship with nature is, so to speak, a domestication of it in his descriptions. Neither in 'Thyrsis' nor in 'The Scholar Gipsy' is there more than 'a graceful wildness';[59] the scene is either a garden or landscape transformed into garden.

In Chaucer's time town and country living were in essentials the same; man was whole because his relationship with nature and his social life were not mutually exclusive experiences. By the eighteenth century the separation had taken place, but the two kinds of living retained their identities; even though the cultivated man of that time was likely to be a townsman by preference, he loved 'the fields in their season'.[60] In Arnold's picture of nature, as in that of so many nineteenth-century writers, we see the country being adopted by the town, made over into the townsman's image of it, and losing some of its wildness in the process. Evidently Thomas sees this as a loss, yet his attitude is not uniformly disapproving or regretful. He writes satirically in *The Country* of the villa men's embellishments of nature around their Surrey residences, where they have 'caused a delicate kind of scenery, semi-rural, semi-urban', and 'the protected wilderness, burrowed under by a railway, lies between trim exotic gardens and ploughland or pasture' (p. 35). But in a series of sketches entitled 'London Miniatures' he discloses a wry but sympathetic feeling for the delicate wildness of countryside on the outskirts of London. He is appreciative of the combination in Richmond Park, for example, of 'the uncultivated and the refined.'[61] It is like other parks in this, but the qualities it has in common with them 'appear to be in greater perfection, because the walls keep in the deer and the peace, but keep out London'. Immediately he recognizes the artificiality of this, but he accepts it as necessary in our age. 'Of course they keep out other things, so that in a sense the park is only half real, as if it were under a glass-case. Without the glass-case, however, it could not exist; it would be destroyed by the life which it now excludes or converts.'[62]

And so Thomas's theory of social and psychological change in England leads, as does Eliot's suggestion that a dissociation of sensibility set in during the seventeenth century, to the notion of a lost order of life. As Thomas's spokesman in *The Country* says, only some 'well-preserved fragments of old England' (p. 7), when a man could belong at the same time to nature and to human society, are left. Old England means also a 'small intelligible England' (p. 6) such as Elizabeth still ruled, in which the 'fifteen or twenty square miles' (p. 7) of native land known intimately may be justifiably regarded as a microcosm of the whole country. Love of one place, a specific locality, is the foundation of patriotism, and patriotism is the veneration felt for an ideal of England. Only where that ideal is closely enough related to the actualities of English life and landscape can locality be an adequate image for it. But England is now not only densely populated and intricately organized, but is many things together that are hard to reconcile. 'What with Great Britain, the British Empire, Britons, Britishers, and the English-speaking world, the choice offered to whomsoever would be patriotic is embarrassing and he is fortunate who can find an ideal England of the past, present, and the future to worship, and embody it in his native fields and meadows or his garden as in a graven image';[63] and robbed of 'the small intelligible England of Elizabeth' we have been 'given the word Imperialism instead', an abstraction for the concretion of things known, which alone can be the nucleus of patriotic feeling.[64]

Thomas was not afraid to refer to the lost order as 'merry England'. This phrase fell into disrepute long before it received its *coup de grâce* from Kingsley Amis in *Lucky Jim*. But Thomas does not use it thoughtlessly. During the course of some meditation on the nature of patriotism he notes that Robert of Gloucester had called England 'merry' at a time when the inhabitants of this island were perhaps first beginning to feel secure in their national identity; 'merry' expressed no more than a man's love for his country and came into use as men felt themselves and the places they knew best to be part of the larger England.[65] It is true, however, that Thomas also uses the phrase with a more objective meaning, though one still linked with the feelings of the patriot. Mr Morgan in *The Happy-Go-Lucky Morgans* was of the opinion that 'they were merry in the old days with little cause, while today, whatever cause there might be, few persons possessed the ability' (p. 220). Mr Stodham then preaches a sermon to prove that England is 'more than a geographical expression' (p. 220). He quotes from

Coleridge's 'Fears in Solitude', 'There lives nor form nor feeling in my soul/Unborrowed from my country', in support of his contention that 'England made you and of you is England made' (pp. 221–2). We have each of us some of the blood and spirit of our great soldiers and poets: 'in proportion as we are good and intelligent we can respond to them and understand them as those who are not Englishmen cannot . . . Deny England, and we deny them and ourselves' (pp. 223–4). To feel this unity of self and country is to feel a merriness without material cause, to be capable of more than personal happiness and unhappiness. To revert to the quotation, from Thomas's spokesman in *The Country*, with which I began this chapter: for those who cannot experience such intensely patriotic feelings *'There is nothing left for us to rest upon,* great, venerable, or mysterious, which can take us out of ourselves, and give us that more than human tranquillity now to be seen in a few old faces of a disappearing generation' (p. 6). Thomas seems to believe that few people after the time of Wordsworth and Coleridge have been able to feel this close bond. Improvements in comfort and health and the rapid acquisition in the nineteenth century of vast quantities of less immediate knowledge have perhaps brought greater ease and power; but, to continue the quotation from *The Country*, 'to be a citizen of infinity is no compensation for the loss of that tranquillity'.

2 The 'Desert Places'

The woods around it have it – it is theirs.
All animals are smothered in their lairs.
I am too absent-spirited to count;
The loneliness includes me unawares.

And lonely as it is, that loneliness
Will be more lonely ere it will be less –
A blanker whiteness of benighted snow
With no expression, nothing to express.

Robert Frost, 'Desert Places'

I

What does it mean? Tired, angry, and ill at ease,
No man, woman, or child alive could please
Me now.   'Beauty'

This is a characteristic mood – some would say the characteristic mood
– of Edward Thomas's poetry. It varies in intensity of expression,
ranging from a diffused brooding sadness to a sharp articulation of
despair; the restless discontent of these lines comes somewhere between
the two. Whether or not it is his principal poetic concern, it is certainly a
major concern; any admirer of Thomas who thinks that his poetic work
amounts to a more valuable achievement than a preoccupation with
such a mood and subject-matter would normally permit must try to
explain why. It will not do to say that the best poems are those that have
no connection with this area of feeling, for this is not so. Nor will an
invocation of Coleridge's name protect Thomas from the charge of
expressing a limited range and an unfruitful kind of feeling. There is
only one 'Dejection Ode'. It would be better to recall Coleridge's
remark, founded on bitter experience, that 'When a Man is unhappy, he
writes damned bad Poetry.' In this connection it is pertinent to note that
in most instances Thomas's is a remembered or recreated depression.

Though we associate depression – to give it a general name – with
Thomas's poetry, 'Beauty' is exceptional in displaying it as nakedly as
this. I take it as my starting-point, however, because we sense that some
such combination of feelings underlies, perhaps initiates, many poems
that are less direct in method. This poem is also unusual in the outright

35

challenge of its question, yet, plainly, a question of this order, albeit unformulated, guides the poet's exploration of his experience in a large number of his poems. Of course, to ask what a state of mind *means* is almost to ensure that the question cannot be answered; there are too many contexts within which the state of mind might be considered. Evidently Thomas knows this and no direct answer is attempted.

This is not to say, as some critics have said, that Thomas, lacking the detachment — and the freedom — of complete self-knowledge, ever presents himself as merely the victim of his temperament. An understanding of the personal condition which prompted the question is implicit, with different emphases and varying degrees of fullness, in most of the poems affected by it. This is true even of the poem ominously entitled 'Melancholy', one of the very few unsatisfactory poems in Thomas's work, which softens the reality of what it depicts (though, no doubt, this has secured it a place in the anthologies). It induces and condones more than it presents and analyses the 'strange sweetness' of abandoning oneself to despair. 'Melancholy / Wrought magic', he confesses, and the poem is partly caught in its spell, but only partly; some of the facts of his condition are clear enough:

> so that if I feared the solitude
> Far more I feared all company: too sharp, too rude,
> Had been the wisest or the dearest human voice.
> What I desired I knew not, but whate'er my choice
> Vain it must be, I knew.

He knows something, if not everything, and the sharp distinctions and firm rhythm of these lines, if not of the whole poem, contain a clear recognition of what it is. 'Wind and Mist' is a much surer achievement, and is therefore more representative of the self-knowledge that informs all his poetry. It is one of several poems in which Thomas or a character representing him talks to a stranger. The Thomas character, here recalling his unhappiness in a house built for him and his family by Geoffrey Lupton, a handsome building on high land with a fine view over a valley of hedged fields, tells a casually encountered sightseer of the mists — at once real mist and the grey mental world ('like chaos surging back') of depression — that in fact continually obscured the view. The perceptions dramatized in this meeting inside the gateway of the house between its erstwhile inhabitant, living in cloud and mist, and the appreciative but ingenuous stranger, who has 'always lived on the firm ground', are, though subtle, also clear and unwavering, and combine with a large measure of self-mockery sufficient self-respect — expressed wryly and sardonically, however — to save it from the complacency of indiscriminately dismissive self-contempt. The poet's understanding of the situation has a moral dimension. Choice of this site for a house, isolated, aloof, perched 'on a cliff's edge almost', is made to yield a psychological significance, one hinting at the solitary's pride and a dreamer's idealism:

> 'I did not know it was the earth I loved
> Until I tried to live there in the clouds
> And the earth turned to cloud'.

There was a garden to be worked and a child was born in the gable room: ' "But flint and clay and childbirth were too real / For this cloud castle" '.

It is another kind of understanding that, discerning more in his melancholy than a peculiarity of temperament, attaches it to a larger context. True, looking back on his memories of life in another house, the speaker in 'The Long Small Room' – this is fictional autobiography – sees himself as sharing the helplessness of 'moon, sparrow, and mouse', involuntary observers 'That witnessed what they could never understand / Or alter or prevent in the dark house': no moral perspective ever leads him to challenge the fatalism of this assertion. Nevertheless his sufferings gain an objective reality from being connected with his professional circumstances, the doom of the literary hack and journalist, whose right hand must continue to crawl

> crab-like over the clean white page,
> Resting awhile each morning on the pillow,
> Then once more starting to crawl on towards age.

And their significance grows momentous when we notice how the shape of the room resembles a coffin (it 'Narrowed up to the end the fireplace filled, / Although not wide'), and how the 'dark house' has become in consequence the close container of a mortal existence. It is not unusual in Thomas's poems for the personal mood to lead to an awareness of the general human condition. 'Rain', his most direct and painful expression of despair, in its first three lines moves rapidly out beyond the personal without losing anything of the personal anguish:

> Rain, midnight rain, nothing but the wild rain
> On this bleak hut, and solitude, and me
> Remembering again that I shall die . . .

At this point, lying awake in the army hut, he ceases to be a lonely individual and becomes all men suddenly remembering that they will die. The circle of meaning continues to expand, rippling out from this centre of disturbance to the last line.

Depression in the extreme forms that he knew in his life rarely enters Thomas's poems with this kind of force; usually it has been tempered with reflection before the poetic imagination has gone to work on it. But an unassuaged mild discontent or melancholy seems to be the medium through which most of his experiences, even the happiest of them, are received. His memory of the 'three lovely notes' sung by 'the unknown bird', in the poem of that title, is certainly a happy memory, yet at first he judges the song to have been 'sad more than joyful'. The paradox bears witness to a strange blend of feelings, characteristic of Thomas. The strangeness is intensified but the paradox dissolved by another distinction: 'but if sad / 'Twas sad only with joy too, too far off / For me to taste it'. The lovely, unidentifiable song of an unseen bird, that sometimes came near but sounded 'distant still', is emblematic of Thomas's dissociation from general living: he recognizes and yearns for a vigour he cannot enjoy, at least not fully.

At the back of the general melancholy and the attacks of depression is this impregnable isolation. The plangent intonings of despair in the opening lines of 'Rain' reach their logical climax with the stark declaration, 'I was born into this solitude'. Nearly always uncomfortable with other people, rarely able to break through his self-consciousness, he confessed to Gordon Bottomley in 1904 that for him 'social intercourse is only an intense form of solitude'.[1] It is the given element, assumed if not stated, of each human situation presented in the poetry. Almost any poem could illustrate this. It is as much part of the – in some ways – peaceful experience of 'It Rains' as it is of 'The New House', where it constitutes the very essence of his misery. 'It Rains' characteristically begins with the poet alone, his isolation emphasized by the rain and the stillness of the scene. It is characteristic too in showing the poet *searching* an orchard, now neglected and overgrown, where he had once courted Helen, thinking 'of two walking, kissing there' – stirring memories, in a scene where 'nothing stirs', of one moment when he had managed to forget his solitude. 'It Rains' nevertheless describes feelings that almost anyone might have. 'The New House' indicates feelings peculiar to Thomas. It is strange but distinctively expressive of his sensibility that on first entering a new house, the house at Wick Green also recalled in 'Wind and Mist', he should feel not hope but 'dread' and find there nothing but a new confirmation of an old familiar solitude. 'I was alone / In the house' is his first thought, from which follows (inevitably for Thomas) anticipation of

> Nights of storm, days of mist, without end;
>   Sad days when the sun
> Shone in vain: old griefs and griefs
>   Not yet begun.

In this house Thomas suffered a nervous breakdown: 'the sun / Shone in vain' indeed. 'Whate'er my choice / Vain it must be, I knew', he writes in the lines of 'Melancholy' already quoted; the word or the phrase runs like a refrain through the poems of this mood. In 'It Rains', too, the poet is 'nearly as happy as possible / To search the wilderness in vain though well' – a phrase which, with a scrupulous detachment, measures the immeasurable, the degree of acceptance of and resistance to an inescapable condition. Solitude and depression are recognized as permanencies in his existence.

II

Although this is so, and although an always unsocial and sometimes melancholy temperament is the dark lens through which he perceives the world, this is not to say that it controls the viewpoint. Poems may start there, literally or in the sense that it is a precondition of their coming into being, but they do not end there. Even in poems most burdened with the poet's hopeless sense of his isolation the poetic impulse is something more than the simple need to record and brood upon the isolation and the burden of it. Self-understanding in Thomas's poems is not a passive or merely clinical process; as my mention of the moral tenor of the characterization in 'Wind and Mist' has implied, the viewpoint is, where criticism is appropriate, a critical one. This is no less true of 'Beauty', the poem with which I chose to open this discussion of Thomas's depressive temperament and its effect on his poetry.

My contention is that, when the limitations of his personality, his melancholy or his solitary disposition, are the theme of his poems, not only is the poetic temper critical but the poet's critical frame of reference is wider than the man's – wider, that is, than one conceivably available to the solitary or melancholic himself. Before proceeding to illustrate this I must, first, make a further distinction and an exception. The frame of reference sometimes includes more than the human values that the word 'critical' normally denotes. A judicative approach suits those poems in which, for example, Thomas's melancholy is presented as that and nothing more. It is less appropriate to those poems that treat the mood as a matching response to a suprapersonal condition. 'The Long Small Room', as we have seen, offers a view not so much of the (limited) personality as of a human destiny. 'Rain', which carries more personal anguish than perhaps any other poem by Thomas, is nevertheless a meditation on the relationship of love and death, the human and the non-human; where 'Beauty' depicts his inability to love as personal failure, here it is neither criticized nor, we must add, condoned but merely stated; in the wildness of that 'wild rain' are forces beyond human control and judgment.

The critical method ranges from straightforward statement to the dramatic mode of 'Wind and Mist' and 'The Chalk Pit'. A typical direct critical statement is this from 'There Was a Time': 'I never would acknowledge my own glee / Because it was less mighty than my mind / Had dreamed of'. Inordinacy of expectation – perfectionism – is the verdict pronounced on Thomas's chronic discontent in these lines, as it is in part the charge laid against the solitary in 'I Built Myself a House of Glass':

> I built myself a house of glass:
> It took me years to make it:
> And I was proud. But now, alas!
> Would God someone break it.
>
> But it looks too magnificent.
> No neighbour casts a stone
> From where he dwells, in tenement
> Or palace of glass, alone.

This is Thomas's image of himself as 'an isolated selfconsidering brain'.[2] Anyone who has experienced prolonged depression would take it to be a metaphor for that kind of isolation in particular. Few sufferers, however, would claim moral responsibility for the condition as Thomas does. The language recalls his account in the essay 'How I Began' of how in his precocious youth he built himself a house of style based on literary models with no materials from spoken idiom; we know that it took him at least a decade to dismantle that imposing edifice. The image, I think, includes all this. The ascribing of his insulation from the general life to a form of pride is a critical interpretation of his disposition frequent in the poems. I have noted it in 'Wind and Mist': the wincing of a past self from the rigours of physical existence is complemented by the desire to be separate and aloof, the building of cloud-castles. The nature of the accusation in that poem is clear enough; the moral grounds for it are perhaps not so clear: despite the uncompromisingly scornful, self-castigating tone of Thomas's persona, we are nevertheless left wondering – intentionally, it seems – whether he can be held altogether responsible for his condition. We are allowed to have no such doubts concerning 'A Lofty Sky' and 'Ambition'. In both poems an ecstasy of *Sehnsucht* is presented with full intensity and irony combined. The same image – a skyward aspiration spurning earth, the flight of the eye upward – an obsessive one in Thomas's writing, dominates them:

Today I want the sky,
The tops of the high hills,
Above the last man's house, . . .
The desire of the eye
For sky, nothing but sky.
I sicken of the woods
And all the multitudes
Of hedge-trees.

'The Lofty Sky'

Idealism – yearning for the infinite singleness and sameness of being, free of the tangle and variety of finite life – entails misanthropy; 'multitudes' joins weariness of earth to weariness of people. The same flight of the eye upward, and a similar desire to still the movement and dissolve the body and multiplicity of life into smoke and cloud, inform these lines from 'Ambition':

And through the valley where all the folk astir
Made only plumes of pearly smoke to tower
Over dark trees and white meadows . . .
A train that roared along raised after it
And carried with it a motionless white bower
Of purest cloud . . .

It is possible, I suppose, to read these poems as neutral renderings of *Sehnsucht*, but when in 'The Lofty Sky' Thomas compares the air to a river and himself to a fish swimming in it I cannot hear the last lines, mimicking as they do, not the parable of the Prodigal Son, but the grandiose gesture of Yeats's 'Lake Isle of Innisfree', as anything other than self-parody: 'and I / Would arise and go far / To where the lilies are'. I think the jackdaw in 'Ambition' 'racing straight and high / Alone, shouting like a black warrior / Challenges and menaces to the wide sky' likewise caricatures with its mad truculence the egoism of the poet's 'ambition'. But ambition for what? he asks, and claims he does not know. As often with Thomas, however, the poem knows more than the poet will admit:

Time
Was powerless while that lasted. I could sit
And think I had made the loveliness of prime,
Breathed its life into it and were its lord,
And no mind lived save this 'twixt clouds and rime.
Omnipotent I was . . .

This is, surely, a Lucifer's dream of usurpation, the pride that comes before the fall, *the* Fall ('But the end fell like a bell. / The Bower was scattered; far off the train roared'). This Lucifer, besides, is a Romantic poet, blurring distinctions between perception and conception,

41

imagining that his work reproduces the act of Creation. It is not the only passage in Thomas's poetry to present the Wordsworthian unitary view – mind and object dissolved into each other – as a delusion, and a seductive one for the solitary who seeks compensation for his impotence in the vicarious power exercised through the mastery of words. 'Yes. Sixty miles of South Downs at one glance,' says the former occupant of the house in the clouds in 'Wind and Mist', 'Sometimes a man feels proud of them, as if / He had just created them with one mighty thought'. Sometimes a man has the illusion of possessing the 'mighty' power that the perfectionist young Thomas of 'There Was a Time' only 'dreamed of'; the title phrase, echoed from both Wordsworth's 'Immortality Ode' and Coleridge's 'Dejection Ode', gives the aspiration its literary source and links this poem with 'Wind and Mist', 'Ambition' and 'The Lofty Sky' in being an exposure of the pride and delusion of Wordsworthian Romanticism. Turning back again to those lines in 'Ambition', one is tempted to find a pun in 'rime', an alternative spelling of rhyme and a rhyme word here. It would be the most apposite criticism of Thomas's *romantic* self, living in his cloud-castle, half believing that his mind had swallowed the solid world and that no contrary reality obstructed free communication between dream and verse.

At the other end of the critical scale from the straightforward statement of such poems as 'I Built Myself a House of Glass' are the dramatizations of 'Wind and Mist' and, more elaborately, 'The Chalk Pit'. In the latter Thomas splits himself into two characters, a romantic and a realistic self, and the poem is a conversation between them. The abandoned chalk pit has a fascination for both of them, though the realist is reluctant to admit it; it is the romantic who sees it as 'strangely dark, / And vacant of a life but just withdrawn'. He carries about with him a memory of the place visited two or three times before, which may, however, be partly imaginary, 'For another place, / Real or painted, may have combined with it' – a composite image, then – and it is clear that the 'emptiness and silence / And stillness' of such scenes haunt him because they externalize, as they correspond to, an *inner* vacancy. The scene is one of several images in Thomas's poetry of, so to speak, posthumous living: the ghost self that in his isolation he continually feels himself to be. Whereas the realist in speculating about the chalk pit's history would 'prefer the truth / Or nothing', and answers his companion's enquiries with facts – 'It is called the Dell. / They have not dug chalk here for a century. / That was the ash trees' age' – the romantic would rather find in its desolation some 'tragical' significance and 'make a tale' of it. But the point of the dialogue form is not that the realist should win all the tricks; the critical direction is not all one way, and the advantage of a dramatic invention is that it encourages flexibility. Maybe this is, as Edna Longley persuasively suggests, 'a portrait of the divided artist', the self-consciously literary, 'fanciful' writer of the early prose, less visible in the later work, confronted by a Thomas who ever since the *Jefferies* book (1909) has been learning to submit 'his imagination to the actualities of a situation'.[3] Yet to make this a dialogue simply between an earlier and a later and therefore truer self – in fact, Mrs. Longley, though she identifies the realist with 'the truer Thomas', is careful not to do this – would be to misrepresent, if only slightly, the total effect of the poem. The proximity of life and death, the human and the non-human, represented concretely in such scenes, intimates real mysteries, to which neither speaker makes a commensurate response. The realist, giving the lie to the other's histrionic mystifications and voicing a 'healthier' attitude, tries at first, with a story of a man who looked for birds' nests not mysteries in the chalk pit, and generally by a breezy matter-of-factness, to empty mystery out of the scene – 'Here, in fact, is nothing at all' – only to be betrayed by his own plainness of language into a truer and indeed more haunting representation of what it is, yet without quite realizing that he has done so:

> Except a silent place that once rang loud,
> And trees and us – imperfect friends, we men
> And trees since time began; and nevertheless
> Between us still we breed a mystery.

The romantic glamourizes and trivializes the mystery by making something too personal of it, but at least draws our attention to its existence. His fault, in the critical perspective of the poem, is not that he finds his psyche reflected in the chalk pit (which seems to be the chief cause of the realist's impatience with him), but that he finds only that and closes his eyes to the impersonal dimension of the mystery which the realist stumbles on, the larger implications of the scene, which have to do with that close conjunction of life and death first noticed by the romantic.

III

Introducing my discussion of the critical orientation of these poems I said that if they begin in moods of anger or discontent or dejection they do not end there; it was at that stage of my argument a way of indicating the measure of self-detachment revealed by a critical approach to experience. But it implies a larger claim, and now is the time to go further in the direction signposted by that remark. Self-criticism plays an important part in 'Beauty' but is barely perceptible in 'Rain'; yet in their plots – the graph of thought and feeling traced by each poem – they are interestingly similar, and in this respect exemplify another characteristic of Thomas's poetry. 'Rain' moves quickly out from and then gradually curves back to the despair dramatized in the desolate scene of the first three lines. In its outward curve, however, the poem not only universalizes the personal mood ('Remembering again that I shall die . . . Blessed are the dead that the rain rains upon'), demonstrating an expansion of self that I noted in my earlier discussion of it, but at its peak, for a moment, releases the poet into a new area of selflessness:

> But here I pray that none whom once I loved
> Is dying tonight or lying still awake
> Solitary, listening to the rain . . .

At the same time as he is declaring roundly that he has 'no love which this wild rain / Has not dissolved except the love of death' he is displaying the very feeling for others that he says he lacks. This does not so much contradict the dominant emotion as locate it on a map of evaluated experience, placing it in relation to a positive movement of feeling by reference to which its limitations can be defined. 'Beauty', too, after its opening description of the poet, 'tired, angry, and ill at ease', moves away from that mood. Beginning in dejection, like 'Rain', it does not, however, curve out and back but continues to expand, culminating in its antithesis, the heart's imaginary enjoyment of what it lacks, a 'home and love'. Yet if this should suggest a facile, sentimental process, it would give a wrong impression of the poem. Even the opening lines, with their forthright naming and curt tone, read more like an accusation than a complaint, and in the next few lines the implied accusation develops into a morally incisive self-dissection:

> And yet I almost dare to laugh
> Because I sit and frame an epitaph –
> 'Here lies all that no one loved of him
> And that loved no one'. Then in a trice that whim
> Has wearied.

The suspended bitter laughter and the epitaph are judgments on the poet's lovelessness, yet they are framed with a self-contempt that is but the obverse of self-pity, and the last sentence, with its shrug of dismissal, turning from the covert gratifications of self-chastisement, opens the way for a more profound image of his condition. The movement is from

44

an 'angry' mood through an angry rejection of it to a natural image that in turn makes possible, if only momentarily, an experience in imagination of the love that fails to sustain him in his life:

> But, though I am like a river
> At fall of evening while it seems that never
> Has the sun lighted it or warmed it, while
> Cross breezes cut the surface to a file,
> This heart, some fraction of me, happily
> Floats through the window even now to a tree
> Down in the misting, dim-lit, quiet vale,
> Not like a pewit that returns to wail
> For something it has lost, but like a dove
> That slants unswerving to its home and love.
> There I find my rest, as through the dusk air
> Flies what yet lives in me. Beauty is there.

These poems illustrate the two principal ways in which the positive nature of the creative impulse expresses itself in Thomas's poetry: on the one hand, by an appeal to values as criteria for measuring his insufficiency and incompleteness; on the other, in the transcendence of personal inadequacy by an act of imagination.

In poems as rooted in personal misery as these are it is notable that the main focus is not on the texture of the experience, vividly rendered though this is in the opening of 'Rain' and in the river image of 'Beauty', but on the experience as an index of emotional and spiritual incapacity in the poet. His condition is perceived less in terms of itself than in terms of the personal and social qualities seen to be lacking, and what is lacking sets the standards by which he comprehends the character and judges the extent of his failure as a human being. Few poems are as close to his suffering as these, but many touch on it lightly, or, as it were, parenthetically. Several contain images of the poet or his state of mind which present him as in some way disablingly incomplete, insubstantial, or enervated. In 'Two Pewits' we see him as a 'ghost', who watches the sport of the two birds and 'wonders why / So merrily they cry and fly, / Nor choose 'twixt earth and sky'; a ghost, that is, in lacking the spontaneity, immediacy, and wholeness of being which constitute their vitality. Thomas is nearly always a divided person having to make a choice between the real and the ideal (earth and sky) or struggling to compose their differences. The exhausted or unworked chalk pit, whose emptiness seemingly expects a ghost-life and corresponds, I have suggested, to the psychic vacancy – the 'absent-spiritedness' (to adopt a word coined by Frost to describe the same state in 'Desert Places') – of the first speaker in that poem, has a parallel in 'The Hollow Wood', in which the hollowness also bespeaks an absence of something. Neither poem gives the image of emptiness an overtly personal significance, but the latent human analogy which the mere fascination exercised by the chalk pit on the two characters discovers for us also makes itself felt strongly in the language of 'The Hollow Wood'. 'In the pale hollow wood', deprived of sun, 'birds swim like fish' and trees live a tortured half-life: 'Lichen, ivy, and moss / Keep evergreen the trees / That stand half-flayed and dying'.

The criteria of living by which Thomas measures his inadequacy in these poems – spontaneous delight and energy, untrammelled expression of one's nature (birds that do not swim but fly), and undivided sensibility – are psychological; I mean simply that they refer to forces within the personality. A label of this kind is a matter of convenience; it assumes a doubtless inadmissible division between inner and outer: a personality is partly, perhaps very largely, constituted by the kinds of relationships it makes or is able to make with the outside world. Personal well-being is also social and 'natural' well-being, and Thomas the 'born' solitary was acutely aware of this. The values invoked in his poems are more frequently social and natural – connection with others and otherness – than (in the narrow sense) personal. I have mentioned the charge of lovelessness in 'Beauty' and the image of love with which the poem ends. This account of the poem needs expanding. The heart released from its sullen prison, and drawn to a particular tree in the vale below, finds there not one thing but two things, 'its home and love', and 'home' itself is not a simple concept. The two words are defined by the contrast between the description of the chill, shadowed, sharply rippled river, an image of (loveless, homeless) abandonment, and the image of the far off tree in the soft 'misting' light of the valley. We have a constellation of related values: natural warmth of feeling (sunlit water) – a giving and a receiving of love – to set against the crossness of the 'cross breezes', a pun to suggest with unobtrusive precision that his malaise, too, has both inner and outer causes (both crossness and being crossed); home, in the sense of rootedness, the nature from which natural feeling derives some of its sustenance, and by extension, since love is the positive moving force in feeling, the only soil in which love can achieve fullness of growth. This natural world is the central value in 'Wind and Mist'. From the winds of uncontrollable violent feeling, the mists of neurotic dissociation from reality, and the cloud-castles of idealism, Thomas appeals to the world outside the enclosed self, the visible and tangible earth and rural England – though less the English landscape than an England conceived as the larger unity of which our individual lives are part:

46

The fields beyond that league close in together
And merge, even as our days into the past,
Into one wood that has a shining pane
Of water.

These values are hedged around, however, with appropriate scepticisms. The lines are spoken not by Thomas's (neurotic) persona but by the (normal) sightseeing stranger who listens uncomprehendingly but kindly and courteously to his tale; they are part of a conventionally patriotic speech, the exaggerated enthusiasm of which is rendered with a certain good-humoured irony. Even in the lines quoted we are meant to separate the serious idea of England as an all-encompassing impersonal reality from the dreamy nostalgia of its expression. The invocation of earth as a standard of sane living is also qualified. 'I did not know it was the earth I loved', confesses the neurotic, but earth is not always easy to love: solid is also hard, and the solid earth, though 'real enough', is painfully real when it means working 'a garden / Of flint and clay'; and the life of earth is 'too real' when it includes the groans of a woman during a difficult childbirth 'while the wind chilled a summer dawn'. And since our simple patriot is the sole representative offered by Thomas of 'Those who have always lived on the firm ground', being realistic can also connote being unimaginative. Again we are invited by the poem to discriminate between kinds of reality and degrees of realism.

The sharply self-critical eye that Thomas turns upon his experience, and the characteristic movement of poems outward and away from the originating personal conditions of enervation and isolation, show that their *imaginative* centre is not in the personal situation but in the positive emotions the lack of which defines that situation. Not only are these positives present as moral landmarks from which the poems take their bearings, but also, almost invariably, they are realized in the texture of the verse: sound, rhythm, and tone express attitudes and a temper that implicitly reveal the capacities supposedly lacking. Edna Longley points out that the opening confession of numbness in 'Tears' ('It seems I have no tears left') is belied by the poem itself, which manifests a 'process of emotional and imaginative thaw' (p. 189). The poem seems to acquire energy as it gathers momentum. The evidence of positive feeling in a poem is frequently more pervasive than that. The normative values of 'Wind and Mist', the common life of earth and, further off, of social relationships (life in common), which are established directly by statement – 'the visible earth / Lay too far off beneath and like a cloud' – and dramatically in the neurotic speaker's mode of address, also invigorate the

47

self-mocking language and fortify the resilience made explicit in its conclusion:

> 'I want to admit
> That I would try the house once more, if I could;
> As I should like to try being young again.'

The tone and language I have in mind are well illustrated by this exchange:

> 'You had a garden
> Of flint and clay, too.' 'True; that was real enough.
> The flint was the one crop that never failed.
> The clay first broke my heart, and then my back;
> And the back heals not.'

'October' hesitates to label as 'melancholy' the mood associated in the poet's mind with the near-suspense of autumn's descent into winter by a spring-like day, but anyone who remembers his first reading of that poem, a reading that failed perhaps to note certain unobtrusive signs, will remember his surprise that the word occurs at all in a poem which registers with such delicate appreciation the fresh life of the scene. In this instance the poet's fullness of response does not contradict so much as blend with the discord between him and the natural cycle also reported in the poem. Feeling, toughness, and responsiveness are the qualities resurrected in these three poems. The verse in 'And You, Helen' ('Household Poem 4, Helen')[4] displays a different kind of quality, one rarely remarked in Thomas's poetry yet frequently to be found in it: poise. It is poise that balances the bantering charm of the conception and the light intimate tone – 'If I could choose / Freely in that great treasure-house / Anything from any shelf' – with the darker implications of what follows, 'I would give you back yourself', and what precedes, 'all you have lost / Upon the travelling waters tossed, / Or given to me', and what the poem ends with:

> And myself, too, if I could find
> Where it lay hidden and it proved kind.

For the light touch with which he handles a subject painful to him and his wife – his own suffering and consequent unkindness to her – is the outward expression of an achieved inner proportion between acknowledgement of and remorse for the wrong inflicted. It is at once the lightness of an accurate mind, which, as it reviews its contemplated gifts, calculates possibilities and measures distinctions, and of a sweet, unselfconscious generosity. In short, the light tone and movement reveal not whimsical evasion but a healthy imagination, tempered rather than weakened by its frequent immersions in the cold waters of misery and conflict.

IV

So far I have spoken of Thomas's melancholy and sense of isolation as ever-present ingredients in the mixture of feelings, attitudes, and thoughts of which the poems are composed: they are an important part – I have suggested that they form something like the substructure – of the mind that creates. I am sure that Thomas, too, knew them to be constants of his personality, and yet frequently the situation in a poem is so focused that what we see, or what we see first, is not lack – inadequacy, emotional impoverishment, or the general negative realities of transience and non-existence – but loss. The condition has been given a pseudo-historical or mythic status: something has 'happened' to dispossess the poet of emotions and relationships he feels he once had, the loss of which has diminished his humanity. A Thomas poem often depicts a search for that lost place or state of being, or simply for his lost self, as in 'And You, Helen' ('Household Poem 4, Helen'); other poems record 'moments of everlastingness',[5] which restore to the poet the home, the mental and emotional powers, and the connections with life that cannot be discovered by conscious seeking.

He is intermittently aware that by translating lack into loss he is making a myth of his condition, and is sometimes critical of this activity. The realist in 'The Chalk Pit', impatient with the histrionic fancy of his companion, who would 'prefer to make a tale' of the deserted scene and is obliged to imagine dark events to account for its desolation, is there an agent of the author's scepticism. But most of the poems 'translate' without apology. Half metaphor, half belief, the myth of dispossession is a way of conveying what is mysteriously inexplicable in Thomas's sense of a personal void, and perhaps could not otherwise be expressed. In 'These Things that Poets Said', for example, the poet or his protagonist wonders whether he has ever loved at all, for now he knows, what as a young man he did not know, that he has never experienced the love described by poets. However, he may have experienced another kind of love:

> Only, that once I loved
> By this one argument
> Is very plainly proved:
> I, loving not, am different.

The mock-logic of this is like the negative proof of God. Being without love, and feeling the pain or dullness of that condition (the understatement echoes Wordsworth's 'and, oh! / The difference to me'), proves its existence; and how can you feel its absence and know it exists unless you have already experienced it? Ergo his lovelessness is a love lost. He does not apologize for such logic, but by the protagonist's almost impudent assurance of manner ('very plainly'), an assurance that brooks no contradiction, the poet deftly exposes the unwarrantedness of such confidence. Between the condition and its expression lies the mystery of what it is and what has caused it. Thomas makes use of a similar disparity in 'When We Two Walked'. The memory of happiness that fills the present void might be a genuine recollection:

> And we that were wise live free
> To recall our happiness then.

But an examination of the preceding stanzas suggests that equally it might not. Here is the first stanza and the beginning of the second:

> When we two walked in Lent
> We imagined that happiness
> Was something different
> And this was something less.
>
> But happy were we to hide
> Our happiness . . .

With a characteristic teasing of the sense this word-play opens a gap in the logic that admits doubt. It is still not certain that, except by contrast with the present, the early period was a happy one; only that a present unhappiness has called up its opposite and given it a body, a time, and a place. The same process is enacted on a larger scale in 'Up in the Wind'. Fragments of information offered piecemeal by the publican's daughter, joined to the poet's speculations, hint at a whole representative social history of diminishing community life, to 'explain', we infer, the disconnected living of the present.

The translation of lack into loss is a way of presenting not merely personal and social incapacities but the mystery of existence itself. For this purpose the archetypal myth of dispossession is the expulsion from the Garden of Eden, which in Jewish and Christian tradition constitutes the Fall of Man and 'explains' his condition; a version of it plays its part in 'Old Man'. But making a story of it is not the only way: 'The Chalk Pit' historicizes the condition but 'The Hollow Wood', while using very similar imagery, does not. Earlier, in pointing to the analogy with a personal barrenness in the descriptions of the two places, I drew attention to a latent or concealed significance common to them; I take them to be related images for the 'desert places' of the soul. But primarily and overtly these places of half-life or desertion represent something less easy to name: not a personal or human void, though that is included, but a non-life at the core of life, or the non-being that precedes and concludes but underlies and may indeed erupt into the realm of being. They are, as it were, minute disjunctions in the flow of time, unoccupied spaces within the territory of human activity, where a man may lose himself for a while, yet they are part of the texture of existence, like the spaces between molecules in the composition of matter. Thus the smothered life of 'dead trees on their knees / In dog's-mercury, ivy, and moss' ('The Hollow Wood') and of 'ash trees standing ankle-deep in brier / And bramble' ('The Chalk Pit'), or the remote submerged life of the hollow wood on the one hand, and the 'emptiness and silence / And stillness' of the chalk pit on the other, exist apart from the poet. Nevertheless he is drawn to the wood's horrors ('Fish that laugh and shriek', 'trees / That stand half-flayed and dying') with a shudder of intimate knowledge, and in the person of the romantic is 'haunted' by the chalk pit because he feels he has been there before and it has some elusive meaning for him. Even the comparison of the poet's feelings, in 'Beauty', to 'a river / At fall of evening while it seems that never / Has the sun lighted it or warmed it', though analogical in form, in effect assigns the human mood to a non-human source, to a dark sunken area of being, eternally unvisited by the sun.

A sense of loss principally motivates the exploration undertaken in 'Old Man'; it is, since Leavis wrote about it in *New Bearings in English Poetry*, Thomas's best-known as well as his most far-reaching treatment of that theme. Moving from reflections on the herb and its names, Old Man and Lad's love, to a description of his daughter plucking feathers from the door-side bush and absent-mindedly sniffing her fingers, the poem reaches its experiential centre with the admission, 'As for myself, / Where first I met the bitter scent is lost'. The loss is a failure of memory. Its significance is first of all personal:

> I cannot like the scent,
> Yet I would rather give up others more sweet,
> With no meaning, than this bitter one.

Where an act of memory recovers meaning, meaning is the restoration of continuity between present and past selves and the self-understanding that accrues; the drive to remember is the drive to integrate personal experience. But why should this particular scent, the 'bitter' scent of this particular herb with these names, rather than another, be the one to compel this irresistible, all-expectant curiosity? The plant itself – the bitterness of its scent and the contradiction of its names – not merely the memories it stirs, is the meaning. A search with such slight promptings, the failure of which, nevertheless, leads to 'an avenue, dark, nameless, without end', hopes to discover more than a personal continuity. 'Wind and Mist' gives a hint of what this might be. 'My past and the past of the world were in the wind', says the former occupant of the unhappy house at Wick Green, trying to convey the absoluteness of the wind's rule, the winds of violent impulse that seized his mind. The 'past of the world' is also in the scent of Old Man (or Lad's love). The question is not merely 'what in my past does this scent recall?' but 'what in the world's past does the unlikeable but haunting bitterness of this herb's scent evoke?' Like its names, Thomas's description of it – 'The hoar-green feathery herb, almost a tree' – makes it both old and young at once: hoary with age, green with fresh, eager, delicate youth. It is the bitter essence of life itself. But its significance extends even further than that. Thomas is not 'playing possum', as C. Day Lewis suggests, when he says that 'the names / Half decorate, half perplex, the thing it is' and 'what that is clings not to the names'; the 'thing it is' includes all life in time – it is reflected in the names, but expands beyond it. 'In the name there's nothing' – so the first line ends; the eye and the voice hesitate for a fraction of a second before continuing into the next – 'To one that knows not Lad's love, or Old Man'. 'Nothing' is repeated another three times: the child shredding the tips of the herb on to the path is 'perhaps / Thinking, perhaps of nothing', and the last eight lines, beginning with two more 'nothing's, form a crescendo of negatives:

> I have mislaid the key. I sniff the spray
> And think of nothing; I see and I hear nothing;
> Yet seem, too, to be listening, lying in wait
> For what I should, yet never can, remember:
> No garden appears, no path, no hoar-green bush
> Of Lad's-love, or Old Man, no child beside,
> Neither father nor mother, nor any playmate;
> Only an avenue, dark, nameless, without end.

At each repetition the word becomes more absolute; 'nothing' grows substantial as nothingness, and after the barrage of 'no's, 'neither's and 'nor's, the last line, without them, though defining a negative condition, also seems to present us with something paradoxically substantial. In the Lord's Prayer God the Father reigns 'for ever and ever world without end' in a positive eternity; there seems no other way of identifying the state conjured by Thomas than as a negative eternity ('nothing . . . without end'). Here lack almost discards its negative implications. Failure to identify an elusive sensation is, finally, a minor episode in a poem of larger ambition and achievement. A pursuit that brings the poet to the threshold of the inexpressible can be labelled neither failure nor success; the divisions between them collapse. Though nothing is found and the journey ends in darkness, for once it was not 'in vain' (though he says it was); for the darkness is also the source of being where life and non-life dissolve into each other.

Although the poem opens with some tentatively exploratory general remarks about the herb and its names, the immediate stimulus for the self-examination and the metaphysical ponderings of the last fifteen lines is not that but the sight of his daughter picking sprigs of it from the door-side bush. Without the child's presence and the poet's attempt to penetrate her mind the poem would lack a perspective. We half perceive the experience through her eyes before we see it through his. In prospective imagination we follow the track of her adult memory back to its source in the scene that we are actually witnessing:

> Not a word she says;
> And I can only wonder how much hereafter
> She will remember, with that bitter scent,
> Of garden rows, and ancient damson trees
> Topping a hedge, a bent path to a door,
> A low thick bush beside the door, and me
> Forbidding her to pick.

Our eyes first take in the general view, pause at the damson trees that mark the boundaries of the garden, then travel in from the garden hedge, curving along the path, to the door and, reaching their destination, the bush of Old Man beside the door, with a motion and a syntax that mimics the homing in of memory on what it seeks. Whether the child will, in fact, remember nothing or something or all of this scene, the poet apparently holds the 'key' he claims he has 'mislaid', the key that by pinpointing time and place unlocks the 'meaning' of the scent. For if some such episode will explain whatever puzzlement lingers in the mind of his daughter as years hence she ruminates on the associations of the herb's scent, then conceivably, as he could provide the key for her, so some other person similarly placed could remove the darkness from his own memory. Such logic, by confining meaning to the personal and draining all metaphysical significance out of the poem, would, of course, make nonsense of it. Yet, since the accounts are made parallel to invite comparison, the logic would be unavoidable if indeed they were comparable only at the level of personal memory. But they are not. I omitted from my paraphrase the very last item in the list, the father 'Forbidding her to pick', which is the ultimate destination of the mind's journey back towards the source of memory. Even without this feature the selection and composition of the other features persuade us to see more here than a cottage garden: not only the arrangement, but certain words and phrases such as 'ancient' and 'bent path', and the way each item – an effect of rhythm, I think – slots into place, in combination, evoke a pastoral archetype, the sort that might have been the subject of a Samuel Palmer etching. The unexpected appearance at the end, however, of the poet as a harsh, admonitory father-figure gives a jolt to the pieces of the picture, which then reform as a primal scene, recalling in particular the Garden of Eden, God's prohibition, and the picking of the forbidden fruit in *Genesis*. The arrival at a definite place and the discovery of a name for what memory has been seeking, the Fall (though it is a racial rather than a personal memory), may still seem a flat contradiction of the negative eternity that opens out before the poet's own search for a meaning. But this is not so. There is a darkness implicit in the mythical sense too; it stretches behind the father, the 'me' that stands sentry at the end of that line, blocking the passage to what is beyond. The mystery of the prohibition is untouched, the meaning and origin of a bitterness already there in the Garden still unknown. The myth makes a story of us – gives expression to the mixed emotions, the wonder and the fear, that we feel about our 'fallen' condition, but does not 'explain' it. What we finally remember is that the child, as she sniffs, perhaps thinks of nothing (already) and may years later merely repeat that experience; in this, like her father, she would 'see and . . . hear nothing', glimpsing the same endless inhuman void.

It is but a short step from this presentment of lack, that has ceased to indicate personal limitation, to a poem like 'Lights Out', that welcomes, or accepts, its dominion. Where 'the unknown' commands and 'all must lose / Their way . . . soon or late', it behoves the individual to go out and meet it. The self he has lost and would, if found, give to Helen ('And You, Helen'; 'Household Poem 4, Helen'), he now seeks to lose:

> There is not any book
> Or face of dearest look
> That I would not turn from now
> To go into the unknown . . .
> Its silence I hear and obey
> That I may lose my way
> And myself.

3   The 'Other Man'

The speakers and characters in Thomas's poetry are solitaries, but his frame of reference is, with a few exceptions, social. He understands himself in terms of the polarity of isolation and relationship and judges himself by social values. There are two selves, the man and the poet; to be more precise, there is the man-in-his-poems, his first person or third person self-characterization, and there is the self-judging, self-extending, self-exceeding poet. This is not the only way in which Thomas reveals his divided personality: sometimes it is externalized as a dialogue between two characters – as, for example, the 'absent-spirited', romantic self and the matter-of-fact, realistic self in 'The Chalk Pit', or between the author and the parody reflection of himself in the man he calls the Other Man in *In Pursuit of Spring*. Although the tension between his solitary temperament, on the one hand, and the social impulse which frequently directs his values and quickens his imagination, on the other, is not usually as visible as these self-dramatizations, I think it is more pervasive, more fundamental than them, and it perhaps underlies all the divided selves that appear in Thomas's work. The most comprehensive representation, in his poetry, of this division is in the long poem 'The Other', the title of which recalls the similarly anonymous alter ego in *In Pursuit of Spring*.

Until recently the most widely held view of Thomas was the one put into currency by F. R. Leavis in *New Bearings in English Poetry*. His approach was largely dictated by a concern to differentiate Thomas's 'nature poetry' (though he refuses to call it that) from that of his Georgian contemporaries; to distinguish his 'descriptions of nature' from those of the Victorian Romantics and their early twentieth-century successors (in 1900 Yeats had disallowed all 'descriptions of nature for the sake of nature').[1] Leavis therefore arrives at this formulation of Thomas's characteristic procedure: 'finally one is aware that the outward scene is accessory to an inner theatre.' His individuality, by this account, consists in the unusual degree of self-awareness displayed in his poetry: precise registering and analysis of sensory impressions serves as a technique for recovering perceptions from 'the edge of consciousness' (p. 69). One implication of my argument in the previous chapter is that, though many of his poems are indeed remarkable for their sensitive introspection, a description of his poetry that makes this its central feature is not only incomplete but seriously misleading. This is most apparent in a common judgment of his limitations, which is not explicit in Leavis's brief account but has been derived from it. Coombes, for example, who in his pioneering study refined and elaborated but kept to the spirit of Leavis's insights, claims that Thomas's self-awareness does not amount to 'complete self-knowledge'; he explains that he was 'a poet who never finally satisfied himself as to the cause of his most characteristic mood' (p. 198), the recurrent melancholy. This characterization is supported from a different point of view by D. W. Harding in 'A Note on Nostalgia', published in the first volume of *Scrutiny* (1932), an essay which he has not reprinted and which, in the application of its psychological argument to an interpretation and assessment of Thomas, he would not now defend. His early opinion is, however, quoted by Coombes: 'In most of the poems there is no recognition of any underlying social cause for his feeling.' The contrary is true. The poet's diagnosis of his 'case' is, in fact (if we remove the word 'unadmitted'), precisely Harding's when the latter writes: 'It is hard not to suppose that the unadmitted craving for an adequate social group lay behind his most characteristic moods' (p. 215). By the time he came to write his poetry the craving was admitted and understood; his self-knowledge was exceptionally clear and penetrating. Moreover, we may say that the core of it is in the large number of poems concerned with the solitary's need for social connection, and his inability to satisfy that need. One of these is 'The Other'. Formally, it is true, 'The Other' is unique among Thomas's poems and would therefore seem to be unrepresentative of his achievement. Instead of coming at its personal theme obliquely, by analogies never overtly metaphorical, half-hinted in the descriptive detail, it is organized as an allegorical narrative; yet in the quest motif which shapes the narrative, in the personal theme itself, and in the sensibility displayed, it is essentially characteristic. The difference is that the approach is more direct, the treatment of his experience fuller than usual, but for that very reason it offers itself, more than any other single poem, as a key to Thomas's poetic world – to the situation the poet finds himself in and to the complex of feelings and attitudes with which he responds to it.

The poem begins with the narrator's emergence from the 'dark wood' of his solitude and melancholy into the light and sounds and sweet smells of a sunny day. The 'happy mood' of release is sealed by his arrival at an inn, where, however, he first learns of the existence of someone like him in appearance who passed that way only the day before. Knowledge that he has a double, another self, breeds a restless desire to know him and he sets off in pursuit. The restlessness destroys his new-found happiness. It is plain nevertheless that in some way the news of the other's existence was engendered by, as it coincided with, the time of well-being that started when the journeying poet reached the 'end of forest'. The other, then, is the poet's contented self made potentially present, whose promise was felt by the poet the moment he escaped from the dark world of his isolation.

The happy mood, and therefore the other self, is associated with the companionship of 'road and inn' (which are here specified as 'the sum/Of what's not forest'). Accordingly the poet looks for him in both places, but for a long time without success. Evidently the other is not the poet's 'real self', as Coombes believes, and as at first he seems to be to the questing poet, but an as yet unknown social self and one complementary to the solitary who roams the forest. But the questing self, it proves, is mistaken in supposing that the casual encounters of 'road and inn' are indeed 'the sum/Of what's not forest', that they constitute all the possibilities of social being. The brevity of the 'happy mood' is one indication of the poet's awareness of this. Although the satisfaction of companionship with strangers hinted at the potential existence of this other than solitary self, as one part of social being implies the existence of the rest, the other's total reality cannot be contained within that kind of relationship. In fact pursuit of him develops in the pursuer a dissatisfaction with the people he meets at inns – 'but never-foamless shores / Make better friends than those dull boors': even solitude, which he had escaped, is preferable (though a critical awareness of the speaker's, the solitary's, arrogance, in this comic dramatization of petulance, is not to be missed). The idea of social relationship must include friendship, love, community; the absence of them, we are left to infer, accounts for the failure of the quest.

In a moment of impatience the speaker returns sulkily to his solitude. I use the word 'returns', but this is different from the forest: in some ways it is a continuation of the original search, only deflected from its human–social goal. 'I sought then in solitude': the logic of the statement points to the continuity, but in what sense can this be the same search merely redirected? We deduce that the speaker is trying to repeat the 'happy mood' which had first prompted the quest. It is happiness, the experience of being at peace with himself, that he is pursuing. What, in fact, he finds, as we shall see, is 'not happiness', but something he was not looking for. Night falls, and Thomas devotes three stanzas to the description of an experience presented many times in his poetry, a 'moment of everlastingness'. Darkness brings what light could never bring, a reconciliation of the antinomies of existence, of the actual and the ideal.

> Had there been ever any feud
> 'Twixt earth and sky, a mighty will
> Closed it.

Briefly he enjoys a sense of harmony, of connection with the universe:

> I stood serene,
> And with a solemn quiet mirth,
> *An old inhabitant of earth.* [my italics]

The thread of common motivation that joins the two quests and makes them one is this need to 'belong': to feel part, in the first case, of the human community, and in the second, of the natural universe. But the core of insight – what makes the poem such a fine demonstration of self-knowledge, inherent in the experience as presented – is where the poet *distinguishes between* the two directions of his search:

> Once the name I gave to hours
> Like this was melancholy, when
> It was not happiness and powers
> Coming like exiles home again,
> And weakness[es] quitting their bowers,[2]
> Smiled and enjoyed, far off from men,
> Moments of everlastingness.

The word 'inhabitant' performs the same service as 'Coming like exiles *home* again': in reminding us that home and habitation imply forms of connection with other people, it calls attention to their absence ('far off from men') from this scene – and makes us aware of this as a paradox. The sense of harmony is purchased at a price – the obliteration of life, in an act like murder:

> A dog barked on a hidden rise;
> A marshbird whistled high unseen;
> The latest waking blackbird's *cries*
> *Perished* upon the silence *keen.* [my italics]

The 'solemn quiet mirth' with which the speaker greets the accomplishment of this moment acquires a grimness appropriate to the mood of one who is aligning himself with the forces of night and death.

The experience has contradictory aspects: 'moments of ever-lastingness' are enjoyed but the enjoyment of them is melancholy – or rather, these moments occur in moods which in the past the poet had thought of as melancholy. The key to this contradiction is the poet's awareness that these sporadic apprehensions of a non-human eternity are, as it were, compensation for the lack of that purely human permanence which is the gift of belonging to a stable and continuous community. The experience is melancholy, from one point of view, precisely because it can only take place 'far off from men', because it *confirms* his solitude.

And so the poet seeks company again. Social fulfilment is desirable, but this development in the story does not set a higher value on the pursuit of it than on the momentary experience of harmony enjoyed in solitude. The quest fails, and there is nothing in the poem to suggest that it might succeed or bring the poet any nearer to the self-completion he is seeking. The quest and its goal have, in fact, only a secondary contingent importance; the primary theme, one might say, is the *pathology* of questing – the malady of discontent that makes pursuit of an 'unseen moving goal' a compulsion in the pursuer ('He goes: I follow: no release').

We are directed to this view of the matter by the consistently ironic rendering of the narrator's progress from inn to inn. The irony can be seen at work, for example, in the sixth stanza:

> I was more eager than before
> To find him out and to confess,
> To bore him and to let him bore.
> I could not wait . . .

This, in its context, captures a quality of incontinence in the speaker's emotion, a childish, desperate excess of need, that suggests that he will not find what he is looking for, and that this is because something in the circumstances of pursuit precludes it. (The same touch of ridicule modifies what might otherwise have sounded as pathos in the poem's last stanza.) The narrator, the poet as quester, is seeking completion of himself. The tone of desire in this stanza and elsewhere in the poem – a pathetic (hopeless) eagerness – tells us that this is out of the question; the element of self-mockery in the tone tells us that knowledge of its impossibility controls the poem's complex attitude. The solitary, whose *sickness* is impoverishment of the social instinct, cannot (by definition) know inwardly the social disposition he is seeking, only that he lacks that disposition and suffers for it. The tone of the reference to the 'dull boors', given a petulance that rebounds mockingly on the speaker, betrays the very condition – isolation and estrangement – he is trying to escape.

The first person narrative, which maintains a delicate balance of involvement and detachment in the poet's relation to his questing self, thus presents us with what amounts to an unromantic interpretation of Romantic *Sehnsucht*. The separation of poet from speaker, which makes possible something like a case-study of the speaker's attitudes, is helped by a series of literary allusions, each of which contributes to a psychological and historical placing of his Romanticism. The lines already quoted – 'but never-foamless shores / Make better friends than those dull boors' – call up the solitudes of 'Ode to a Nightingale', the 'magic casements, opening on the foam / Of perilous seas'. And the lines that follow, those which begin the fourth stanza, refer to Tennyson's 'Ulysses':

> Many and many a day like this
> Aimed at the unseen moving goal
> And nothing found but remedies
> For all desire. These made not whole;
> They sowed a new desire, to kiss
> Desire's self beyond control,
> Desire of desire . . .

The manner of allusion to Keats produces a joke – the incongruous juxtaposition of 'dull boors' with the large, vaguely resonant 'never-foamless shores' makes it precisely that – against Romantic withdrawal, displaying it as merely the sulkiness of a frustrated social instinct. The second passage strips Romantic aspiration of the heroic pretensions with which Tennyson had endowed it ('nothing found but . . .'), and then proceeds to diagnose its illness (as Eliot was to say a few years later, 'the only way to cure romanticism is to analyse it'). Romantic desire is as intense as it is vague; the combination indicates its prime characteristic, inordinacy. Lack of an attainable goal that would satisfy all his needs generates in the romantic a contempt for partial satisfaction, the limited but possible, and an ambition obsessively preoccupied with an unknown ('unseen') and unknowable ('moving') wholeness of being.

Thomas thus exposes to critical analysis Romantic habits of mind to which he knew himself to be intermittently addicted. There is point in remembering that he was a younger contemporary of Hardy; like him he was accustomed to view life with a more compelling sense of human limits than was normally exhibited by the poets of the early nineteenth century. Neither Hardy's nor Thomas's work is the worse for this sceptical realism, anticipating as it does a tone characteristic of a later period. But comparison with the best Romantic poetry in other respects works to their disadvantage. The image of human potentiality presented by Hardy, as Donald Davie has argued (*Thomas Hardy and British Poetry*), is in comparison with Wordsworth's a diminished one. Thomas was himself sharply conscious of the gulf dividing his perspective from a Wordsworthian unitary vision, and this consciousness reveals itself in the speculative presence of 'a mighty will' composing the difference between 'earth and sky', reality and dream, which recalls (if I am not mistaken) 'On Westminster Bridge'. We are meant to reflect that the time for such confident statements has passed. The affirmation is immediately compromised, as it has to be for Thomas, by what follows:

> the crocketed dark trees,
> A dark house, dark impossible
> Cloud-towers, one star, one lamp, one peace
> Held on an everlasting lease.

The unified scene is presented as the self-conscious creation of an archaizing Gothic imagination, an 'impossible', even sinister production of the poet's fancy, rather than as a genuine revelation.

With one more literary echo, a reference in the penultimate stanza to Herbert's 'Redemption', Thomas completes his limiting definition of (what the comparison helps us to see as) his spiritual condition. Diagnosing in himself a sensibility enfeebled by a negative Romanticism, this critical percipience is not counterbalanced by any positive expectations of commitment. He has declared his incapacity for the affirmations of positive Romanticism. The reference through Herbert's poem to the Christian revelation now introduces what is for the Western world historically the ultimate measure of the narrator's uncertainties. Christ, who was *banished* from the world by man's sin, forgave and forgives him. 'Seek and ye shall find': hunted by 'thieves and murderers' (Herbert's words), he is at the same time the object of the opposite kind of pursuit, opening himself to those who seek redemption. These paradoxes are at the centre of Herbert's poem. In all respects the quest narrated by Thomas is antithetical.

> That time was brief: once more at inn
> And upon road I sought my man
> Till once amid a tap-room's din
> Loudly he asked for me, began
> To speak, as if it had been a sin,
> Of how I thought and dreamed and ran
> After him thus, day after day:
> He lived as one under a ban
> For this: what had I got to say?
> I said nothing. I slipped away.

Thomas's 'man', while he speaks of the narrator's pursuit 'as if it had been a *sin*' (in this more like the 'thieves and murderers' than the speaker of Herbert's poem), is an accuser not a saviour. Pursuit only ensures loss; the other lives 'as under a ban': seeking is not finding.

The solitary in Thomas's poem has set his sights lower than Herbert's Christian: he aims at relationship with another part of himself, not with something beyond self. This is one reason for the quest's predestined failure: the person who needs saving is not saved out of his own inadequate resources. The second reason brings into sharper focus the disabling modesty of the speaker's ambition. Because his escape from the prison of solitude is connected in his mind with the gregarious pleasures of 'road and inn', his most intense experience of relationship with others, he is under the illusion that 'road and inn' are 'the sum / Of what's not forest'; in pathetic gratitude for the moment of release described in the first stanza he seeks to restore the 'happy mood' of that kind of association, to the exclusion of other kinds. Ignorance of more demanding forms of social communion condemns him to seek his social identity precisely in those places where he, an inveterate solitary, will not find it – in the tap-rooms of roadside inns. He has indeed *nothing to say* to one who speaks 'loudly' amidst the 'din' of such gatherings.

As I have set out the poem, there are two modes of action, inwardly and outwardly directed, each viewed by the poet with severely critical reservations, and with no final choice made between them: the first, a social quest conducted in a spirit of Romantic desperation and bound to fail, the second, an introspective search which leads to a state of mind, a sense of identity with nature, of questionable value. I have depicted a condition of arid stalemate; but in doing so I have slightly misrepresented the second experience. Descriptions of it are frequent both in the poetry and the prose. It was supremely important to Thomas; evidently many of the poems originated in some such mood. The two stanzas in which it is again presented may, in fact, be said to constitute a representative Thomas poem or at least an account of how such a poem arrives. However, in the following (ninth) stanza, from which I quoted earlier ('Once the name I gave to hours / Like this was melancholy . . .'), he makes a crucial distinction, between the poetic present and his non-poetic past. *Once* he thought of such hours as 'melancholy', but, it follows, he thinks so no longer; and this is clearly because now, as not before, they have borne fruit. The restored powers, 'Coming like exiles home again', are poetic, and the broken reticences, 'weaknesses quitting their bowers', are poems; and with poems comes insight. 'Melancholy' is now felt to be not the word for this mood, but neither is 'happiness'. The poems help him to see that the 'moments of everlastingness' are, as I have suggested, surrogates for a sense of community; they do not enable him to make good the loss of that sense. The hovering definition – not melancholy, not happy – gives us Thomas's balanced evaluation of the moments and the poems recording them. They both testify to the potentiality of a full social existence, of a 'belonging' to nature that does not exclude a 'belonging' to human settlements. That is their value and their limitation. On the one hand, social fulfilment is only negatively present – an implied norm, not an experience actualized in the poem. On the other, these glimpses of a non-human eternity occur under conditions the absence of which explains the speaker's failure to discover an analogous human permanence: they therefore provide an insight into the nature of the less ephemeral social relationships. I have not yet quoted the last three lines of stanza nine:

> And fortunate my search was then
> While what I sought, nevertheless,
> That I was seeking, I did not guess.

These lines are the core of the poem. By this standard the quest cannot but fail. Belonging precludes seeking; it happens without personal effort, or personal effort can only confirm what has already come about.

In its allegorical method 'The Other' is not typical of Thomas's poetry, but if it is characteristic in other respects, as I believe it is, then this analysis of the poem would suggest that the usual critical account of the poetry needs to be modified and supplemented. In depth and objectivity the self-understanding revealed is, it seems to me, exceptional. Thomas is far from showing uncertainty as to 'the cause of his most characteristic mood' (Coombes). His melancholy is confidently given the social context tentatively offered as an explanation by D. W. Harding: the poem at once dramatizes and comments upon his supposedly '*unadmitted* craving for an adequate social group'. While the focus, the instance, is undeniably personal, the kind of attention the poet turns upon his experience gives it a wider bearing. We derive from concrete and specific detail a general understanding of social deprivation and social need; the personal case – casting it in the form of fable ensures this – is made to seem representative.

It is well known that a sense of loss pervades Thomas's writing. It is not so widely acknowledged that, whatever evasions he practised in his earlier prose, by the time he came to write his poems he knew *what* had been lost. As presented in 'The Other', it is at once the capacity for firmly based, lastingly satisfying relationships and the sort of social groups where such relationships could be formed – two aspects of the same situation. He is without illusions: he recognizes equally the inescapable compulsion to search for social gratification and the impossibility of success. The poet's relationship to the speaker in the poem is either one of self-mocking identification or one of ironic detachment. Whichever way it is read, this kind of tough scepticism is not what critics normally find in Thomas, and yet it is characteristic and a part of what is to be appreciated in his poetry. The poet remains critically alert as he evokes that moment of peace and apparent harmony, the experience 'far off from men' of what is evidently felt as an epiphany. But however equivocal its message, however tenuous the fulfilment, many of Thomas's poems attend upon, owe their existence (as stanza nine tells us) to, moments like this. The core of self-knowledge and self-acceptance has been reached in the recognition that his scope is limited to what can be accomplished by withdrawal from, rather than co-operation with, society. The narrative tacitly assumes the unavailability to the poet of all but the shallowest and most transient of social experiences.

I have emphasized Thomas's introspective penetration, and especially, in his understanding of himself, his consciousness of limits. But there is more to the poem than self-knowledge. What seems to be promised in that moment of emergence from the forest into the world of men is fulfilment of the poet's social needs; what he in fact experiences is the shallow sociability of a tavern-haunter: this is what he knows, and that he has to live with the presumption of failure. But this disparity between expectation and outcome, and the dissatisfaction which prevents him from abandoning the search, imply the possibility of other, as yet unexplored, kinds of relationship. This is confirmed by Thomas's refusal to endorse the *misanthropy* of those hours, conducive to no matter what revelations, spent in sullen retreat from the frustrations of his social adventure. The poem's complex achievement is, while registering admissions of personal inadequacy and sparseness of social opportunity, to *affirm* nevertheless the human values by which he himself is judged to be a failure. He sees himself always in relation to the potential self still being pursued in the last stanza: 'I try to keep in sight / Dreading his power but worse his laughter'. The laughter, though contemptuous, speaks eloquently of the once glimpsed, carefree existence from which he is exiled, but the prospect of which governs his actions.

4 The traveller's home

I have argued that, though Thomas characteristically appears in his poems as a solitary, disconnected from general human living, many of the poems also disclose a recoil of feeling against isolation and self-consciousness and a counteracting drive to restore connection with the world of others. The moral perspective in them is invariably self-critical, bringing to bear standards of personal integration, of social and natural relationship, upon the experience of alienation (dissociation, self-consciousness, void). That the outward movement exists has been sufficiently demonstrated. In this chapter I aim to give a more substantial picture of the *presence* of these values in Thomas's poetry.

Whatever the channels of influence may have been, their ultimate source is Wordsworth. By general agreement among nineteenth-century critics, he was the last poet, in Arnold's words, 'to see life steadily and to see it whole'. We should say, rather, that he was the last poet to make the attempt, for it seems clear to us that the achievement was, even in the decade of his best work, a precarious one. The philosophy *per se* does not interest us, as it interested the Victorians; our bias is psychological, and reading (for example) the First Part of *The Excursion*, we are more likely to remark the *tension* between the Pedlar's 'philosophical' serenity and the tale he tells of unrelieved suffering than the serenity itself. This view of Wordsworth is for the modern reader no belittlement of his achievement, since conflict, ambivalence or tension is what he expects to find in large as well as small poetic ventures. If it is only with difficulty that the centre of Wordsworth's poetic world holds, and its parts withstand centrifugal forces, the fact that it holds at all is, for an age wary of such undertakings, all the more impressive.

Both the aspiration to a totality and unity of vision and the strain on the Romantic poet of attempting such a vision, the poet's necessarily precarious hold on it, are discernible in his claim, made in the Preface to the *Lyrical Ballads*, that the poet 'is the rock of defence of human nature; an upholder and preserver, carrying everywhere with him relationship and love'. (The implication of strain in this famous announcement has, I think, gone unnoticed; but if the basic social instincts are in *need* of defence and must moreover depend for their survival on the poets, who have themselves deserted the social centres to live at the outposts, so to speak, of civilization, then the situation is indeed grave and the remedy proposed correspondingly desperate.) In relationship and love Wordsworth included every kind of interaction with the external world, every association that serves to integrate inner and outer, subjective and objective experience; 'the great *social* principle of life' named in *The Prelude* (1850, Book II, 389) is not merely the human instinct for fellowship but the whole range of man's impulsions to seek connection with his universe. He has his first experience of this binding agent through the mother, when 'with his soul' he 'Drinks in the feelings of his Mother's eye' (Book II, 236–7); the 'most watchful power of love' (Book II, 291), passed in this manner from the mother to the infant, for him in turn 'irradiates and exalts / Objects through widest intercourse of sense' (Book II, 239–40). It is this wedding of feeling to perception that makes man a true 'inhabitant of earth' (Thomas's phrase in 'The Other'): 'No outcast he, bewildered and depressed', therefore, but 'An inmate of this active universe' (Book II, 241 and 254); indeed the fusion is perhaps what makes it *active*. Owen Barfield, repudiating the Cartesian epistemological assumptions which, he alleges, underlie much of modern philosophical and scientific thought, has frequently, in presenting an alternative theory, spoken of a 'participatory consciousness'; Wordsworth, supremely, made this consciousness his theme.

Thomas himself may have recognized in Wordsworth the ultimate source of his values. On more than one occasion he refers to the famous lines in Book XI of *The Prelude*, which convey the excitement aroused in the poet and similar enthusiasts by the French Revolution in its early stages ('Bliss was it in that dawn to be alive', 108). In the paragraph which describes the appearance of a promised land that France, transfigured by the light of love and hope, presented to idealists – a France irradiated, he might have said, by revolutionary fervour – Wordsworth writes that the revolutionaries 'Were called upon to exercise their skill. / Not in Utopia,'

> But in the very world, which is the world
> Of all of us, – the place where, in the end,
> We find our happiness, or not at all!

Thomas, it is true, misquotes it as 'the earth where we have our happiness or not at all', but without distorting the sense. For Wordsworth means not merely the human world but everything that Thomas means by earth – every manifestation of natural life – and he in fact switches immediately to Thomas's word 'earth', following his assertion with a confession:

Why should I not confess that Earth was then
To me, what an inheritance, new-fallen,
Seems, when the first time visited, to one
Who thither comes to find in it his home?

In the half-apologetic, half-defiant tone of these lines there is a hint that
we are to understand such extravagant sentiments to be a secularization
of what is properly a religious hope – the Christian's hope for his eternal
inheritance, the prototype for which is the promised land of the
Hebrews. The religious charge of feeling that belongs to the ideas of
inheritance and the promised land has been transferred, however, to the
word 'home'.

Love, earth, and home thus inter-related, which constitute the Wordsworthian unity, are the values that Thomas inherited. Occasionally, as
we have seen in 'Beauty', a poem shows the three similarly fused into
one. In the four Household Poems – 'If I Should Ever by Chance', 'If I
Were to Own', 'What Shall I Give?', and 'And You, Helen' (1,
'Bronwen', 2, 'Merfyn', 3, 'Myfanwy', 4, 'Helen') – the values, though
essentially indivisible, are distinguishable from each other, so that one
may properly speak of a relationship between them. There is a poem for
each of his three children and the last is addressed to his wife, Helen; in
each poem Thomas playfully makes a gift, appropriate to the recipient,
of certain familiar places, villages and parts of the countryside. The
giving of nature symbolizes the giving of himself, his natural feeling for
them, as the poems are themselves gifts, acts of love.

Nature can stand for natural feeling because love of nature and
human love are closely linked, are perhaps ultimately the same emotion.
This perception is implicit in much nature poetry and some love poetry,
as Thomas himself suggested in *Feminine Influence on the Poets* (p.
77),[1] but it is most fully explored by Wordsworth and is central to his
naturalist faith – a faith that informs even the light, delicate word-play
of Thomas's 'hedges that lovers / love' ('If I Were to Own'); one is
reminded of the association of love with nature in 'As the Team's
Head-Brass' and 'Lovers'. The final poem in this sequence ends with the
word 'kind': the last gift of himself – 'if I could find / Where it lay
hidden and it proved kind'. All these poems, being symbolic gifts of
himself, exhibit the tender kindness he could not always show in daily
life. The other sense of 'kind' is also implied: the finding of his loving
self would also be the finding of his natural self.

The place-names that fascinated Thomas, that he delighted to list,
and that provided a recurrent topic for rumination in his prose, themselves witness man's intimate feeling for the places in which he dwells:
they are, he says, addressing them in 'Words', 'dear / As the earth which

you prove / That we love'. The roll-call of Essex names in the first two of those poems displays this proof. Both a sense of life's fullness and of human possession are suggested by the names ending in 's' – 'Skreens, Gooshays and Cockerells / . . . Rochetts . . . and Pickerells, / Martins, Lambkins, and Lillyputs' – while the contrast between the sturdy solidity of 'Codham, Cockridden, and Childerditch' and the dreamy mellifluousness of 'Roses, Pyrgo, and Lapwater' suggests the diversity and extent, ranging from vigorous relish to entrancement, of man's feelings for the country he inhabits.

Man *locates* himself in place and seems simultaneously to possess and be possessed by nature. The reciprocity of the relationship distinguishes it from possession in the sense of ownership. The offer made in the first poem, beginning 'If I should ever by chance grow rich', to buy the Essex villages for his elder daughter, is conditional on a chance acquisition of wealth the notion of which is only fancifully entertained; a man cannot by owning lands truly possess them; the riches involved in man's relationship with nature are riches of feeling. To live *in* the world and belong *to* it is to have a loving relationship *with* it. Making the country-side your property separates you from nature, like the rich 'queen / Who once on a time sat in Havering Bower / Alone, with the shadows, pleasure and power' ('What Shall I Give?'; 'Household Poem 3, Myfan-wy'). Thomas's bequest to his younger daughter, therefore, is no more than 'her own world', the world of her daily experience, and Steep, the village which contains it and which is already hers because she lives there. You truly possess only what has become part of you; your 'own world' is not the world you own but an inner and an outer world dissolved into each other. You are as much at home in it as the birds that also live there – 'pewit, woodpecker, swan, and rook' – and with which you share a common land; this is the real 'commonwealth'[2] of crea-tures, the 'social' relationship that binds man to all natural life.

Love that is at once or by turns a human love and (in the sense that it 'irradiates and exalts objects') a *natural* love, is in Thomas's poetry the central value, from which others arise. The recoil from solitude and self-preoccupation in 'Rain', for example, and the outward movement of feeling that culminates in a prayer for the lonely and the suffering ('But here I pray that none whom once I loved / Is dying tonight or lying still awake / Solitary'), even as it seems to make love a thing of the past, is itself a movement of human love; it is the same instinct, though directed to a natural object, that sends the poet's eye, in 'Beauty', homing down unswervingly to a particular tree in a 'misting, dim-lit, quiet vale'.

It is no less central for Thomas than for Wordsworth and Coleridge.

The difference between him and his Romantic predecessors lies in the degree of self-assurance that accompanies the affirmation. Faith is a not unsuitable word to denote the confident temper of the Romantics, even if it is not a simple faith. In Wordsworth's best work his idealism is severely tested by a contrary recognition of evil and suffering, but it cannot be said to waver and is never muted. Coleridge's poetry, it is true, has more in common with Thomas's: they share the experience of isolation and a sense of failure, and both practise an intimate kind of writing in which 'confessional' revelations of misery are made, without Wordsworth's proud reserve. Yet, when all is considered, Coleridge is nearer to his contemporary Wordsworth than to Thomas. The significance of Coleridge's despair is the larger for the largeness of positive ideals from which his failure is judged to be a falling away; 'dejection', his word for this state of mind, carrying the suggestion as it does of being cast down from the mountain heights of aspiration, is the precise word for it. More modest words are favoured by Thomas: he is 'tired, angry and ill at ease' in 'Beauty', and the Keatsian 'melancholy' is used because it is a faintly depreciatory word with an atmosphere of self-indulgence about it. Thomas's sense of his values is refracted through an agnostic, self-doubting intelligence, and his appeal to them, by way of hints and ironies, is oblique and tentative. Yet the scepticism and hesitancy result from self-knowledge, not uncertainty about the values themselves. It is evidently a matter of regret to him, in 'That Girl's Clear Eyes', that he and his fellow-soldiers were 'sealed' in the 'tombs' of themselves – only subsequent reflection supplies the 'social' responsiveness lacking to them at the time – yet the diffidence that conceals his allegiance to his 'social' values is clearly due, here as elsewhere, not to doubt of them but doubt of himself, to an overwhelming sense of personal frailty. It is not in his power, he confesses in 'And You, Helen', to guarantee that the self he has lost, if restored, would be 'kind' to her, yet the admission is made in tender, loving terms. In a poem held back from the first Collected Poems, 'No One So Much As You', he charges himself with an inability to return the love she feels for him; he can but accept hers and record gratitude for it. Nevertheless, though he depicts himself as a 'pine in solitude', it is, in the vignette of the last line, a pine 'cradling a dove': the image, like the tone of the poem, expresses tenderness, if no more than a protective tenderness. Although he wonders in 'These Things that Poets Said' whether the love celebrated by the poets, whose authority he never doubted in youth, had ever existed, 'For certainly not thus, / Then or thereafter, I / Loved ever', it is notable that he wants to retain the word to describe something he had felt once and feels the lack of now, for 'I, loving not, am different'. There was, it seems, a time of unshadowed and unquestioned love in Thomas's life, and such a feeling cannot be lost; the image of it continues to dominate the poems, and despite his sense of incapacity and failure the emotion continues to nourish them. 'It Rains' is characteristic in its subtle blending of diffidence and assurance. The poet returns to a scene of youthful love-making, an orchard now neglected and overgrown, and is 'nearly as happy as possible'

> To search the wilderness in vain though well,
> To think of two walking, kissing there,
> Drenched, yet forgetting the kisses of the rain.

The literal search is, of course, bound to be 'in vain', but as an act of memory and imaginative repossession it is not. The poem is about the loss of love, but in its delicate interweaving of present sadness and past happiness, expressing allegiance to an emotion no longer felt, it not only avoids bitterness but begins to restore the emotion, and in a landscape which embodies his recognition of present loss and hopelessness manages to conjure up an image of love and affirm its power. Not only sexual happiness is in question here. 'Forgetting the kisses of the rain' is more than a pretty thought. Rain is represented in *The South Country* as an 'immense dark force' 'possessing the whole earth at evening, smothering civilization' (p. 281), and invariably, as in the poem 'Rain', counterpoints and confirms the poet's solitude; the *obliviousness* of lovers to rain therefore bespeaks the healing power of love, the power to make man at home on earth: the kissing harmony of lovers brings about a similar harmony of man with nature.

The two harmonies are closely associated in Thomas's poetry. We may say that for him as for Wordsworth they are creations of the same urge to escape solitude and make connection with the world beyond self, 'the very world, which is the world / Of all of us', the common medium of human existence. And that world includes both the human and the natural. Love is the unifying force, healing divisions whether between man and man or man and nature. I have suggested that in Wordsworth's view love informs man's desire 'to find in [earth] his home'; more precisely, love is the craving for relationship, and home, a sense of belonging, is its satisfaction.

Three poems bear the title 'Home', but they are not the only poems to explore the subject; the search for home and the poet's chance discovery – always it is an experience of serendipity – of a place that feels to him like home, though he may not call it that, is a recurrent theme. It was the preoccupation of the constitutional outcast, for whom the rarity of the experience was its value; his interest was motivated more by aspiration and glimpses than by steady knowledge. At the same time he knew or felt himself to be, despite daily attachments, a rootless, homeless person, and that feeling was not always regretful. By comparison with W. H. Hudson, for example, whose aim according to Thomas was 'to be still, somewhere in the sun or under trees where birds are',[3] Thomas was by nature not a settler but a traveller. At times his restlessness needed the satisfactions of a nomadic kind of existence. There are poems dominated by a nostalgia for home and poems that primarily express or celebrate the joys of wanderlust. Few, however, are exclusively one or the other: the momentary experience of belonging or the yearning for a settled state, and the enjoyment of or craving for the exaltations of a nomadic freedom, confront or modify each other in most of the poems that explore these feelings.

The home feeling is frequently dramatized in this way: the poet arrives at a familiar or unfamiliar place and experiences an unusual sense of identity with it. The place is an English village or stretch of country and what he finds there is a quintessence of Englishness, but although Thomas smuggled two of these poems, 'The Manor Farm' and 'Haymaking', pseudonymously into his anthology *This England*, traditional rural England is not in itself the subject. The heart of the experience in each case is the sense, whether declared or not, that this chancing upon a fragment of England is a coming home. Its momentary perfection has the intensity of a revelation. Upon seeing for the first and only time the outwardly unremarkable river valley described in 'I Never Saw that Land Before', the poet is convinced that 'some goal / I touched then', and this states what is implicit in the other poems of arrival. That England rather than a group of people – a landscape with a history rather than a family or community – should attract such feelings is partly due to Thomas's confessed discomfort as a social being; but chiefly it is because Thomas's theme is attunement to the conditions of natural existence more than it is the finding of a congenial society. It is arguable, of course, that the source of Thomas's – and of Wordsworth's – concern with man's relation to nature was a prior estrangement from social life.

Home – in the second of the poems with that title – is the experience of community with the (mainly) natural life around:

> Often I had gone this way before:
> But now it seemed I never could be
> And never had been anywhere else;
> 'Twas home; one nationality
> We had, I and the birds that sang,
> One memory.

A labourer passing his cottage, 'his tread / Slow, half with weariness, half with ease', is mentioned in the last stanza, but as part of the scene; all that the poet shares with him is the contentment of returning home after completion of the day's work. Work and rest are natural complementary satisfactions, and home is comprised of 'familiar' sights and sounds and weather: the sound of sawing, 'The April mist, the chill, the calm' and 'The thrush on the oak top in the lane'. The memory Thomas shares with the birds is sensory, not cultural. And unexpectedly its roots seem stronger, deeper, more inscrutable; it is almost as though his purpose in claiming 'one nationality' with the birds is to undermine the social and political meanings of ordinary patriotism.

Home in this poem is a village 'familiar / And pleasant', but, seen with unfamiliar eyes, 'strange too'. In 'I Never Saw that Land Before' it is the reverse – an unknown country, visited once only, which yet awakens feelings of recognition and love in the poet:

> Yet, as if by acquaintance hoar
> Endeared, by gladness and by pain,
> Great was the affection that I bore
>
> To the valley and the river small,
> The cattle, the grass, the bare ash trees,
> The chickens from the farmsteads, all
> Elm-hidden, and the tributaries
> Descending at equal interval . . .

Yet in their opposite ways these two poems insist on the same quality of strangeness. The strangeness in the experience is the element of epiphany: more is revealed than an ordinary love of one's country. And yet it reveals that too, in the latter poem with a whole-heartedness exceptional in Thomas. The scene is homely, and at the same time, in its smallness and order, an epitome of England. Here are the few intimately known acres which for the Englishman embody his 'idea' of England. Indeed this partly explains, though only partly, the poet's sense of discovery, the feeling on arrival that he had briefly touched 'some goal' then. Beyond that, however, the poem tries to convey a further discovery: the total identity of human experience with its natural setting. This identity occurs when a landscape has been the scene of man's key experiences, and is thus indelibly stamped for him with the full range of his emotions – 'Endeared, by gladness and by pain'. Between the poles of gladness and pain lies a world of feeling; their specific association with the landscape is indicated in the third stanza, where Thomas, continuing to itemize its contents, finds pain as well as beauty in it:

> The blackthorns down along the brook
> With wounds yellow as crocuses
> Where yesterday the labourer's hook
> Had sliced them cleanly; and the breeze
> That hinted all and nothing spoke.

When Thomas asserts that Jefferies was 'the human expression' of his native Wiltshire and Gloucestershire, 'emerging from it, not to be detached from it any more than the curves of some statues from their maternal stone' (p. 9), his praise is more than fanciful. He had in mind, I think, a real relationship, one that is imaged even more suggestively in this stanza. The description of the breeze, integral with the landscape and yet sufficiently independent of it to be its voice, its consciousness, prepares for a quietly phrased poetic manifesto:

> and if I could sing
> What would not even whisper my soul
> As I went on my journeying,
>
> I should use, as the trees and birds did,
> A language not to be betrayed;
> And what was hid should still be hid
> Excepting from those like me made
> Who answer when such whispers bid.

This implies certain ideas about language and symbolism in poetry, and has bearings on Thomas's practice that will be examined in Chapter 10; the source of these ideas, however, is a discovery about the nature of meaning. Thomas's poetic ideal is not merely the outcome of personal diffidence and reticence nor even a defence of his peculiarly oblique use of imagery: it has implications for the whole imaginative means of knowing. Meaning is inherent in, not an interpretation of, our experience of nature. Nature and human feeling have a meaning in common, the language for which therefore must be – according to which way you look at it – natural phenomena humanized or human feeling naturalized. Either way it is a language which, avoiding the 'translation' of experience, arises out of and speaks for an intrinsic, indissoluble relation between thing and feeling, a humanized or spiritualized reality. It is the expression of what Owen Barfield has called 'participatory consciousness'; I referred to the idea in my earlier discussion of Wordsworth. It also plays an important part in Charles Davy's *Towards a Third Culture*, in which he distinguishes it from the 'onlooker consciousness', the mental outlook which, according to a theory of evolution of consciousness that he shares with Barfield, has prevailed in the West since the Renaissance.

'The Manor Farm' presents another 'fragment of England'; not only as it appears to the senses, however, but also as it is perceived by the historical imagination:

> The church and yew[4]
> And farmhouse slept in a Sunday silentness.
> The air raised not a straw. The steep farm roof,
> With tiles duskily glowing, entertained
> The midday sun; and up and down the roof
> White pigeons nestled.

Here is a piece of traditional England – asleep in the past. The last word, 'nestled', focuses the general mood of the poem and forms the whole scene into a historically located image of home, a historically founded accommodation of man to nature, making neighbours of roof and sun, roof and pigeons, of 'church and yew / And farmhouse'. Not only is nature humanized, but in 'entertained' an appropriately civil relationship is hinted at; natural and social harmonies are identified.

The sense of homecoming in 'Home' and 'I Never Saw that Land Before' is an unexpected grace of the moment; it gives the feeling a quality of epiphany. However its very momentariness and unaccountability also suggest its precariousness and assure its transience. A special concurrence of circumstances is similarly responsible for the discovery made in 'The Manor Farm' – the revelation of a February spring – yet the experience feels more solid; the rhythms of the poem are firm, the voice, eschewing melancholy or wistful inflections, is robust. A sense of belonging which adds a temporal to a spatial aspect is perhaps a more substantial thing: the self is enlarged into both nature and history. Even this, however, does not entirely explain the uncharacteristically confident mood of this poem. Reality – the reality of the weather, the place, and the history it holds – is extended with conscious hyperbole into the ideal: the seasons of time, asleep 'in a Sunday silentness', are exchanged for 'a season of bliss unchangeable / Awakened from farm and church where it had lain / Safe under tile and thatch for ages'. Noting this shift of emphasis, I must qualify what I have said about history in the poem. Its mood responds to a feeling not so much for the past as for the immemorial. Being at home on earth implies here something more than being tied to a particular place and tradition, may even not require it. 'The Winter's cheek flushed as if he had drained / Spring, Summer, and Autumn at a draught / And smiled quietly': humorous annotations notwithstanding – the 'season of bliss unchangeable' is also a blissfully tipsy rustic's defiance of time – Thomas affirms a placeless and timeless condition. Home means this too, but without any tacit reservation, in 'Haymaking'. Like 'The Manor Farm' it captures a traditional scene, in a moment of mid-morning rest and stillness:

> The tosser lay forsook
> Out in the sun; and the long waggon stood
> Without its team; it seemed it never would
> Move from the shadow of that single yew.

And thus the still moment begins to stretch into timelessness. Again what moves him is not a vision of continuity with the past but a sense of the immemorial awakened by it: 'All was old, / This morning time, with a great age untold'. The concluding lines take this further:

> Under the heavens that know not what years be
> The men, the beasts, the trees, the implements
> Uttered even what they will in times far hence –
> All of us gone out of the reach of change –
> Immortal in a picture of an old grange.

Almost *sotto voce*, in the parenthesis, the lines tell us that this living scene, the meaning it conveys, is as changeless as death is changeless. It is longer than the span of individual lives, and to feel oneself to be part of it is one way of conceiving everlasting life.

What I have said of 'Home' and 'I Never Saw that Land Before', that the sense of homecoming is an unexpected grace of the moment, is equally applicable to the other two poems of arrival. These epiphanies occur only when heralded by auspicious omens and under specially favourable conditions. The weather which precedes the discovery of the haymaking scene has precisely the aura of good omen about it:

> After night's thunder far away had rolled
> The fiery day had a kernel sweet of cold,
> And in the perfect blue the clouds uncurled,
> Like the first gods before they made the world
> And misery, swimming the stormless sea
> In beauty and in divine gaiety.

The suspended action of a mid-morning break – men and horses, waggon and implements as motionless and seemingly ageless as the farmer's 'white house crouched at the foot of a great tree' – provides the favourable conditions that disclose the latent meaning of the scene. In 'The Manor Farm' they are the spring-like warmth and the 'gilding beam' of a mid-winter sun and the almost perfect stillness in which the revelation of 'church and yew / And farmhouse' takes place. 'Haymaking' is explicitly framed as a picture, but in both poems the scene is transfixed in a timeless moment of stillness. 'Moments of everlastingness', as he tells us in 'The Other', played an important part in the release of Thomas's imagination, and I shall be discussing them in greater detail in Chapter 6. It suffices to note here that only by such special dispensations is the poet ever able to feel identity with a place.

II

The stillness, the rootedness, the home feeling expressed in these two poems and elsewhere, comprise an experience unique to the traveller: this is the paradox, the peculiarity, of the situation. The poet 'happened' on these places in his walks. He 'came down', for example, from somewhere outside to make his discovery of 'the old Manor Farm, / And church and yew tree opposite'; he had not seen them before. Accustomed to the role of stranger, at best an appreciative *onlooker*, suddenly he finds himself to be a *participant* in the essential life of the scene. The 'blessedness' in the experience (to use the appropriately Wordsworthian term) is in proportion to its gratuitousness; it is for this reason that the scene, 'irradiated' with the glow of the poet's welcome, is pictured in such unflawed perfection. In a reading that takes cognizance of this aspect of the occasion in 'Haymaking', one inconspicuous detail becomes significant: 'Only the scent of woodbine and hay new mown / Travelled the road'. Nothing and nobody else 'travelled' – the quiet surprise sprung by the word, its unexpectedness as a metaphor for the faintest movements of air, calls up its more usual associations: no more wandering of the endless roads in pursuit of unknown vanishing goals. All these timeless moments are interludes of peace and stillness; naming, for exclusion from this scene, the *traveller's* restlessness lightly touches upon what threatens its perfection. It is only a touch; it does not disturb the confident mood of this poem. Both in 'Haymaking' and in 'The Manor Farm' Thomas, with unusual singleness and tenacity, retains firm possession of the home feeling. His hold upon it is less secure, however, in 'I Never Saw that Land Before'. There the traveller's viewpoint is made explicit and controls the poem:

> I never saw that land before,
> And now can never see it again;
> Yet, as if by acquaintance hoar
> Endeared . . .

That 'as if' directs the presentment of the experience and leads to the conditional wishes expressed in the last two stanzas. Even in 'Home' ('Often I had gone that way before'), which names the feeling, its status is precarious. Though this village has been in fact 'endeared' by long acquaintance, the sense of rootedness suddenly bestowed upon the poet is likened to the emotion of a *revenant* – 'I had come back / That eve somehow from somewhere far' – who experiences at the same time attachment and detachment, the familiarity and the strangeness of the place.

Clearly the escape from isolation into a feeling of close identity with a village or landscape, recorded in these poems, is essentially the exile's experience tinged with the special emotions of the exile – wistfulness, intense gratitude, the brief joy of sudden illumination. The 'strangeness' that partly reflects the epiphanic quality of the experience – strange in the sense of wonderful – also expresses, in the other sense of the word, the estrangement of the habitual wanderer. The viewpoint is never that of the established and contented home *dweller*. Since that is so, it is not surprising that in several poems Thomas's nomadic impulse should be given freer rein and the satisfactions of wanderlust should become a value in their own right, although when this happens it rarely goes unchallenged. In 'The Manor Farm' the affirmation of a traditional way of life is modified but not challenged by the nomadic consciousness of the questing poet. But where wanderlust is allowed, as it were, a speaking part in a poem, the two sets of values are brought into open confrontation. Thus the carefreeness and exhilaration of a day's expedition into unknown country, described in ' "Home" ', is set against the homesickness which overtakes him and his companions and draws them back. Home is the central theme of the poem. Recalling an incident of his army life – his companions are fellow soldiers – its main purpose, as the quotation marks in the title suggest, is to give a meaning to the word; he distinguishes between the need-enforced temporary comradeship of barrack routine and the deeper relationships that grow from common roots:

> Between three countries far apart that lay
> We were divided and looked strangely each
> At the other, and we knew we were not friends
> But fellows in a union that ends
> With the necessity of it, as it ought.

Yet the opening description of the expedition is not merely subservient to this theme: it does more, for example, than give the walkers a reason for homesickness.

> Fair was the morning, fair our tempers, and
> We had seen nothing fairer than that land,
> Though strange, and the untrodden snow that made
> Wild of the tame, casting out all that was
> Not wild and rustic and old; and we were glad.
> Fair too was afternoon, and first to pass
> Were we that league of snow, next the north wind.

These lines, adding a second motif to the poem, balance the bleakness of the scene against the joy of exploring unfamiliar ground. The two motifs are indeed interwoven, and the poem makes an unobtrusive pattern of correspondences – contrasts and parallels between this landscape and the impermanent environment of army camp, on the one hand, and between it and the familiar landscapes of each man's native country, on the other. Negatively, the strangeness and coldness of the snow-covered land correspond to the unfriendliness of the camp's 'cold roofs', the substitute home to which the walkers return, and the element of strangeness in army friendships. Positively, the lifetime's shared experience of place which constitutes true home is paralleled and contrasted with the travellers' experience of a virgin landscape, the tameness of the known with the wildness of the unknown: while it lacks the enrichment of human association, the wild scene has the glamour of the untouched and unstaled; the snowfall is seen as a cleansing, a 'casting out' of all that would sully nature's pristine purity. Thus, although in this poem the attractions of a rooted life outweigh those of nomadism, the strength of the nomadic impulse in Thomas is clearly demonstrated.

'The Sheiling', which commemorates a visit to his friend Gordon Bottomley's house on the edge of the Lake District, the house named in the title, similarly juxtaposes a wild and a homely scene; this time home is literally a household and by extension the artistic milieu it epitomized. Perhaps few readers would see this juxtaposition as being also a confrontation of values; for the poem celebrates Bottomley's successful cultivation of a civil humanity and the arts in a barren soil. Certainly the poet comes to praise, but without discourtesy or disloyalty to his friend, he also keeps a careful distance from what he praises. His description of the home that Bottomley has created in this unbenign spot incorporates veiled but firm reservations. The poem expresses a correspondingly quiet but appreciative response to the wildness of the surrounding country – 'A land of rocks and trees / Nourished on wind and stone' – that calls to mind the 'rocks and stones and trees' of Wordsworth's 'A Slumber Did My Spirit Seal'. Edna Longley comments in her notes to 'The Sheiling': 'Barren or mountainous regions are on the frontier of [Thomas's] poetic territory (perhaps because spiritually too close), remote from the softer centre and sanctuary of his "South Country" '[5]. This is true; it is only adding a distinction and drawing out a possible implication of that parenthetical remark to suggest that his 'poetic territory' is not, as might be inferred, single, but discontinuous: that there is more than one Thomas, and the one who chooses the 'South Country' is the Thomas who wants from nature a home or place to settle, while the other Thomas, whose instincts are those of the wanderer, feels an affinity with the wilder scenery of Wordsworth's Lake District and of Wales (as in 'The

Mountain Chapel'), and with the less homely parts of England's southern counties ('Up in the Wind'), or with that landscape stripped or made strange by snow.

Again, as in 'Haymaking', the unexpected placement of the word 'travelling' alerts us to the existence of this second set of sympathies. Here is the third stanza:

> Safe resting there
> Men hear in the travelling air
> But music, pictures see
> In the same daily land
> Painted by the wild air.

Men seek shelter from the winds in this bare 'land of stone', but the bleakness of the region is given no menace by 'the travelling air'; the grave beauty and serenity of the phrase, on the contrary, conjures a vision both of freedom and of an alternative peace, possibly more enduring than the security provided by the house. This stanza celebrates the transformation of the wild by the artistic imagination as a benevolent, humanizing act of home-making, but in equivocal terms. 'Men hear . . . But music': that can be read as praise or as insinuating some limitation of perception. To hear *nothing* but music in 'the travelling air', see *nothing* but pictures in the daily appearances of the land, would be, in the latter reading, to hear and see none of its harshness, to find only sweetness (melody and beauty) in it or to find something which is not there at all. When 'the wild air' turns painter, the thought, so uncharacteristic of Thomas, draws our attention to the artifice in this artistic transformation.[6] The representation of 'The Sheiling' as a haven of the arts begins in the preceding stanza:

> And all within
> Long delicate has been;
> By arts and kindliness
> Coloured, sweetened, and warmed
> For many years has been.

The arts that oppose a 'coloured' and 'warmed' reality to the (implied) greyness and 'cold heart' of this stone land are the arts of mitigation. The opposition, like the word 'delicate' to describe the refining influence of a cultivated life, is unique in Thomas's poetry, and evokes Yeats; there is something Yeatsian also in the tone and formal austerity of the poem — even the marmoreal quality partly created by the identical rhyme words is Yeatsian — and one imagines that these echoes are called up by some actual sympathy between Gordon Bottomley's and Yeats's cultural ideals. But they are as foreign to Thomas as the conceits of the third stanza are foreign to his style, and I think this is intimated, whether consciously or not, by the faint air of quotation in both stanzas. It is not irrelevant to recall the 'untrodden snow' of the landscape in '"Home"', which 'made wild / Of the tame', thereby renewing its potency; for these conceits, by taming the wildness (and 'taming' seems justified), reverse that effect. Bottomley's creation of a sanctuary for civilized living involves – and I believe this is the deepest, covert significance of the poem – a shutting out of certain invigorating influences, sources of life that have, for example, 'nourished' the 'rocks and trees'. The very indoor quality of that key phrase 'arts and kindliness' – the association of the nature in 'kindliness', a word that *is* characteristic of Thomas, with the vocabulary of a softening aestheticism – points to what is lacking: openness, freedom and spontaneity, the seemingly boundless possibilities of life suggested by 'travelling air'. Is there not even a faint reminiscence in stanza three of the magic that transformed Prospero's isle, 'full of noises, / Sounds, and sweet airs that give delight and hurt not'? Though there is no precise verbal echo, it is surely not fanciful to see a resemblance between the role of the arts cultivated in 'The Sheiling' and the effect upon Ferdinand of Ariel's music: 'This music crept by me upon the waters, / *Allaying* both their fury and my passion / With its sweet air' (my italics). If this is so, it would confirm the hinted characterization of Bottomley's art as a civilized enchantment which, like Prospero's, creates 'sweet' illusions in the wild air.[7]

'Travelling' is evidently a potent word in Thomas's vocabulary; it exercises a strong attraction upon him, as almost an alternative way of life. But even when he is echoing the carefree, jaunty inflections and sentiments of roving songs like 'The Lincolnshire Poacher' and 'The Maid of Amsterdam', as he is in the two poems entitled 'An Old Song', or 'Rio Grande', as in 'Early One Morning' ('Song 3'), he does not lose the complexity of self-awareness which distinguishes these poems from anything written by the Georgian poets in a superficially similar mood. Despite the prevalence of the traveller's viewpoint in so many of his poems, few of them are whole-hearted celebrations of nomadism. Nor do the few poems of this type – 'The Signpost' is perhaps the most substantial of them – lack any of Thomas's usual subtlety of tone and poise of attitude.

But the first thing to say about 'The Signpost' is that it does give unreservedly positive expression to the intoxication and yearning of wanderlust. Even on a chill, pale, frosty day, the impulse to break loose, to abandon the human warmth of familiar places and people for the solitary delights of exploration, proves irresistible. Wild clematis is given its country name, 'traveller's-joy', to identify the impulse, and a suggestion of its trailing sinuous delicacy is sketched in such a way as to catch the exact quality of lightness and release that goes with yielding to the impulse: 'The smoke of the traveller's-joy is puffed / Over hawthorn berry and hazel tuft'. The poet pauses before a fingerpost wondering which way to go, displaying a characteristic vacillation, which Frost said he was parodying in 'The Road Not Taken'. But Thomas here does not think of it as a weakness. Two voices comment. The first speaks, as Edna Longley defines his attitude, 'for the absolutism of youth in requiring an immediate and unqualified decision':[8] 'You would not have doubted so / At twenty', it says. The second voice, 'gentle with scorn', is that of the mature Thomas: 'At twenty you wished you had never been born'. And winning the exchange with that riposte, the voice of maturity virtually takes over the poem. When the first speaker wants to 'know' (precisely and undeniably) what it would be like 'To be sixty by this same post', and the other responds with laughter at this youthful desire for assurances, the poet adds, 'I had to join his laughter'. The only certain knowledge we have, the second speaker goes on, is that we shall die; death will cure all uncertainties:

> Whatever happens, it must befall,
> A mouthful of earth to remedy all
> Regrets and wishes shall freely be given;
> And if there be a flaw in that heaven
> 'Twill be freedom to wish, and your wish may be
> To be here or anywhere talking to me
> No matter what the weather, on earth . . .
> With a poor man of any sort, down to a king,
> Standing upright out in the air
> Wondering where he shall journey, O where?

The indecisiveness in Thomas which amused Frost is thus transformed into a strength. To inhabit the region between 'regrets and wishes', to be without finalities or expectation of anything like a 'remedy' for life, is at least to have no illusions, which is the sort of strength Keats believed to be definitive of the poetic character;[9] but it is also more than that. As against the intransigence of his youthful self (matched only by the relentlessness and rigidity of death), it represents openness to different possibilities. A life perpetually on the move, propelled by a question never to be finally answered, could in another context suggest a life without firm purpose, but here the exultant rhythms and the words – 'Standing *upright* out in the air' – are clearly affirmative, and 'wondering' signifies not doubt but vitality, to be wonderingly alive. The sardonic contrast between the rule of death, whose 'mouthful of earth . . . shall freely be given' (but never withheld), and the true freedom of choice enjoyed by the traveller, leaves room for no other alternative to the 'heaven' of immunity from 'all / Regrets and wishes' than this of the totally unattached life fed by ceaselessly changing impressions.

But few of Thomas's poems renounce connections so unequivocally. As, in several poems, a nomadic impulse modifies the assertion of home values, so this nomadism in its turn is implicitly questioned in the poems that in some measure celebrate it. 'Early One Morning', for example, ostensibly chants a hymn of praise to wanderlust, but the treble of praise is accompanied by an at first almost inaudible bass murmur of unease that grows louder as the poem proceeds.

> Early one morning in May I set out,
> And nobody I knew was about.
>> I'm bound away for ever,
>> Away somewhere, away for ever.
>
> There was no wind to trouble the weathercocks.
> I had burnt my letters and darned my socks.
>
> No one knew I was going away,
> I thought myself I should come back some day.
>
> I heard the brook through the town gardens run.
> O sweet was the mud turned to dust by the sun.
>
> A gate banged in a fence and banged in my head.
> 'A fine morning, sir,' a shepherd said.
>
> I could not return from my liberty,
> To my youth and my love and my misery.
>
> The past is the only dead thing that smells sweet,
> The only sweet thing that is not also fleet.
>> I'm bound away for ever,
>> Away somewhere, away for ever.

From the outset the folksong zest and gusto gives off a hollow echo – in the refrain, for instance, with its repetitions and diminuendos and its large vague enthusiasm. The build-up of negatives in the first three stanzas, expressing the poet's thankfulness for his deliverance from all binding associations, at the same time gives uncomfortable emphasis, as it were unwittingly, to the fact itself: the prospect that is invitingly trouble-free is by the same token empty of people, of relationships. As this implication begins to dawn on the consciousness of the poem, a wistfulness for the past supposedly disowned breaks into the third stanza. The ruefulness of 'I thought myself I should come back some day' suddenly exposes a childishness in the voice which directs our attention to a note of bravado in the preceding lines. From here on this undercurrent of disquiet presses to the surface of the poem. The conflict of feelings is represented in stanza five by the double action of the banged gate: first it conveys the poet's robust decisiveness and signifies his liberation, and then, as it echoes in the head, it shuts with the dead finality of banishment and irreversible loss. Conflict becomes ambivalence in the sixth stanza in the double sense of 'could not': it combines with its plain sense, 'I was unable to', the colloquial meaning, 'I could not bring myself to', which goes with a shudder and a grimace of distaste, and accords with the overt feeling of the poem. Thomas has discovered voluntary freedom to be at the same time involuntary loss, a sentence of exile; in one view his 'liberty' is release and enlargement, in another it is a diminishment of life. This prepares us for the final, contradictory, reluctant admission that although it is a 'dead thing', the past – its 'misery' no less than remembered 'love' – 'smells sweet' (sweeter, maybe, than the 'mud turned to dust by the sun'), and that, moreover, its sweetness is the only enduring thing in a transient life.

This poem is not so much a confrontation between the values of relationship and nomadic freedom, as a celebration of nomadism that, almost despite itself, betrays the paradoxes of freedom and bears witness to the strength of human ties. Nevertheless reflection upon those paradoxes discloses a series of (unpointed) balances and antitheses. On the one hand, the appeal of travelling is experienced as both a liberation and a compulsion; on the other hand, the poet's links with the past are represented as both a sweetness and a constriction: each is a bondage and each has its charm. A further enrichment of the pattern is that, while travel has the sweetness of life (mud, as Vernon Scannell points out,[10] is a life-breeding substance), which yet turns to 'dust' in the sun, the past's sweetness is a 'dead thing' which yet lives on in memory.

'Roads' takes yet another approach to the theme of nomadism. It celebrates the conditions and the act of journeying in unflawed tones of enchantment, and on first reading it seems more like 'The Signpost', a hymn to wanderlust, than 'Early One Morning', with its sombre, questioning undertone. The roads he loves, that interlace the landscape of England and Wales, are many things, but the sum of their allurement is that they lighten the burden of living. Winding, seemingly endless, indeterminate, offering perpetual surprise and promise, they are watched over by 'Helen of the Roads', the Welsh goddess whose carefree spontaneous laughter he hears 'When the thrush cock sings / Bright irrelevant things', and their loneliness is alleviated by the ghostly company of previous travellers whose footsteps are as light as Helen's; the free buoyant life they symbolize is contrasted – it is where the meandering course of the poem's thinking unexpectedly emerges – with the captive life of the training camps in war-time Britain: 'Now all roads lead to France / And heavy is the tread / Of the living'. The joy of unbounded wandering is the ruling emotion, and unlike 'Early One Morning' the set of the poem is affirmative; yet, as nearly always in Thomas, there is a backdrop of darker implications. Even as he is explaining his love of roads, extravagantly endowing them with a kind of eternal life, he is also speaking of life's transience:

> Roads go on
> While we forget, and are
> Forgotten like a star
> That shoots and is gone.
>
> On this earth 'tis sure
> We men have not made
> Anything that doth fade
> So soon, so long endure.

The Shakespearian echo, a characteristically de-ritualized, stripped, yet elegantly riddling version of the lines in Ariel's dirge – 'Nothing of him that doth fade, / But doth suffer a sea-change / Into something rich and strange' – solemnizes the ambiguity of feeling.

The need to find an image of everlastingness in the aimless life of the roads betrays the awareness of transience that feeds it; similarly, though Thomas gives us the solitude of the nomadic way of life emptied of many of its terrors, the reality of loneliness is not exorcised from the poem. Its presence as a deprivation, however disguised, darkens the affirmative mood; but it does not destroy it. In this its position is as far from 'Early One Morning' as from 'The Signpost'. The roads, he says,

> are lonely
> While we sleep, lonelier
> For lack of the traveller
> Who is now a dream only.

To speak not of people but of roads as lonely, at night when no one travels them, is to transform the idea of loneliness, for the roads constitute thereby an alternative society: the ghosts of previous travellers, who 'make loneliness / With their light footsteps' press', in imagination 'keep [him] company / With their pattering',

> Crowding the solitude
> Of the loops over the downs,
> Hushing the roar of towns
> And their brief multitude.

The ghostly company of the dead merely compensates, however, for the lack of social fulfilment. By smuggling in a comforting if attenuated connection with humanity Thomas has tried to bestow upon the wanderer a form of the home-dweller's experience. We have here neither a confrontation between the two sets of values, as in 'The Sheiling', nor the espousal of one set compromised by self-contradiction, as in 'Early One Morning', but a fusion of the two. They even exchange characteristics. 'Roads go on' but it is men who have made them 'so long endure'; though the span of the individual life is brief, the species is immortal:

> The hill road wet with rain
> In the sun would not gleam
> Like a winding stream
> If we trod it not again.

The sense of continuity that belongs in a rooted existence has been transferred to the nomadic experience; correspondingly transience is associated exclusively with the noisy gregarious life of the towns 'And their *brief* multitude'.

Poems which either express an unqualified sense of belonging or celebrate with complete insouciance the nomadic life are rare in Thomas's work. Whereas the poems of homecoming imply the traveller's perspective, the message of freedom and spontaneity loudly proclaimed in the poems of wanderlust, such as 'Early One Morning' or 'Roads', is almost invariably accompanied by a murmuring awareness of loss and transience and never quite silences the undervoice of nostalgia for the home lost or never possessed. It is true that 'Roads', by incorporating some of the characteristics of settled living into its portrayal of the nomadic life, attempts a rapprochement between these conflicting feelings, but the result is a blurring of distinctions rather than a resolution of the poet's ambivalence. Though ambivalence of feeling permeates all of these poems, comparisons between them reveal that in Thomas's disposition the yearning and search for a home, on the one hand, and the enjoyment of the traveller's freedom, on the other, do not contradict so much as complement each other.

'Good-Night' is a revealing poem in this regard, in that, unlike 'Roads', it makes plain (and makes play with) the interdependence of these opposing sentiments. It is yet another poem of homecoming, a version of the experience presented in 'I Never Saw that Land Before'. After a day's walking the poet enters a strange town. The birds that have kept him company, the skylarks 'that sang over the down' and the 'suburb nightingales', have been left behind,

> But the call of children in the unfamiliar streets
> That echo with a familiar twilight echoing,
> Sweet as the voice of nightingale or lark, completes

A magic of strange welcome . . .
The friendless town is friendly; homeless, I am not lost;
Though I know none of these doors, and meet but strangers' eyes.

The quality and intensity of feeling in these lines, the sweetness and 'magic' of the occasion, are largely in response to the poet's consciousness of what the experience is not – the exile or estrangement which, it is implied, is his normal condition. But the paradoxes of those last two lines and the half-concealed oxymoron in 'a magic of strange welcome' not only tell us that the occasion is exceptional but pinpoint the nature of its exceptionality. The last stanza completes the poem's definition of it. It begins: 'Never again, perhaps, after tomorrow, shall / I see these homely streets', and ends, insisting again on the paradox: 'But it is All Friends' Night, a traveller's good-night'. As the greeting is, precisely, the 'traveller's good-night', so the goodness in that 'good night' is of the kind only to be felt by a stranger, for whom it is a rare and therefore precious experience. The home feeling is both more intense and less durable than the sense of identity with a place enjoyed by the person who truly belongs there; it is, however, the limit of what is available to the constitutional outcast. (It is in keeping with this characterization of Thomas that his most moving image of home – a home-on-earth as against the forces of night – is the inn, the substitute home of the traveller, which offers 'food, fire and rest' to the poet in 'The Owl'.) The town is hospitable; it greets him, or seems to greet him, as both a friend and a stranger. Since that is the meaning of hospitality, it could be said that there is nothing paradoxical about the last line. But this is to ignore an implication of the phrase 'All Friends' Night'. It indicates that this is no routine kindness but a special amnesty for the wanderer, like All Souls' Night for the restless spirits.

I described the oxymoron effected by the coupling of 'strange' with 'welcome' as half-concealed. This is because Thomas is playing on two (related) senses of 'strange', and the primary sense here is not 'foreign' but 'wonderful' or 'unusual'; the second sense lies dormant until awakened by the word's echo four lines later in 'strangers' eyes'. Then the paradox comes to life – or, perhaps one should say, to half-life, for we are less conscious of a tension between incompatible notions than of a transfiguring effect. By exploiting the ambiguity of 'strange' the poet manages both to admit the substitution – the transference of homeliness to the strange and unfamiliar – and, with a verbal magic that supports and expresses the 'magic' of the occasion, to suggest a mood that transcends the traveller's condition, raising loss into possession, exclusion into communion, exile into homecoming.

The interdependence of homing and nomadic, of social and solitary, inclinations, is displayed most characteristically in the encounters with strangers which are a common feature both of Thomas's prose and of his poetry. They commemorate the moments of casual friendship without ties, peculiar to the traveller's experience, and range from the ordinary to the extraordinary. At one end we have the entirely natural occasion of relaxed and leisurely talk between poet and ploughman in 'As the Team's Head-Brass'; at the opposite end are all those encounters which are, like the unfamiliar town in 'Good-Night', transfigured by the circumstances. This is so with the girl whose brief intrusion on the poet's solitude is recalled in 'The Mill-Pond'. On that day 'ages ago' Thomas sat by the mill-pond taking in sight and sound, chiefly conscious of the noise of the weir close by, half-attentive to the distant sounds of thunder. However, ignoring the warning sign of an approaching storm – seemingly mesmerized by the continuing brightness of the day and the roar of the water – he still dangled his feet and 'teased the foam / That slid below', heedless of the water's turbulence as of the thunder, until the girl, 'Dressed all in white', made her appearance: ' "Take care!" she said – ages ago'. The poet was startled and angry; that was all, but

> Then the storm burst, and as I crouched
> To shelter, how
> Beautiful and kind, too, she seemed,
> As she does now!

'Now' is war-time and the remembered storm prefigures the larger personal and national disaster to come. By those words then the poet–solitary was, as it were, released from the spell, the sinister attraction, of disaster, and re-absorbed into life; now, against the growing darkness of both settings, she stands out in her white dress as symbolic of all that is 'beautiful and kind', that makes life precious and inspires resistance to the forces of death (in the prose passage quoted by Edna Longley as a source for the poem Thomas speaks of 'the farmer's daughter in a white dress' as 'a Lady May').[11] As in 'Good-Night' the houses and streets gave him 'strange welcome', so here the girl's kindness to the poet is, in both senses too, a *strange* kindness (more wonderful, that is, for being the act of a stranger); the beauty of the girl – and of the occasion – is what the poet's gratitude has added ('how beautiful . . . she *seemed*'), a transformation of memory and imagination. The precise nature of the transformation, the transcendence of paradox, in such poems as this, is conveyed most directly by 'Over the Hills'. This is the poet's wistful recollection of a time when he happened upon a 'new country' and entered an 'inn where all were kind, / All were strangers'. In the faintly mythic (once upon a time) atmosphere surrounding this episode the negative connotations of 'stranger' are suspended, and 'kind stranger' seems to define a new species of relationship, not less than but surpassing ordinary friendship. All these encounters are with 'kind strangers'; in most of them the relationship is aureoled with an atmosphere of the marvellous.

5 Naturalism

Edward Thomas *is* a nature poet, but we cannot call him that. 'Nature poetry' as a term ceased to be merely descriptive of content and became a pejorative label for poetry specializing in certain attitudes – moralistic and sentimental attitudes – among the new critics of the twenties and thirties, when the kind of poetry to which it had been applied fell into disrepute. This was poetry written in the Wordsworthian-didactic and Keatsian-aesthetic modes, and in particular poetry expressing a simple-minded, enfeebled naturalism. The phrase has never lost the taint of its former undesirable associations, and for tactical reasons critics writing about Thomas and wishing to dissociate his work from the diluted romanticism of Victorian and Georgian nature poetry have either shunned the label or, unable to do without it altogether, have defensively surrounded it with anxious explanations and disclaimers. Coombes was understandably concerned therefore that Thomas should not be regarded as 'just another pleasant nature poet' (p. 13).

Yet the original Nature poet (and here it needs the capital) was Wordsworth. It is an irony of literary history that the term should have acquired from Wordsworth's own more trivial productions and those of his imitators this disabling association with pleasantness; for 'nature poetry' in the sense in which Coombes uses it, applied critically or neutrally to the work of its first practitioner, misses its deepest significance and ignores its best qualities, and indiscriminate repetition of that description has encouraged a simplified and sentimentalized conception of nature's role in his poetry. 'The great social principle of life', the phrase from Book II of *The Prelude* quoted in my last chapter, with all that it signifies in Wordsworth's thought, gives some idea of what that role is. It was never a merely external nature; the 'nature poems' of Wordsworth, and of Coleridge, were nearly always 'human nature' poems too; if the tradition which sprang from Wordsworth had not finally run into the shallows of Georgianism, this distinction, used by Coombes to suggest the more complex interest of Thomas's poetry in comparison with that of his contemporaries, would not have been necessary. As it is, we lack a term that would even approximately characterize the central preoccupations of Wordsworth's and Coleridge's poetry.

Since I see Thomas as an independent inheritor of these preoccupations, I specifically need a term that acknowledges this relationship. Although I may not now call Thomas a nature poet, I may surely at this stage, without fear of misunderstanding, call him a naturalistic poet. For Wordsworth the trinity of love, earth and home, values whose presence I have traced in Thomas's poetry, was encompassed by the one word 'Nature', and it would be perverse to avoid it entirely. Naturalism has the added advantage when applied to Thomas of being antithetical to supernaturalism. In *The Prelude* Wordsworth did not consistently take the (in this sense) naturalist position which he seems to hold in the passage quoted in the last chapter ('the very world ... where, in the end, / We find our happiness, or not at all'); but, as his fondness for the lines suggests, Thomas did. Thomas was by no means a 'simple-minded' naturalist, but this is only to say that his *understanding* of his values was not a simple one; it left room for an uncertainty, a consciousness of their limits, which distinguishes him from the militant upholders of a philosophical naturalism.

In his concern with the values of love, home and nomadism Thomas was committing himself to a movement out of self, affirming a relationship with otherness; these are values that transcend a narrowly defined naturalism, though the 'other' is always associated with the life of nature, as it exists in man and outside him. For poems that appeal to these values, the need for some term such as naturalism is perhaps less apparent than it is for poems which directly celebrate the life of nature and the life of man as part of nature. Where the first kind of poem brings to its experience a desire for relationship with nature, the second embraces the life of nature – it displays, we might say, an affirmative naturalism.

It is easier to illustrate what I mean by this than to talk about it in the abstract. Natural life is in the first place the wild – instinctive and spontaneous – life of animals: of weasel, crow and magpie, for example, 'beasts / And birds' whose amoral ways are sardonically admired in 'The Gallows'. Birds are Thomas's favourites, especially the inconspicuous and commonplace birds neglected by other poets; the ordinary life of nature has a stronger attraction for him than its exceptions. Among the songsters, for instance, he prefers the thrush over the nightingale; he shares this preference, it is true, with other post-Romantic poets, but he is alone in celebrating (as he does on more than one occasion) the chattering busy nonchalance of starlings ('The Barn' and 'The Mill-Pond') and in 'Sedge-Warblers', for their hardiness and tenacity, the 'small brown birds' of the title, with voices 'quick, shrill, or grating'.

Very similar qualities of natural life are embodied, Thomas believed, in folk art and folk speech. They played a decisive part both in his development of a poetic voice and idiom and in the shaping of his later prose style. 'If I am consciously doing anything,' he wrote to Eleanor Farjeon in January 1915, 'I am trying to get rid of the last rags of rhetoric and formality which left my prose so often with a dead rhythm only' (p. 110). The re-telling of the legends collected in *Celtic Stories* (1911) and *Norse Tales* (1912) evidently contributed to that endeavour as much as did the editorial advice of Edward Garnett and the re-reading of Jefferies for the critical study which appeared in 1909. Some of his best prose is to be found in his stories for children, *Four and Twenty Blackbirds* (1915), witty, humorous, fantastic derivations and explanations of proverbial sayings. It is not surprising therefore that, with George Sturt's gardener Bettesworth in mind, he should tell his brother Julian that he aimed at a style 'as near akin as possible to the talk of a Surrey peasant'.[1] He was thinking of his prose when he said that, but the ambition was realized more strikingly in the verse. The country voice that speaks in 'Women He Liked' ('Bob's Lane') reflects in idiom, tone and rhythms the manner and sensibility of the character it commemorates:

> Women he liked, did shovel-bearded Bob,
> Old Farmer Hayward of the Heath, but he
> Loved horses. He himself was like a cob,
> And leather-coloured. Also he loved a tree.

The energy transmitted by the idiomatic syntax of the first sentence, the staccato drive of the short sentences, the hearty relish enacted in the fractional pause that separates the pronoun from its verb in 'he / Loved horses' – all express the poet's participation in the folk qualities of his character. The same gusto, directness and toughness are to be heard also in poems where dramatic appropriateness does not explain their presence. In these the poet assumes the collective voice preserved in ballads and traditional songs and stories; without being imitations at all, they are as close to the spirit of folk art as the best of Hardy's poems in this vein. 'The Gallows' is an attractive example; take the second stanza:

> There was a crow who was no sleeper,
> But a thief and a murderer
> Till a very late hour; and this keeper
> Made him one of the things that were,
> To hang and flap in rain and wind,
> In the sun and in the snow.
> There are no more sins to be sinned
> On the dead oak tree bough.

The influence is less conspicuous in 'There's Nothing Like the Sun', but for that very reason the result is perhaps finer, for the personal voice is not absorbed by the folk voice but blended with it.

> There's nothing like the sun as the year dies,
> Kind as it can be, this world being made so,
> To stones and men and beasts and birds and flies,
> To all things that it touches except snow,
> Whether on mountain side or street of town.

The sentence has a shape and movement characteristically expressive of Thomas's way of thinking; the list in line three – the surprises in some of the items and their ordering – and the careful balancing of opposite possibilities in the last line bear his hallmark. But it would be difficult to distinguish what is traditional from what is individual in the idiom and mood of the first line, or the plainness and colloquial rhythm of the second (so unconventionally colloquial that Thomas had to accentuate the line for Eleanor Farjeon's ear), or the humour of the fourth. This blend or alternation of voices is characteristic of the whole poem. As R. George Thomas and Edna Longley have noted, Thomas had a deep and informed interest in folk song; a few of his poems echo or allude to some of his favourites. The first of the two poems entitled 'An Old Song' ('I was not apprenticed nor ever dwelt in famous Lincolnshire') takes its refrain and adapts its jaunty rhythms from 'The Lincolnshire Poacher', both to counterpoint its carefreeness with the enforced constraint of his own working routine and as a way of sharing in the zestful, liberated life expressed in the music and in the words, especially of the refrain, 'Oh, 'tis my delight of a shiny night in the season of the year'. This is life *in* nature and *of* nature: roaming, poaching, seeking 'nests, wild flowers, oak sticks, and moles', but also the buoyant, spontaneous quality life has for a man who is open to his feelings, 'a man that sings out of his heart'.

The instinctive life of animals, the life of spontaneous feeling in men, is life unconfined and undivided. The description of the 'two pewits' that 'sport and cry' in the evening twilight, in the poem named after them, is a description of wholeness and perfect freedom. In flight and voice, they blend merriment and pain; the word 'cry', used four times in a poem of fifteen lines which rhymes throughout on that one vowel, dissolves the distinction. 'Plunging earthward, tossing high', free to move anywhere between earth and sky, they draw opposites into a unity, just as the two birds themselves move and sound as one. Measured against their absolute rightness of instinct and physical perfection, the poet–observer's existence is made to seem unreal, and the poet is present in the poem only as a 'ghost who wonders why / So merrily they cry and fly / Nor choose 'twixt earth and sky'. Yet the life of man lived in accord with nature can have nearly the same rightness and perfection. The poet in 'An Old Song', who, with the melody of 'The Lincolnshire Poacher' on his lips, 'sings out of his heart', has by his openness and spontaneity also attained wholeness and freedom of being. The aptness of the song to all occasions and moods signifies the all-embracing unity of being that is focused by it. This is conveyed stylistically in the repeated pairing of alternatives: contented or restless, 'at home or anywhere', indoors or out and, if out, 'on shiny nights or dark', alone or in company and whether his companion was 'friend or dear', the song expressed his feelings, 'joy or sorrow', equally. The poem not only celebrates a spontaneous and instinctive wholeness of personality, it also displays a buoyant impatience with social divisions and constraints:

> I roamed where nobody had a right but keepers and squires,
>   and there
> I sought for nests, wild flowers, oak sticks, and moles, both
>   far and near;
> And had to run from farmers, and learnt the Lincolnshire song;

and though he 'never took up to poaching', he admits to having 'thrown away a chance to fight a gamekeeper' with a whimsical sigh of regret. The prohibition that turns a crow into 'a thief and a murderer', in the second stanza of 'The Gallows' (quoted above), is the keeper's, and the keeper in that poem stands for all that opposes or confines natural, free life: the 'weasel [who] lived in the sun / With all his family' along with the inordinate magpie that had both 'a long tongue and a long tail', the crow, and 'many other beasts / And birds' have been taken from their 'feasts' of natural life by this representative of law and limit.

In the 'commonwealth'[2] of nature man is equal and at one with all creatures. In the first stanza of 'For These' Thomas expresses gratitude for the gift of his 'kingdoms three': 'The lovely visible earth and sky and sea / Where what the curlew needs not the farmer tills'. Life so regulated is reciprocal and harmonious; the order of precedence, with the curlew's needs having priority, is merely natural fact, but, with an effect of mild impudence, is here endorsed by the poet. The same reversal of what is from man's usual viewpoint the right and 'natural' order occurs again in 'The Barn', when with sly humour the poet pretends to believe that the barn was 'Built to keep corn for rats and men'.

The sun is equally kind, 'this world being made so, / To stones and men and beasts and birds and flies'. Not only are all things thus made equal in nature, but natural life, life 'in the sun', is all we have to pit against death: 'There's nothing like the sun', we are reminded in the last line of that poem, 'till we are dead'. The threat of death enhances the value of life and sharpens man's enjoyment of it. Both this poem and 'The Gallows' celebrate that tenacity of physical existence and gratitude for its pleasures which are instinctive in animal and human life; both are vigorous appreciations of living in and for the moment, and affirmations of physical life at all costs.

The life of nature is manifested, and valued by Thomas, in animals and in the general folk life. The latter makes its appearance in poems which salute the musical and poetic folk traditions, and in a style which intermittently draws on the 'peasant' idioms, rhythms and feeling peculiar to such countrymen of the old order as Bettesworth. The folk life is most conspicuous, however, in the nomadic solitaries, the 'natural men', who frequent Thomas's prose books as well as his poems. His name for one of them, Jack Noman, in 'May the Twenty-third', acknowledges what is true for all of them – the mixture of the real and the mythic, the individual and the generic, in the composition of these folk characters. Jack arrives on a day when Spring is turning into Summer, 'the first day that the midges bit', as if he were an emanation of the season – 'welcome as the nightingale', and, it seems, for the same reasons. In many ways he and the environment are of a piece:

> He was tanned like a harvester,
> Like his short clay pipe, like the leaf and bur
> That clung to his coat from last night's bed,
> Like the ploughland crumbling red.

There is a suggestion in the line that introduces him, 'Old Jack Noman appeared again', that he incarnates the spirit of rural England: he has been before and will come again; Jack, like Robin, is a traditional name for the English folk hero. The unnamed man in 'Man and Dog', a jack-of-all-trades who has worked all over the country – 'navvying on dock and line / From Southampton to Newcastle-on-Tyne', 'hoeing and harvesting / In half the shires where corn and couch will grow' – thereby epitomizes the folk life of England. But 'Lob' gives us the richest portrait. Lob, a name for 'the hobgoblin (Hob) or Robin Goodfellow' in English folklore, is applied by Thomas to 'a mythological figure able to sum up the English character and the character of England as they have evolved through time, in landscape, and in language':[3] he carries in him the essential history of the land; he is the continuous thread of its life, the source of its poetry and the racy humour of its tales, the creator of its proverbs, as of the names of its villages and the local names of its plants and animals. Gipsies, though not solitaries, play a similar role in Thomas's writing; 'their mystery', he declares in *George Borrow*, 'is the mystery of nature and life'.[4]

They also share with the folk archetypes an ambiguous relationship to England. Where the gipsies are 'foreigners but native as the birds', as Thomas says in *George Borrow* (p. 237), Lob and Jack Noman are walking embodiments of the land and its people who are yet in some ways outcasts from its community. The point of combining in them the opposite qualities of nomad and settler is to create an ideal mixture. Lob is the half-wild, unconfined yet steadily continuous spirit of England; the gipsies, while seeming to exist outside the law, form something like an alternative society. But the stress is on wildness: Jack offers stolen cowslips with a wicked grin, while the woman in 'The Gypsy' unites 'grace / And impudence' and her brother performs 'a rascally Bacchanal dance' on the mouth-organ, to the accompaniment of stamping feet and tambourine. They are, as it were, the wild source of natural living. Like Lob the Romany is identified with vitality itself:

> The gradations of the dark
> Were like an underworld of death, but for the spark
> In the Gypsy boy's black eyes as he played and stamped his tune;

the spark redeems the darkness. (When Thomas concludes 'The Glory' with the complaint that he is 'fast pent'[5] in his condition, and the self-accusation, 'I cannot bite the day to the core', he is measuring his uncertainty and discontented seeking against the norm of spontaneous unconfined living, the immediacy, sense of freedom and sureness, set up by poems like this.)

The gipsies come to beg, but Thomas is concerned to show them as 'impudent' rather than mercenary. The gipsy woman is content with the pipeful of tobacco she wins from the poet and rejoins her group before he can 'translate to its proper coin / Gratitude for her grace'. She is as careless of gains as the Romany is generous with his musical entertainment: 'And I paid nothing then, / As I pay nothing now with the dipping of my pen / For her brother's music'. Their vitality is a *love* of life, an uncalculated giving of themselves, and the poet's remark about payment expresses a mild shame that he could not match their abundance with an equal love and vitality. The same connection between a love of life and a self-giving generosity is made in 'May the Twenty-third' and 'Women He Liked' ('Bob's Lane'). When the archaic 'shovel-bearded' Bob Hayward, who loved horses and trees ('For the life in them he loved most living things'), planted an obscure lane with elms, we are meant to feel that the gift was a natural and inevitable utterance of his love. His immersion in life is implicitly contrasted with the dissociation of the modern 'travellers' who do not even see the lane, but from the distance, in space and time, of their 'slow-climbing train', only hear the stormcocks singing in it. In 'May the Twenty-third' Jack

Noman gives away the stolen cowslips that the poet will not buy from him: 'I don't want to sell. / Take them and these flowers, too, free'. And his own question to the poet – 'Perhaps you have something to give me?' – invites the same comparison between abundance and meagreness of life that presents itself to the speaker in 'The Gypsy'. Jack's love of life is more like that of the gipsies than Farmer Hayward's, impudent and devil-may-care, but it blends easily with an attitude of praise and thanksgiving – 'The better the day . . . / The Lord couldn't make a better, I say; / If he could, he never has done'. Thanksgiving and literal giving are very close.

Lob 'has been in England as long as dove and daw'; his origins are pre-Christian and his nature in all ages is essentially pagan; in saying that he '*Christened* one flower love-in-idleness', thus creating a disparity between the giving of the name and the name given, the poet has made the pagan flavour of the act more rather than less pungent. The gipsies arrive 'a fortnight before Christmas', so that, with the proximity of gipsy fair and Christian festival, Thomas may again hint at a comparison between pagan vitality and its Christian alternative. If, for the poem's purposes, Christmas is no more than the simple faith expressed in the story of the oxen and the 'Christmas corpses to be' of 'pig, turkey, goose, and duck', then 'Not even the kneeling ox had eyes like the Romany' is persuasive, and there is no difficulty in associating life with the gipsies and death with Christianity in its popular forms. When applied to poems such as these, naturalism, along with its other senses, is the antonym of supernaturalism. The contrast between the two visions of life is incidental to 'Lob' and is perhaps only a light presence in 'The Gypsy', though more central to the meaning of that poem; it is used more seriously, however, in 'March the Third' and 'Swedes'. In the latter the life of nature is celebrated in contradistinction to the afterlife which is the hope of most religions. 'Swedes' is a short poem and needs to be quoted in full:

> They have taken the gable from the roof of clay
> On the long swede pile. They have let in the sun
> To the white and gold and purple of curled fronds
> Unsunned. It is a sight more tender-gorgeous
> At the wood-corner where Winter moans and drips
> Than when, in the Valley of the Tombs of Kings,
> A boy crawls down into a Pharaoh's tomb
> And, first of Christian men, beholds the mummy,
> God and monkey, chariot and throne and vase,
> Blue pottery, alabaster, and gold.
>
> But dreamless long-dead Amen-hotep lies.
> This is a dream of Winter, sweet as Spring.

Half-concealed in these lines is a comparative assessment of two kinds of renewed life – seasonal rebirth and resurrection to life after death. Most obviously it is a comparison of edifices, the living-mortal swede pile with the Egyptian monument to death and immortality. Thomas's comment on the inordinate aspirations of a Pharaoh is implied in the answer given to 'Blue pottery, alabaster, and gold', the dead artifacts of human yearning, by the living, 'tender-gorgeous', colours, 'white and gold and purple', of nature at its lowliest. The reader is encouraged to make a further comparison by the mention of 'Christian men'. As the farm labourers have 'Let in the sun' upon the winter darkness of the swede pile, so the boy's discovery of a Dynastic tomb lets in the light of a later, Christian age to 'lighten the darkness' of the Egyptian world; superimposed upon the first simple analogy is this between the light and dark of nature, on the one hand, and the polarities of Christian revelation and the tomb-dark mysteries of Egyptian religion, on the other. Nature in 'Swedes' is the cycle of the seasons; in 'March the Third' it is twelve hours of sun and birdsong, nature's yearly blessing on the poet's birthday – so the woman speaker with a fond extravagance maintains. 'Swedes' opposes the values of nature and religion; 'March the Third' entertains the notion of a new *blend* of the natural and the holy to replace the Christian unification of life. 'This singing day' happens every year and comes as nature's perfect offering, but 'when it falls on Sunday' its perfection seems more-than-perfect; it is therefore welcomed by her – and the poet too, presumably – as 'this unnamed, unmarked godsend',[6] for 'godsend' hovers lightly and ironically between the literal sense of grace and the idiomatic sense of luck. In token of this new harmony the musics of nature and religion are made to exchange qualities:

> And when it falls on Sunday, bells
> Are a wild natural voice that dwells
> On hillsides; but the birds' songs have
> The holiness gone from the bells.

Thomas's response to nature and to zestful, spontaneous–instinctive living in animal and man is often enthusiastic, sometimes rapturous, but rarely sentimental; even his portraits of half-mythic characters like Lob and Jack Noman have absorbed too much of their folk toughness and humour to be vulnerable to such a charge. Life is typically, for Thomas, a blend of opposites, both 'Lad's love' and 'Old Man' (for example); its mystery is the mystery of the herb whose 'bitter scent' is not likeable yet compels an involuntary, inexplicable love; it has a tantalizing fascination and attracts not enthusiasm so much as a helpless allegiance. The life prized in 'The Gallows', against the keeper's destruction of it, includes pleasure and pain, *is* pleasure-and-pain: these are the polarities of a single life, as the light and dark in 'Swedes' are the polarities of one world. Signs of their presence are on the face of the natural man who every spring comes looking for birds' nests, in 'The Chalk Pit' – 'At orts and crosses Pleasure and Pain had played / On his brown features' – and mark him as the antithesis of the affectedly literary, self-dramatizing first speaker in that poem, who cannot decide whether the chalk pit *he* remembers was a 'real or painted' place. They define the reality faded from the anaesthetizing, levelling memory of the past: 'Pleasure and pain there have no sting . . . Remembered joy and misery / Bring joy to the joyous equally; / Both sadden the sad' ('Parting'). The resilient fitness for all conditions of the natural world of the homely, otherwise unremarkable sedge-warblers, commends them to the poet. Their 'realism' also exposes the partiality and illusion in the human dream of perfection. For the poet is led by the beauty of a river, 'of such radiance racing clear / Through buttercup and kingcup bright as brass / But gentle, nourishing the meadow grass', to imagine a corresponding unearthly beauty, 'divine and feminine, / Child to the sun'; only when 'rid of this dream' and its 'poison' does he see the water for what it is; the sedge-warblers then enter the poem to preside over this new vision and preference. Not seeking the heights but 'hanging' low 'on willow twigs', they yet sing longer than the skylark, a 'song that lacks all words / all melody, / All sweetness almost'; yet, as he would rather have the 'bitter scent' of Old Man than 'others more sweet', so this song is dearer to him 'Than sweetest voice that sings in tune sweet words'. And the reason is the same: the instinctive wisdom of their song, like the mystery of the herb, is that, blending opposites, it expresses the wholeness of life – 'Quick, shrill, or grating, a song to match the heat / Of the strong sun, nor less the water's cool'.

Life, as composed of pleasure and pain, is accepted wryly or neutrally in these poems, but positively welcomed in others.

> And April I love for what
> It was born of, and November
> For what it will die in,
> What they are and what they are not:

the poet's appreciation, in 'The Thrush' of each month's uniqueness is intensified by awareness of its contrary. Absence gives value to presence, lack enhances the worth of possession. In 'November' ('November Sky'), the unlovely 'mixture of earth and water, / Twig, leaf, flint, thorn, / Straw, feather' characteristic of that month, which is 'Condemned as mud' by most men, is praised by Thomas precisely because it stands in distinct contrast to the light of skies that are 'Clean and clear and sweet and cold'; while the sentimental dreamer 'imagines a refuge there / Above the mud, in the pure bright / Of the cloudless heavenly light', the realist

> loves earth and November more dearly
> Because without them, he sees clearly,
> The sky would be nothing more to his eye
> Than he, in any case, is to the sky;
> He loves even the mud whose dyes
> Renounce all brightness to the skies.

In the last two lines there is a hint that earth and sky partly correspond to the real and the ideal seen as complementary opposites of natural existence. Thomas's realism renounces the *fugitive* imagination, but not the desire itself for the unattainable, a desire which, in tension with the actual, sharpens the poet's relish of things as they are.

Affirmation of values passes naturally into, and is often inseparable from, the application of critical standards; poems celebrating the life of nature may be aimed critically at some character's or the poet's own avoidance of reality. Thus, in 'The Watchers', the carter's communion with the life of his horse meets its antithesis in the inn visitor's dissociation from what he sees, and praise by the second speaker in 'The Chalk Pit' of the man who searches painstakingly for birds' nests each year becomes a judgment upon the first speaker's romantic mystifications. 'Sedge-warblers', too, is both an affirmative poem and a poem critical of the idealism of a dreaming self. But 'The Lofty Sky' and 'Ambition' are purely self-critical; the values directing the exposure of the poet's *Sehnsucht* are no more than invisible presences in the margins; in these two poems we have a critical rather than an affirmative naturalism. The same is true of several other poems. There is no overt presentment of values in 'It Was Upon'; the judgment upon the poet's *Sehnsucht* (again) is merely inherent in the associations of the language used. 'The lattermath / Will be a fine one', the stranger had said one July evening, looking out over the country at the rich second crop of grass, and the younger Thomas had responded with characteristic excess: 'Flushed with desire I was. The earth outspread, / Like meadows of the future, I possessed'. The promise of 'a second Spring' has prompted a dream of power; the words recall the mixed promise expressed in the last lines of *Paradise Lost* and the temptation of Christ in the wilderness. Even without the succeeding reference to the stranger's words as 'an unaccomplished prophecy' – the future actually in store for Thomas and England was the war – this is enough to locate the emotion and identify the illusion in it. Temptation is allowed to exercise a more immediate, more seductive attraction upon us in 'The

Brook', lacking, as it does, the intervention of morally slanted words like 'flushed' and 'possessed'; self-judgment is buried deeper and can be missed in a first reading of the poem. The poet, seated by a brook, shares his solitude with a butterfly, and his contentment seems innocent enough:

> As if never a cart would pass again
> That way; as if I were the last of men
> And he the first of insects to have earth
> And sun together and to know their worth.

Yet the yearning for an absolute solitude murmurous in those mildly worded 'as if' clauses, a wish to preserve for ever in suspended time the pleasures of 'sight and sound' and guard them from all human intrusion, is not far removed from the hectic desire to command the future confessed in 'It Was Upon'.

But in his self-critical poems Thomas's values are usually explicit. Where natural life is the standard, these are various aspects of natural reality. Such poems differ, however, from 'November' ('November Sky') and 'The Thrush', which affirm the life of nature, in presenting that reality negatively, as a limiting condition, invoking it with a chastening intention as a curb on the ambitious spirit: it is a nettle to be grasped, a reality to be endured rather than celebrated. In 'Liberty', for example, the poet, in the roles of both dreamer and critic, first records his fantasy of an absolute freedom from confining circumstances and then adds a scathingly sceptical commentary; in conclusion he confesses a fond but half-grudging commitment to an imperfect mortal life, a life of contraries, a life ultimately not subject to human will:

> And yet I still am half in love with pain,
> With what is imperfect, with both tears and mirth,
> With things that have an end, with life and earth,
> And this moon that leaves me dark within the door.

Here, we might say, the reality to be endured is both limiting and liberating; for acceptance of human limitation – being ignored and, as it were, nullified by the non-human – is at the same time a release from the prison of self. 'The Glory' captures a related and also characteristic mood in its full complexity. 'The glory of the beauty of the morning' 'tempts' the poet, as so often, to seek a perfection of life equal to 'the lovely of motion, shape and hue' and to go in quest of 'something sweeter than love', a 'happiness I fancy fit to dwell / In beauty's presence'. The lovely, which deserves greeting and admiration, here raises the mirage of something beyond love and the lovely. Implicit in the language is a judgment upon the inordinacy, the illusion, and the mere vague discontented restlessness ('In hope to find *whatever it is I seek*') that informs the questing compulsion. The complexity of this poem is that the critical standard applied – acceptance of the limits of life – does not have the last word. On the one hand, he can ask, 'Or must I be content with discontent?' and reinforce the realistic assumptions prompting that question with a wry, unexpected analogy, 'As larks and swallows are perhaps with wings' – a comparison that effectively 'clips the wings' of human aspiration, since the ability to fly, especially the climbing and darting flight of these birds, is a natural image for freedom from limits. On the other hand, exposure of the fancy and illusion that feed a craving for 'something sweeter than love' fails to subdue the last rumblings of rebellious dissatisfaction with a time-bound condition:

> Or shall I perhaps know
> That I was happy oft and oft before,
> Awhile forgetting how I am fast pent,
> How dreary-swift, with naught to travel to,
> Is Time?

One line in particular in this poem highlights the difference between the affirmative poems and the poems that display a critical naturalism. It comes almost exactly half-way through the poem, and pictures a lovely, earth-bound delicacy to set against 'The glory of the beauty of the morning' that sings so rapturously of perhaps unearthly promise in the opening. It is how he imagines the beginning of his quest for a superhuman 'Wisdom or strength to match this beauty'. 'Shall I now this day,' he asks, 'start / And tread the pale dust pitted with small dark drops?' This is, as it were, where all journeys begin, whatever their anticipated destinations, and the homely vignette is a reminder and a gentle admonition aimed at his inflated aspirations. In lifting such humble, inconspicuous sights to the eyes' attention this one line does what 'November' does throughout; yet the moods of the two poems are quite distinct. Here the feeling is certainly appreciative: answering the tiny exquisiteness of the scene there is a precision and delicacy of touch in the sound and movement of the line; but it lacks the gusto of 'November'. It has more in common with the explicit counter-romanticism of 'But These Things Also', which notes tiny, bleak tokens of a winter not yet turned spring with a loving attention that is nevertheless directed by a spirit of ascetic self-denial:

> chip of flint, and mite
> Of chalk; and the small birds' dung
> In splashes of purest white:
>
> All the white things a man mistakes
> For earliest violets . . .

6 Imagination

There are for Thomas two modes of imagination. The first, the subject of my previous two chapters, creates values by judging the self's limitations, or by delivering the poet from 'self-consciousness' and making sympathetic connection with the common life. The second, which I will examine in this chapter, transforms reality and enables him momentarily to transcend the self's limitations. The poems of 'moral' imagination are self-judging or self-expanding; the poems of metamorphic imagination are self-transcending or self-transforming. Time rules in the one and is suspended in the other.

Birdsong is a traditional image for poetry, and birds feature frequently in Thomas's poems as, in part, metaphors for both kinds of poetic imagination. The choice of birds, however, is not always traditional. The undistinguished, hardy sedge-warblers are the subject of one poem, and the insouciance and resilience of chattering starlings are admired in 'The Mill-Pond' and 'The Barn'. These are the common virtues; birds also symbolize for Thomas the rarer qualities of poetry. Though he pretends to think of thrushes as among the 'lesser things' in 'The Word', their song is used elsewhere to represent the transcendent imagination, notably in 'March' and 'The Green Roads'. In 'March' they defy mortality: 'So they could keep off silence / And night, they cared not what they sang or screamed'. There is also a question of special knowledge. 'Something they knew – I also, while they sang', which explains the opening line, 'Now I know that Spring will come again': they have prescience of the year's end, and, by analogy, of the spirit's regeneration. In 'The Green Roads' one creates with its tune an alternative eternity to confront the eternal darkness and enigma of the forest:

> In the thicket bordering the forest,
> All day long a thrush twiddles his song.

'Twiddles' is echoic but also a brilliantly evocative word. Suggesting normally an idle, time-filling activity, in juxtaposition with the menace of the forest, into which all green roads disappear, it enlarges its range to include a sense of placid, heedless, unwitting bravado on the part of the 'twiddler'. It is no accident, I think, that this reminds us of the gentle, unemphatic, self-deprecating yet unflinching, unflagging voice of Thomas's poetry. The last lines of 'Haymaking', which set the poem's picture of changeless life against the changelessness of death, come to mind:

> The men, the beasts, the trees, the implements
> Uttered even what they will in times far hence –
> All of us gone out of the reach of change –
> Immortal in a picture of an old grange.

Thomas's critical books reveal a mind that had thought persistently and individually about the language of poetry and the nature of the poetic imagination. The relevant passages of general reflection occur not only in the studies of the poets Maeterlinck, Swinburne and Keats, but also in the books on Jefferies and Pater. It is not surprising therefore, with these behind him, that some of his poems should be partly or wholly about poetry – the nature of words, the poet's relation to his material, the peculiarities of his own imagination. When he writes about the imagination it is nearly always what I have called the metamorphic imagination. A preliminary look at some of these poems will prepare the way for discussion of the poems which display this kind of imagination in action.

In 'Aspens' even the melancholy that permeates his poetry is cast as a transformative agent.

> All day and night, save winter, every weather,
> Above the inn, the smithy, and the shop,
> The aspens at the cross-roads talk together
> Of rain, until their last leaves fall from the top.
>
> Out of the blacksmith's cavern comes the ringing
> Of hammer, shoe, and anvil; out of the inn
> The clink, the hum, the roar, the random singing –
> The sounds that for these fifty years have been.
>
> The whisper of the aspens is not drowned,
> And over lightless pane and footless road,
> Empty as sky, with every other sound
> Not ceasing, calls their ghosts from their abode,
>
> A silent smithy, a silent inn, nor fails
> In the bare moonlight or the thick-furred gloom,
> In tempest or the night of nightingales,
> To turn the cross-roads to a ghostly room.
>
> And it would be the same were no house near.
> Over all sorts of weather, men, and times,
> Aspens must shake their leaves and men may hear
> But need not listen, more than to my rhymes.

Whatever wind blows, while they and I have leaves
We cannot other than an aspen be
That ceaselessly, unreasonably grieves,
Or so men think who like a different tree.

His poetry 'grieves', and 'ceaselessly', but there is no self-pity here; his melancholy is presented in those last two stanzas not as a burden but as a kind of grit and stubborn honesty, acknowledged and endured. Assenting to the conditions of its making and obeying its necessity are the courage of poetry: 'Aspens *must* shake' and 'We cannot other than an aspen be'. Men may think his grieving unreasonable, but its persistence, 'whatever wind blows', impervious to changes of 'weather, men, and times', if it is a limitation of temperament, is also proof of stamina and an assertion of independence; the last line breathes a diffidently expressed but none the less firm defiance of those whose taste is merely different. Melancholy was 'the foul rag-and-bone shop of the heart' for Thomas, as 'lust and rage' perhaps were for Yeats, and poetry was the 'ladder' on which he climbed out of it to find an antithetical self.[1] Although the perpetual 'rain' which is the inner weather of Thomas's poetry gives a darker tint to whatever experiences are reflected in it – its 'talk' nearly always has a murmuring undertone of sadness – yet, echoing the robuster noises of the day's activities, it manages to re-create a busy general life (a spectral version of it) in the mind, transforming his grieving loneliness into a ghostly society, 'a silent smithy, a silent inn', making within an 'empty' non-human universe divided between beauty and terror – 'moonlight' and 'thick-furred gloom', 'nightingales' and 'tempest' – a human interior of voices talking together. Dimmed or muted, this reflection of reality nevertheless holds its own in the daily world. Its 'whisper . . . is not drowned', but with a quiet insistence imposes its own coherence upon life's randomness – 'The clink, the hum, the roar, the random singing'. Which is to say that 'over' means both 'above' and 'about'. 'Over all sorts of weather, men, and times' (in every kind of circumstance and upon all subjects), the rustling voice of the aspens is to be heard commenting, shaking their leaves as poets shake their heads in doleful judgment; composing the differences of people, times, and conditions under the one sound of whispering leaves or the one covering of fallen leaves. Poets shake their heads over (about) a miscellany of subjects and bring a kind of unity to them by giving them one voice, and poets stand sadly aloof shaking poems over the world, but their 'rhymes' live on through all sorts of weather and times and are heard by all sorts of men in various times.

Aspens 'whisper'; every reader will recognize this as a description of

Thomas's poetic voice. He hardly ever raises it; when he does, as in 'This is No Case of Petty Right or Wrong', he is liable to strike a false note. He speaks in an undertone and his thought moves obliquely or underground; it is evasive, making an unhurried meandering progress on the surface and going off in unexpected directions, at times seeming to disappear altogether, leaving, as it were, an invisible murmur of meaning. In 'I Never Saw that Land Before' he permits himself to dream of a language of such reticence that it would not even 'whisper [his] soul':

> I should use, as the trees and birds did,
> A language not to be betrayed;
> And what was hid should still be hid
> Excepting from those like me made
> Who answer when such whispers bid.

Evasiveness and reticence seem appropriate words to describe this quality of voice and thought, and a further refinement of it, a hermetic secretiveness, seems to be the ideal expressed here. But in using such terms I do not mean to ascribe his poetic practice and aspirations to a mere personal diffidence. Though the language postulated is one that will secretly convey the poet's soul, it is the language not the soul that he is anxious to protect from betrayal. The imagery of the poem makes it plain that what is in need of protection is a particular relation between words and the things they signify: the trees and the birds, whose 'language' the poet emulates, are like the breeze in a previous stanza, 'That hinted all and nothing spoke', and the breeze is both free-floating and a part of the landscape, linked to it as consciousness and speech are to the body. It is language whose implicitness testifies to an identity of word and thing, of mind and world: it speaks, rather than speaks about, the world – its meaning 'hid' in the sense of inherent in its images; any interpretative attempt to separate the words from what they signify would indeed be a betrayal, a revelation that would not so much 'give away' as falsify the wholeness of meaning. (Critical 'translation' of poetic meaning cannot be avoided, however; my own effort of interpretation here is necessary but not therefore exempt from such a charge.) Thomas is, of course, stating a personal ambition, but his poetry only carries to one extreme an implicitness which is intrinsic to poetic thought; and although the metaphors of concealment and betrayal particularly suit the elusiveness of his kind of poetry, the ideal is for all poetry. The lines quoted – they are the closing stanza – depict with a fine accuracy and suggestiveness the kind of knowing mediated by the imagination and the means of transmitting or sharing that knowledge peculiar to the imagination. This is true even of the last two lines, with their personal reference to 'those like me made', which would seem to restrict the audience sought by Thomas for his poetry to a very small band of fellow spirits. If this is what he meant, his expectation was certainly based on experience. Robert Graves once declared pessimistically if proudly that he wrote poetry only for poets; Thomas could not count on even that many readers. In his lifetime sympathetic readers of his manuscript poems were to be numbered perhaps on the fingers of one hand; editors, fellow poets and friends were unable to provide the intelligent and sensitive response that would have made a different expectation realistic. But if the lines do have this meaning, they also have, like the preceding lines, a reference beyond the personal situation. When language identifies word and thing the relation between poet and reader is similarly close, a relation of communion rather than communication. The mood of these concluding lines is in fact far from pessimistic. Thomas is imagining a special kind of invisible community that poetry creates, a finer bond of sympathy between people than any that exists in ordinary societies.

The power of words is the theme of several passages in Thomas's criticism; Edna Longley quotes the most interesting of them in her commentary on the poem 'Words' (pp. 279–81). It may be true, as she tentatively proposes, that this poem is 'the most modest tribute ever paid by a poet to his medium'; in the opening lines, for example:

> Out of us all
> That make rhymes
> Will you choose
> Sometimes –
> As the winds use
> A crack in a wall
> Or a drain,
> Their joy or their pain
> To whistle through –
> Choose me,
> You English words?

The poet, it is implied, is one who assumes a posture, in Edna Longley's phrase, of 'alert receptivity' (p. 279) to the potentialities of words, who does not use words but is used by them, does not choose but is chosen. This suggests possibly a moderate estimate of his own poetic gifts, but not, certainly, of the poetic vocation. Rather, the images of almost self-abasing deference playfully mimic the attitude of the votary to his god; in humbling himself the servant magnifies his master and in so doing exalts his service. The petition combines modesty with a sense, or hope, of election; he is a vehicle for but no less a maker of 'rhymes'. 'I know you', he continues, with the confidence surely of an initiate. What he knows is that words contain all the qualities of life – 'light' and 'tough', 'sweet' and 'strange', 'old' and 'young':

> But though older far
> Than oldest yew, –
> As our hills are, old, –
> Worn new
> Again and again.

They are commensurate and coeval with the full span of earthly reality. The poet gives himself to the language, a suprapersonal order to which he learns to belong, and where, joining the 'dance' of words, he is at once 'fixed and free'. All the contrary qualities of existence are in words; winds whistle joy or pain almost as though the difference between them hardly matters or hardly exists, merely because they have found expression. They not only express joy and pain, the long-lasting and the new-minted, the familiar and the strange, but they have the same range of qualities as life has and attract the same range of responses as life does. To use them or to belong to them, possess them or be possessed by them, is therefore to have the power to reconcile contraries. In a convenient shorthand I have spoken of an identity of word and thing in poetry; this does not mean that language is a mere reflection of reality. 'Words never consent to correspond exactly to any object,' Thomas wrote in *Feminine Influence on the Poets*: 'the magic of words is due to their living freely among things' (p. 85) – as freely as man their inventor. 'Earth' is 'dear' to us and words 'prove/That we love' it: they reflect not the world but our feelings for it; or rather, they dissolve all distinction between subjective and objective perception, expressing the quality, which is to say our sense, of life.

Words add human feeling to what they signify. They name neither a purely objective nor a purely subjective reality but an 'interfusion' of both. 'The word' that thrushes learn every spring, however, that stays in the memory when more 'significant' names like those of 'the mighty men' and 'most of the stars' have been forgotten, is an unattached 'empty thingless name'. 'Empty', that would seem to discredit it, and in fact enhances the mystery of its memorableness, is later changed to 'pure' – 'A pure thrush word'. 'Clear / And tart', like the 'bitter scent' of Old Man it points beyond the human world – 'the name, only the name I hear':

> While perhaps I am thinking of the elder scent
> That is like food, or while I am content
> With the wild rose scent that is like memory,
> This name suddenly is cried out to me
> From somewhere in the bushes by a bird
> Over and over again, a pure thrush word.   ('The Word')

The elder scent is like food and the wild rose scent is like memory, but this is *like* nothing; not empty but pure, the word is its content, or it names something pristine and ultimate, the unnameable. It is what the title says, *the* word, as it were nature's surrogate for the eternal Word, the Logos of St John's gospel.

The existence of a 'thingless name' raises the possibility of a reality beyond words, inexpressible. The act of naming is the primary act of the verbal imagination, but it fails of its purpose if it is a naming of the unnameable. Imagination as Wordsworth conceived it, not merely verbal, unites man with and thereby transforms the natural world; for it is surely by imagination that 'the discerning intellect of Man' is 'wedded to this goodly universe / In love and holy passion'. But Thomas sometimes sees naming as a divisive not a unitive act. Where Wordsworth 'proclaims / How exquisitely the individual Mind . . . to the external world / Is fitted: – and how exquisitely too . . . / The external World is fitted to the Mind; / And the creation . . . / . . . which they with blended might / Accomplish',[2] Thomas is occasionally aware that human words are only loosely attached to what they denote: of the herb called Lad's love or Old Man he confesses that

> the names
> Half decorate, half perplex, the thing it is:
> At least, what that is clings not to the names
> In spite of time.

Indeed they may come between man and his perceived or 'created' world. 'October' is a poem that shows linguistic imagination as just failing to transform external reality. The autumn scene 'has grown fresh again and new / As Spring' but the slowed wheel of the seasons has not quite stopped; the elm tree still 'Lets leaves into the grass slip, one by one'. 'Earth is beautiful' and is felt to be beautiful but the poet is not happy or cannot convince himself that he is happy. He can neither suspend time nor 'turn / In alternation of violet and rose, / Harebell and snowdrop, at their season due' – that is part of what the poem is saying, but not all; it is not only time and the human condition that trouble him, but a personal disposition to label as melancholy the indefinable feelings aroused in him by a scene like this. It could be that he has an unhappy disposition; 'Now I might / As happy be as earth is beautiful, / Were I some other . . .' is one possibility. A second is that this might indeed be happiness, or if not

> who knows?
> Some day I shall think this a happy day,
> And this mood by the name of melancholy
> Shall no more blackened and obscured be.

This suggests not just that it is a wrong name, but that words are always an imposition upon experience; the name masks and distorts the reality of mood and day, and the failure of imagination is directly linked with the failure of language to express the unitary world of man and nature.

The limits of language are also treated in 'Women He Liked' / ('Bob's Lane'). Two acts of naming occur and parallel each other. The first is the explicit theme of the last half of the poem: an explanation of how a certain track lined with elms came to be called 'Bob's Lane', after the Bob Hayward who had planted them. The second is mentioned in passing, with a sly lack of explanation: the archaic title for Bob, 'Old Farmer Hayward of the Heath', in fact supplies an attractive but fanciful etymology for the Sussex town Hayward's Heath. He liked women but loved horses and trees; 'For the life in them he loved most living things, / But a tree chiefly'. He is a sturdy Bettesworth character whose love unites him to the natural world, who in one respect – 'He himself was like a cob, / And leather-coloured' – had come to resemble it. His planting of the elms was both an expression and a commemoration of that love. Perhaps the word 'commemoration' provides a clue to the significance of the puzzling sequel:

> Many years since, Bob Hayward died, and now
> None passes there because the mist and the rain
> Out of the elms have turned the lane to slough
> And gloom, the name alone survives, Bob's Lane.

There is, of course, nothing puzzling about the literal degeneration of the lane; it is only unexpected as the (almost anti-climactic) conclusion to a poem apparently celebrating natural vitality in a human being. The poem does celebrate the life created by the union of love and its object, but the point made is that it eludes naming. The difference could perhaps be expressed as the difference between natural imagination, in which love marries nature and generates a world, and linguistic imagination. This creative life continues only as long as Bob Hayward himself is alive; the love that keeps it in being is anterior to words and is wordless. Naming, however, is an act of love too, as 'Words' says, and for its 'thicket' and 'nightingales' the track deserved a name; but, remarks Thomas with a resigned sigh, 'To name a thing beloved man sometimes fails'; not always but sometimes, and when he does fail his failure symbolizes the disparity between words and the living reality they try to accommodate. Words identify a livingness only when it is past its prime; hence the lane acquired its name in the aftermath – a name which, moreover, tied its life to the man, whose death therefore doomed it to a soulless afterlife. It is as though naming betokens a recognition not of 'the thing it is', its full life, but of its passing, the loss of it; it becomes a substitute for the condition itself. Invariably this is true of place names. Hayward's Heath, whatever else it is, is no longer a heath; the name commemorates what it once was and is no longer.

'Old Man', 'October', and 'Women He Liked' ('Bob's Lane'), in conveying Thomas's consciousness of a reality beyond words, indicates the finiteness of the purely linguistic imagination but does not radically challenge its value and powers. At least the name, Bob's Lane, survives to entice a poet to seek the reality it commemorates; Old Man and Lad's love may not contain the essence of the plant they name, 'and yet,' the poet can say, 'I like the names'. But Thomas can be more sceptical than this of imagination, as of anything else. It would be more accurate to say that he is aware – from self-examination chiefly – of delusions fostered by the misuse of imagination. I have already noted it in the theatrical fancies of the first speaker, portraying a younger self, in 'The Chalk Pit'. There it is opposed to the matter-of-fact, sceptical mind of the second speaker, above all to his trust in what his eyes show him; whereas the romantic looks inward and finds 'ash trees standing ankle-deep in brier / And bramble', playing parts in a mental drama, his practical companion appeals to the facts: 'But see: they have fallen, every one, / And brier and bramble have grown over them'. The visitor to the district remembered by the second speaker is added to the opposition. He searched for birds' nests, not mysteries, and 'The wren's hole was an eye that looked at him / For recognition' – a striking figure to convey the primacy of objects in his vision. Thomas celebrates respect for the facts (whole vision depends on it) in 'The Thrush' –

> I *must* remember
> What died in April[3]
> And consider what will be born
> Of a fair November –   [my italics]

and clear seeing in 'November' ('November Sky') –

> Another loves earth and November more dearly
> Because without them, he sees clearly,
> The sky would be nothing more to his eye
> Than he, in any case, is to the sky.

And he practised both as a poet. He is often critical of the sentimental romantic in himself, and the poems that are dialogues between two aspects of his personality, voices or actual characters, are usually, as in 'The Chalk Pit', confrontations of the romantic and the realist or factualist. Equally characteristic of Thomas's manner are the poems which indirectly expose rather than openly criticize the delusions of imagination. Thus 'She Dotes' half reveals and pityingly half conceals the consoling fantasy of the woman crazed by the death of her lover – a mad, shy willingness to suspend disbelief in miracles:

> Yet she has fancied blackbirds hide
> A secret, and that thrushes chide
> Because she thinks death can divide
> Her from her lover.

More sinister is the moonlight's metamorphosis, in 'The Wasp Trap', of the wasp jar into a seeming star. It is the way of moonlight, as of the imagination, to make the lovely – 'lakes / And meadows' – lovelier. But it is undiscriminating; it changes the unlovely into something no less lovely. The lethal jar swings in the tree, and the poet prays with perfect ambivalence that it may keep its false but star-like appearance: 'long may it swing / From the dead apple-bough / So glistening' – the sentiment poised with horrible tremulousness between 'dead' and 'glistening'.

II

These poems explore approvingly or critically the Romantic idea of imagination as a species of 'magic'. The motivation of many of the poems that display the metamorphic imagination at work is also, in this sense, Romantic. They are essays in self-regeneration, seeking to transcend the temporal and spatial limits of circumstances and personal disposition and to create images of a unity of man and world; they belong to what Thomas thought of as 'moments of everlastingness' ('The Other'). A particular form of this self-transcendence is expressed in those poems which, by connecting the poet to a past or present suprapersonal reality, give him imaginative possession of some order or condition outside his immediate experience. In Chapter 4 I used the term 'epiphany' to describe this quality of experience in some of Thomas's poems. As I said there – my examples were 'I Never Saw that Land Before', 'Home', 'The Manor Farm' and 'Haymaking' – the power of the transformative act of imagination is usually released by some rare conjunction of circumstances; often the listing of them precedes the main narrative or description as auspicious signs prefiguring the occasion. The signs may be something exceptional about the season, or the time of day, or the weather. Sometimes the specialness of these favourable conditions consists in the coincidence and reconciliation of opposites; in this they may be suitable preludes to the idyll, or seemingly timeless moment, or perfection of being, to be presented in the body of the poem.

In his poems about imagination Thomas's attitude varies from the modestly celebratory to the sceptical; the poems displaying the transformative imagination at work in his experience show a comparable range. It is as well to begin an examination of these poems with recognition of Thomas's pervasive scepticism. The experiences recorded are never more than momentary glimpses vouchsafed to the poet but inaccessible to the man; sometimes not only are they brief and fragile but what they reveal is questionable. In 'It Rains' the poet seeks and, in a visit to a scene of his early courtship, finds, a lost love.

> It rains, and nothing stirs within the fence
> Anywhere through the orchard's untrodden, dense
> Forest of parsley. The great diamonds
> Of rain on the grassblades there is none to break,
> Or the fallen petals further down to shake.
>
> And I am nearly as happy as possible
> To search the wilderness in vain though well,
> To think of two walking, kissing there,
> Drenched, yet forgetting the kisses of the rain:
> Sad, too, to think that never, never again,
>
> Unless alone, so happy shall I walk
> In the rain. When I turn away, on its fine stalk
> Twilight has fined to naught, the parsley flower
> Figures, suspended still and ghostly white,
> The past hovering as it revisits the light.

He is seeking imaginative repossession of what is in reality irrecoverable – 'And I am nearly as happy as possible / To search the wilderness in vain though well' – and the exquisite metaphor of the last sentence 'figures' the apparent success of his enterprise. The enabling conditions are a moment of flawless stillness and the twilight that seems to suspend the recovered past in a timeless, dimensionless limbo. The stillness and twilight make possible this revival of past feelings, but the incongruity of that word 'revival' to denote what actually happens – the disembodiment of the past – and the imperfect happiness of the occasion identified with fastidious precision – 'I am nearly as happy as possible' – point to a less satisfactory aspect of the experience. The moment of exquisite stillness is also an interlude of immunity from pressure and responsibilities, an escape from life as much as a pursuit of it. The scene in its glittering fragile perfection, epitomized by 'the great diamonds / Of rain on the grassblades', has other, sinister implications, which grow more insistent as the poem proceeds. The perfection sought and found seems too perfect. The virgin stillness, we are gradually made to realize, is maintained at the expense of life. The grassblades unbroken, the leaves unshaken, the orchard untrodden – a condition evidently so soothing to the poet depends upon the exclusion of people, notably the very lovers whose former disturbance of the scene stands for the happiness he has lost. The shock of conflicting evaluations comes early, in the confrontation arranged by the line-division between the two halves of 'the orchard's untrodden, dense / Forest of parsley'. During the unfolding of this description the orchard changes from itself into what it later becomes, a 'wilderness': life's potentialities have been neglected; love, untended, has failed to bear fruit; from the scene fenced in by memory's idolatry actual life has withdrawn itself. The parsley stalk, already fine, has been refined out of existence, and its pale flower appears to float in the air without roots: the past hovers with spectral insubstantiality. The poem stresses the paradox of the timeless moment the rich endowment of such moments cannot be separated from the emotional poverty implicit in the need for them. Yet only thus, only by grace of these momentary respites from time and disturbance – this is the pathos of the situation – can Thomas transcend the lovelessness of the present. And only in solitude, in sequestered, peopleless scenes like this, can he re-experience the lost connection with general living. *Only in imagination* – the emphasis in this poem is on limitation – can his lost love be restored; to possess vicariously, palely, insubstantially, what his life lacks, he is condemned to pursue the very experiences which betray, and confirm, his actual dispossession.

At the opposite end from the guarded affirmation of 'It Rains' is the exhilaration of 'An Old Song', the second of the two poems with that title, both of which declare a sense of kinship with the folk songs they quote, echo and reflect upon. A still, windless, uninterrupted vista of sea and sand, and a striking effect of after-sunset light – a horizontal ray dividing the clouds and stretching 'Like a straight narrow footbridge bright / That crossed over the sea to me' – combine with the involuntary memory of a sea shanty, 'The Maid of Amsterdam', to create a moment of transport ('I walked elate, my bridge always / Just one step from my feet'). In 'It Rains' Thomas seeks and finds a connection, if an attenuated one, with his own past. In 'An Old Song' he enters into a suprapersonal reality. The solitary ('And no-one else in the whole world / Saw that same sight') experiences immediate identity with the life of nature and the body of mankind: 'The sailor's song of merry loving / With dusk and sea-gull's mewing / Mixed sweet', and he becomes part of that blend as he joins in with the sailors' chorus, 'I'll go no more a-roving / With you, fair maid'. The civilized modern poet, one who feels bound to acknowledge and perhaps deprecate the 'lewdness' of the song in his appreciation of its 'wild chorus', finds his source in the unconfined wildness of the English folk tradition.

In several poems, England itself, an immemorial and rural England, is the general life and larger reality restored by the poet and inhabited by him for the duration of the poem. I have mentioned in another connection the *immemorial* quality of the England mirrored in 'Haymaking' and 'The Manor Farm': 'All was old, / This morning time, with a great age untold', and 'A season of bliss unchangeable / Awakened from farm and church where it had lain / Safe under tile and thatch for ages'. The same image of England is presented in 'May the Twenty-third', personified, as we have seen, in the half-real, half-legendary figure of Jack Noman: both vagrant and archetypal countryman, whose very walk seems to epitomize the folk life of England ('Who could say if his roll / Came from flints in the road, the weather, or ale?'), arriving each year in late spring, with 'his cresses from Oakshott rill / And his cowslips from Wheatham hill', he shares in the agelessness of the seasons and the landscape.

I speak of something restored, but in these three poems we have not so much the sober celebration of historical continuity as the defiance and defeat of time. 'May the Twenty-third', 'Haymaking', and 'The Manor Farm', no less than 'It Rains', are examples of a type of poem very common in Thomas's work, which presents an idyll, either as a goal reached or as a scene transfixed in suspended time. Often the motifs work together, as they do in 'It Rains', and also in 'The Manor Farm', though there the goal is not the reward of seeking but a gift of serendipity. One February Sunday the poet, while walking, chances upon an old farmhouse, set by a church and yew-tree of equal age. The scene is lit by a wintry mid-day sun; this seems to endow it with special significance, and with the stillness and silence at once transforms winter into 'a season of bliss unchangeable'. A final mention of the one sound to break the silence, the sound of cart-horses 'swishing their tails / Against a fly, a solitary fly', by drawing attention to this mundane irritant, a tiny flaw in the moment's perfection, in fact humorously sets a seal on the scene's apparent immunity from change and disturbance. Unlike 'It Rains', 'The Manor Farm' pictures an almost flawless idyll.

But the real imperfect world is not forgotten. A notable feature of the poem's plot is that there are two stages in the establishment of the timeless moment. First comes the mid-winter sun's defiance of the season, melting the ice; the poet treats its spring-like promise with an affectionately contemptuous scepticism. His attitude to it changes, however, when to this illusion is added the vision of a past world caught in its immutable essence by the sunglow and the 'Sunday silentness':

Nor did I value that thin gilding beam
More than a pretty February thing
Till I came down to the old Manor farm,
And church and yew-tree opposite, in age
Its equals and in size.

The distinction between the two stages is not between the false and the true, rejection of the one and acceptance of the other. The spuriously 'gilding beam' of a freak sun is at first dismissed as valueless; yet the 'glow' which the village scene acquires would not exist without it. By admitting into the poem, barely, the notion of a false spring, Thomas as it were inoculates the deep reminiscent glow of the experience against a more virulent scepticism. The lightness of touch that sometimes tempers the hyperbole of these moments has a similar function; the poems call for a willing suspension of disbelief and coax the reader into this state by displaying an open, self-amused connivance in the illusions practised. These jaunty lines from 'May the Twenty-third' epitomize the mood of many of the idylls:

Today ere the stones were warm
Five minutes of thunderstorm
Dashed it with rain, as if to secure,
By one tear, its beauty the luck to endure.

A 'dash' of reality and nothing grander than 'luck' suffice to 'secure' the conditions in which the imagination may work its magic.

'Adlestrop' is perhaps the best-known, though by no means the best, example of the idyll in Thomas's work. Yet, while it is a slighter achievement than most of the idylls, it is none the less an attractive poem and worth some attention. It records an express train's brief unscheduled stop at a country station, the silence and emptiness, a view of fields, the song of a blackbird. The preparation for the experience of timelessness – in a note for the poem he refers to 'an extraordinary silence between two periods of travel'[4] – is simpler than that of 'May the Twenty-third' and 'The Manor Farm'. Those poems candidly display their stage-management of the occasion, set the moment in the quotation marks of an amused if indulgent self-awareness; 'Adlestrop' lacks that kind of sophistication, yet the unassumingly prosaic conversational tone of the opening, the bare disjointed notation of the event, and the fragmentary rhythms, have a comparable effect. The sheer ordinariness of the occasion, the very lack of incident –

It was late June.

The steam hissed. Someone cleared his throat.
No one left and no one came
On the bare platform. What I saw
Was Adlestrop – only the name . . .

– similarly disarms the reader's critical vigilance and exposes him to the full force of the 'extraordinary' sequel:

> And willows, willow-herb, and grass,
> And meadowsweet, and haycocks dry,
> No whit less still and lonely fair
> Than the high cloudlets in the sky.
>
> And for that minute a blackbird sang
> Close by, and round him, mistier,
> Farther and farther, all the birds
> Of Oxfordshire and Gloucestershire.

As the poet unites himself with the English folk tradition in 'An Old Song', and captures the essence of an immemorial England in such poems as 'The Manor Farm' and 'May the Twenty-third', so in 'Adlestrop' a scene glimpsed in a brief moment from a stationary train seems to open upon an ever-widening prospect of England's central counties. These are common sights of the English countryside, but the moment is visionary; the language of addition ('*And* willows . . . *and* grass, / *And* meadowsweet, *and* haycocks dry') suggests a rippling movement out into never-ending space; where the eye stops the ear takes over. Again it is an ideal England mirrored in the stillness and solitude of the poet's mind, where there are no distinctions between earth and sky. Yet it is related to a view of patriotism expressed by Thomas more than once. The implication of a passage in *The South Country* (p. 71) is that patriotism is the veneration felt for 'an ideal England', but that each man's ideal (or idea) of England is based on knowledge of a very small part of it. In *The Country*, he accepts 'fifteen or twenty square miles' (p. 7) of intimately known native land as large enough to be justifiably regarded as a microcosm of the whole country.

The entry of self by an act of imagination into some larger reality, or the imaginative repossession of something lost, which are ways of describing the theme that connects 'It Rains', 'The Manor Farm' and 'Adlestrop', are sometimes aspects of a more general movement of the metamorphic imagination. An alternative description of 'Adlestrop', for example, would be that in seeking to heal division between self and not-self it presents images of oneness and wholeness. They can be interpreted as a series of paradoxes. Here is a part of England that contains or yearns to contain the whole, an emptiness that contains fullness, a solitude which is also a crowdedness, a stillness that utters itself in birdsong; perhaps also we have a word, a name, that in some sense contains concrete reality. Certainly we can say either that association of the name with the scene combined with the experience of pause – a sensation as of time suspended – to generate the revelation of that moment, or that the name released the potential of this interval in time.

All the idylls present 'moments of everlastingness'. Stillness is especially characteristic. The halted train and 'No one left and no one came' of 'Adlestrop' correspond to the picture-like stillness of 'Haymaking' – 'The men leaned on their rakes, about to begin, / But still. And all were silent' – which has a quality of eternity: 'the long waggon stood / Without its team: it seemed it never would / Move from the shadow of that single yew'. Nothing moved in that mid-morning break; only scents 'Travelled the road'. Frequently the stillness – the stillness of immobility or silence – is set in strong relief by a slight, trivial movement or sound: the tiny disturbances of 'one small wave that clapped the land' in 'An Old Song' and the swishing tails of the cart-horses in 'The Manor Farm' have the same function as the hiss of steam and the noise of throat-clearing in 'Adlestrop'. Thomas's note, quoted above, mentions a pause of 'silence between two periods of travel'; many of the poems explore the quality of such interruptions in the regular flow of time. 'Interval', in its title, names the experience, and speaks of a moment of 'stormy rest' between a 'wild day' just gone and a 'wilder night' to come. As often in Thomas's work, the moment of respite occurs in the transition from day to night, an ambiguous time of 'brief twilight' between opposite conditions in which neither rules. In 'Sowing' it is 'a long stretched hour', but in this instance it gratifies more than the desire for a 'temporary' reprieve from time.

> I tasted deep the hour
> Between the far
> Owl's chuckling first soft cry
> And the first star.

The word is 'between', but the stanza evokes the satisfaction not of disengagement but of unity. The distance between the associations of owl and star is lessened, in the first place, by the ambiguous description of the owl's cry, which blends soft and sinister, laughter and pain, the feelings of predator and victim. And then, as though enacting the length of the 'stretched hour', the owl's cry seems to stretch out along the length of that third line, filling up the interval that separates owl from star and finally joining them. 'It was a perfect day / For sowing'; he has tasted since then the perfection of evening twilight; and now night comes with rain, 'Windless and light, / Half a kiss, half a tear, / Saying good-night'. There is no timeless moment in 'Digging', but it resembles 'Sowing' in this rendering of the world as a blending of opposite conditions. The poem celebrates the sense of smell, which dissolves distinctions between wild and tame, joy and pain, life and death:

scents dead leaves yield,
And bracken, and wild carrot's seed,
And the square mustard field;

Odours that rise
When the spade wounds the roots of tree . . .

The smoke's smell, too,
Flowing from where a bonfire burns
The dead, the waste, the dangerous,
And all to sweetness turns.

In the last two lines of the poem he turns suddenly from the smell of earth, remembering appropriately Keats's 'To Autumn', to the robin that 'sings over again / *Sad* songs of Autumn *mirth*'. The larger, suprapersonal reality into which the poet of transformative imagination steps, whether it is love or the folk tradition or his 'native land', is ultimately this one world breathed through the nostrils or glimpsed at twilight and in rare moments of stillness.

7 World's end

Thomas's perception of nature is frequently interwoven with his perception of himself. This has been a commonplace of criticism since Leavis drew attention to it in *New Bearings in English Poetry*: 'the outward scene,' he wrote, 'is accessory to an inner theatre' (p. 69). Leavis carefully avoids saying that nature is only a metaphor for feeling; for it is plain that 'the lovely visible earth and sky and sea' ('For These') is also frequently Thomas's theme. Moreover this is not Wordsworth's universal nature but the lovingly observed landscape of England. *This England*, the England celebrated by John of Gaunt in *Richard II*, is the title of an anthology put together by Thomas in the early months of the war. Increasingly in his later prose, and then in his poetry, his imagination was engaged with an idea of England: a pre-industrial rural England, both wild and cultivated, of pre-historic and historic foundations, a land of hills, valleys and streams, of gardens, orchards, fields and woods, of farms and villages, possessed by a 'commonwealth'[1] of wild creatures, labourers and wandering men. Almost all of Thomas's values are in some way associated with this image of England.

It is also an endangered England, one about to disappear from men's consciousness. Poems that affirm these values invariably present them in the context of imminent loss, as belonging to a dying order of life, a world coming to an end. The pervasive theme of loss in Thomas's poetry is usually discussed in exclusively psychological terms; yet it has both a personal dimension – the lost love in 'It Rains' is a representative expression of it – and this social–historical dimension, where it appears as a deterioration of national character or loss of national identity. Frequently, indeed, personal and general loss are felt and presented as aspects of the same situation; the poet's sense of personal debility is at times hardly distinguishable from his consciousness of social or cultural enervation.

I have explored the personal dimension of this theme in Chapter 2; in the first part of this chapter I shall be examining the historical dimension, the assumption in Thomas's poetry that he is living at the end of an era. But if we can say that personal failure and cultural decline were habitually associated in Thomas's mind, it is also true that the sense of personal and historical loss is a manifestation of his sensitivity to the transience of all things. Most of Thomas's perceptions take place within a larger awareness of the dark, non-human, insentient world outside the circle of light created by human consciousness, memory and desire; this is the metaphysical dimension of the theme. Thomas's preoccupations with historical loss and ultimate, absolute loss are connected, and so this chapter will end with a consideration of the metaphysical theme.

I *The passing of England*

Thomas wrote all his poems in war-time and nearly half of them as a soldier training and instructing in various English camps and barracks; he seems to have written no poems during his few weeks of active service in France. Apart from three epitaphs there are no war poems in the usual sense of the word: no poems written in anticipation or from experience of battle. Many of his poems draw on moods and scenes recollected from his pre-war travels in the southern English countryside. Yet these are not exercises in memory for their own sake; he was not trying to forget the war, nor is it forgotten. William Cooke was right to draw attention to oblique references in a number of poems and the tacit presence of the war in many others, but he gives the phenomenon not too much but the wrong emphasis. It is true that the memories almost always came to Thomas (one suspects) coloured and altered by his present consciousness of an England at war, but this does not make them war poems. Thomas's response to the war stems on the one hand from his feelings about a spent England, sapped of vitality, living in the aftermath of its strength – not war but specifically England at war is what concerns him – and on the other from his general awareness of the dark side of existence. The catastrophe when it came only licensed and reinforced an inveterate bias of sensibility by providing it with the objective situation it was formed to apprehend and interpret.

The subservience of the war theme to the larger theme of an enfeebled, superannuated England is plainly discernible in three poems which, having in common the same image of sudden disaster, would seem at first glance to tell against the case I am presenting. 'Fifty Faggots', 'The Barn', and 'As the Team's Head-Brass' all use the image of the tree (or trees) cut down. The destruction of the elm in 'As the Team's Head-Brass' and the clearing of brushwood in 'Fifty Faggots' are explicitly linked to the war: in the former 'the blizzard felled the elm' on the night the ploughman's mate met his death in France; in the latter

Thomas makes a loose association of the faggots, winter and war as he conjectures that

> they must
> Light several Winters' fires. Before they are done
> The war will have ended, many other things
> Have ended, maybe, that I can no more
> Foresee or more control than robin and wren.

The war is not mentioned, however, in 'The Barn', and it may or may not be implied in the anticipated fate of the old but healthy tree that overhangs the barn – 'Tomorrow they cut it down'; it is more significant that the tree is again an elm, in Thomas the quintessentially English tree, and its fortunes are sardonically contrasted with that of the dilapidated barn, for the sake of which perhaps the elm tree is to be sacrificed:

> They should never have built a barn there, at all –
> Drip, drip, drip! – under that elm tree
> Though then it was young. Now it is old
> But good, not like the barn and me.

> Tomorrow they cut it down. They will leave
> The barn, as I shall be left, maybe.

Whether or not there is a link with the catastrophe of war, or whether the cause is chance, an external agency or human choice, is secondary in significance to the actual felling of England's elm. Moreover the blizzard of war, in 'As the Team's Head-Brass', only completes what decay has begun: 'The blizzard felled the elm whose crest / I sat in, by a woodpecker's round hole, / The ploughman said'; where a woodpecker has been the tree is already dying or dead. War is seen at once as a random disaster and as the culmination of a natural process; disaster is in the foreground, but other alternatives are present and the poem does not decide between them. In 'Fifty Faggots' the relationship between the two possibilities is reversed: the thinning of underwood would encourage the growth of the remaining trees, and only comes to seem ominous here in the dark hints about endings that crowd the last lines of the poem (quoted above).

These three poems share little else other than the common symbol (if that is the word);[2] in form and style they are very different. They each focus a different facet of their theme, the virtually posthumous life of a dead England; even the images they present of the condition of England vary. 'Fifty Faggots' emphasizes general transience and the common helplessness of bird and man, and the elegiac tune dominates: 'There they stand, on their ends, the fifty faggots / That once were underwood of hazel and ash / In Jenny Pinks's Copse'. 'As the Team's Head-Brass' plays several tunes – solemn and whimsical, wistful and amused, hopeful and resigned; it is a poem of oppositions – love and war, peace and destruction, talk and silence. The image of destruction is the whole of 'Fifty Faggots', barely more than a parenthesis in 'As the Team's Head-Brass'. In one respect, however, they stand together and in contrast to 'The Barn': the England represented in them as dead or threatened is a simple entity. In 'The Barn' there are two Englands, one healthy and one not, as there are two differently depicted Englands in 'The Combe' and 'Women He Liked' ('Bob's Lane') and several other poems. 'The Combe' distinguishes the 'Briton' from the 'English', identifying a comparatively recent vein of Englishness with the deliberate savagery of hunting, and setting it against the original primordial darkness of the 'ancient' combe, where the hunted badger, its 'ancient' denizen, still burrows. 'Women He Liked' ('Bob's Lane') takes a shorter historical view: the earthy Victorian squire Bob Hayward, life-loving, a planter of elms, is the 'natural' survivor of a 'natural' England; the train-travellers that pass by hearing the stormcock in Bob's Lane but not seeing the elms he planted are the rootless, dissociated inhabitants of a later, effete England. The elm has a similar significance in 'The Barn'. With a wry wit the poet includes himself in the superannuated order figured in the dilapidated barn – the tree 'is old / But good, not like the barn and me'; a barely perceptible gesture of self-deprecation similarly accompanies his attachment of himself, in 'As the Team's Head-Brass', to the decayed elm felled by the blizzard – 'the elm whose crest / I sat in, by a woodpecker's round hole'.

The outbreak of war and the ensuing protracted examination by Thomas of its impact on him and his thoughts about the England he loved, a process of troubled introspection that led a year later to his enlistment in the Artists' Rifles at the age of thirty-seven, almost certainly clarified and extended the self-knowledge already apparent in his prose writings. More than that, a sharp insight into the ambivalence of his feelings and in consequence a less simple view of the character of England and Englishness seems to have developed during that period; one expression of it was the conception, which I have begun to illustrate, of a divided England. The strongest evidence for this development is in one of his earliest poems, 'Tears'. It presents images of traditional England – a fox-hunting scene and the changing of the guard in the Tower of London – and hints at certain 'truths' embodied in them, truths unnamed and difficult to translate but which concern both England and previously undreamed-of ambiguities in Thomas's patriotic response. But if, in the words of 'Tears, Idle Tears', he is 'thinking of the days that are no more', he is thinking more energetically than Tennyson; it would be pleasant to believe that the opening lines are a 'dry' plain comment on the lachrymose plangency of Tennyson's 'divine despair'.

> It seems I have no tears left. They should have fallen –
> Their ghosts, if tears have ghosts, did fall – that day
> When twenty hounds streamed by me, not yet combed out
> But still all equals in their rage of gladness
> Upon the scent, made one, like a great dragon
> In Blooming Meadow that bends towards the sun
> And once bore hops: and on that other day
> When I stepped out from the double-shadowed Tower
> Into an April morning, stirring and sweet
> And warm. Strange solitude was there and silence.
> A mightier charm than any in the Tower
> Possessed the courtyard. They were changing guard,
> Soldiers in line, young English countrymen,
> Fair-haired and ruddy, in white tunics. Drums
> And fifes were playing 'The British Grenadiers'.
> The men, the music piercing that solitude
> And silence, told me truths I had not dreamed,
> And have forgotten since their beauty passed.

Motifs already noted in the three poems examined above are to be found here too. This is a vanished or vanishing England. The 'beauty' of whatever 'truths' the scene holds for the poet has indeed 'passed'; perhaps not for ever, perhaps only for the poet, but 'passed' is a strong word to end with and suggests an irrevocable finality; the word 'whispers' possibilities rather than states certainties. The poem seems to exist in the 'silence' of aftermath. Again, like 'The Combe', 'Tears' pictures an England divided against itself; however the line between the different strains of Englishness is not so easily drawn. The remembered scenes are alike not merely in their almost postcard representation of traditional England, but in less predictable ways, which set up a disturbing counter-current to nostalgic emotion. The ugly implications of unity in the hounds – 'all equals in their rage of gladness . . . made one' – throws its shadow of dark meaning over what, without this collocation, would be an innocuous phrase, 'in line': though singly these are guileless young countrymen, together they constitute a destructive force and have been taken from their shires and lined up for that purpose. Murder that gratifies the instincts of the huntsmen is the trade of the soldiers. The first scene is a revelation of collective emotion, the second of the collective will. The overt stress, it is true, falls on the glamour of these English occasions; even the dragon is as much a gloriously heraldic as an ominous presence. Much of the 'charm' of the courtyard scene on this warm spring morning lies in its contrast with – its tacit repudiation of – the grim 'double-shadowed Tower'. Yet the dead past of the Tower with its dark history is not so lightly banished; it has obvious if undisclosed connections with the present, embodied so picturesquely in the line of soldiers and the martial music. The continuity witnessed here has both bright and dark threads. It is one England, and, as we are shown, a united England; but there seem to be two *images* of England, one superimposed upon the other, which are felt to be incompatible. It would be dangerous to try to be more definite than this: a Thomas poem is a composition of such fine nuances that exposition can easily simplify and coarsen the total effect. Perhaps we can say that whatever strain in the national character sent the Hunt trampling over Blooming Meadow, which 'once bore hops' (the curve of the phrase, as in 'Fifty Faggots', bears an elegiac cadence), is now at work again fashioning soldiers out of the no less blooming 'fair-haired and ruddy' countrymen of England. In each case the poet's quiet grief, audible as a faint undertone of sadness, is for *rural* England, the England that was most dear to Thomas; either the rural way of life or an idea of its quintessential Englishness is menaced – but oh so picturesquely! – by the dragon of war. But it is menaced from within: he sees the war not as an external cause but as the culmination of an internal process.

It becomes clear that there are actually more than these two aspects of England in the poem: we have a military and a civil, a past and a present, perhaps a patrician and a plebeian England. The tension of incompatible emotions in the poet is commensurately more acute than in 'The Combe' or 'The Barn'. A power to feel, disclaimed in the opening line, does in fact return and grow during the course of the poem, as Edna Longley remarks; but, I would add, the feeling restored is not the simple patriotism he says he has lost. Tribute is paid to the 'beauty' of hitherto unsuspected 'truths' conveyed by the ceremony in the Tower courtyard, truths that are, by implication, latent in the hunting scene too. They are in part revelations concerning the poet's feelings for the 'beauty' of the English tradition, for he is susceptible to the glamour in these handsome demonstrations of its collective identity. These feelings are, however, tinged with uneasiness at the thought of the '*rage* of gladness' (my italics) that in the event has been the unifying factor. The title, after all, is 'Tears'; and although the tears he could not shed would have expressed a joy in England's beauty intensified by foreknowledge of its passing, a more bitter truth, undercutting the stately decorum of elegy, is also brought to recognition in the poem. All the pain of it is packed into one word, 'piercing': the music pierces him with love of England and grief for its passing, but also grief for a flaw of violence in its make-up (as in that of all nations and all men).

The part that Thomas gives himself in these poems about a doomed England corresponds exactly to the part he sees himself playing in some of the exclusively personal poems. To take one example, the past in 'It Rains' is 'ghostly' and yet more alive than the present, the poet's former self more alive, even in 'ghostly' memory, than the self that now searches the neglected orchard and sadly commemorates his courtship. Having no real tears but only 'ghosts' of tears to shed, Thomas casts himself in 'Tears' as a ghostly survivor in the ghostly afterlife of a once vital tradition. The grief he feels for the impurities in England's composition is at the same time grief for his own inability to grieve any more, or at least to grieve in simple elegy and unflawed nostalgia. This imagery of posthumous living really belongs to the character of solitary which he assumes in most of his poems. 'With me, social intercourse is only an intense form of solitude', he confessed to Bottomley,[3] and in the poetry he seems to regard his isolation as symptomatic of or analogous to a general breakdown of relations, an absence of vital connections that corresponds to the absence of life evoked in such scenes as the 'chalk pit', 'vacant of a life but just withdrawn', 'the emptiness and silence / And stillness' of which 'haunt' the first speaker in that dialogue ('The Chalk Pit'), an English scene that recalls the 'silence' of the Tower courtyard in the earlier poem.

There is a paradox at the heart of all these poems. The sense of imminent loss has sharpened the immediate reality, and intensified the poet's appreciation, of what he wants to call English, whether imaged as the 'ancient' badger or a copse of hazel and ash or the English elm. The paradox does not call for comment until it presses into the language of the poem, which is the case with 'Tears'. It is a paradox closely associated with the dual status of solitude in Thomas's poetry. What he said about it in a despairing mood to Bottomley is not the whole truth. A limitation of personality it may be; but it is also – this is a central recognition in his poetry – the medium through which he transcends that limitation. His deficiencies as a social being were not, of course, to be *explained* historically by the condition of England, but Thomas discerned a relationship between them. Equally he saw a link between the poetic rewards of a lost national identity and the poetic rewards of solitude. As the reality of England faded, the nearer it seemed to approach extinction, the more urgently was Thomas spurred to the imaginative realization of an ideal England. Similarly his very remoteness from the reality of social experience seems responsible for the central position which social values have in his poetic world. Thomas speaks of the 'charm' of the courtyard scene, and all the enchantment of that moment is concentrated in the brief statement, 'Strange solitude was there and silence', a key sentence, the words of which are played over again in the concluding lines. The martial music – all that it implies of a nation at war and a belligerence glorified by tradition – is alien to the solitude and silence in which he most intensely feels *his* connection with England. It is 'strange' that solitude should co-exist with the presence of soldiers; that is one meaning, but the word also brings with it the submerged suggestion that the poet is there among them as a stranger, for the solitude is his. His affection for the countrymen turned soldiers is strong but he has no direct relationship with them. It is as though they and he breathe a different air, and the atmosphere of isolation that surrounds Thomas necessarily interposes itself between him and them. Debarred as he was by temperament from direct enjoyment of social life, there were moments such as this – moments of intensely experienced apartness – that nevertheless awakened in him a heightened imaginative and reminiscent response to the general life.

The 'truths' about England and Thomas's feelings expressed in 'Home' ('Often I had gone this way before') are similarly complex. It may not be immediately obvious, indeed, that this *is* a poem about the lost England of the past, an England without a future. The first two stanzas proclaim the poet's rediscovery of his nationality, a renewed sense of belonging to a particular locality and country. In 'Tears', feeling which was supposedly deadened is regenerated during the course of the poem; in 'Home' the rebirth of feeling is announced as a fact in the opening lines.

> Often I had gone this way before:
> But now it seemed I never could be
> And never had been anywhere else;
> 'Twas home; one nationality
> We had, I and the birds that sang,
> One memory.
>
> They welcomed me. I had come back
> That eve somehow from somewhere far:
> The April mist, the chill, the calm,
> Meant the same thing familiar
> And pleasant to me, and strange too,
> Yet with no bar.

The speaker has discovered in himself an unsuspected vein of feeling that connects him with a particular locality and, beyond that, with a particular nation. To have 'one nationality' is to have 'one memory' – that is part of its meaning. He is speaking of what goes to make up a national identity; the only companions in memory mentioned here are the birds, and they share consciousness merely of a place and its seasons, but they are joined in the last stanza by a labourer trudging home, and memory adds to its store the *human* sounds and activities of that place. All this is included in the meaning of 'home': home is where one belongs, and the gist of these stanzas is that a sense of belonging has returned to the poet.

Yet if this is so, there is something not quite right about it. Against the assurance that now 'it seemed' he 'never had been anywhere else', we have to weigh the admission that he had been away 'somewhere far'. In 'seemed' we hear a murmur of self-distrust, and we glimpse something fragile and possibly untrustworthy in an occasion that unaccountably 'somehow' restored a sense of belonging – which might, then, just as unaccountably disappear again. The feelings revealed are not those of a man who securely belongs but of a *revenant* who experiences at the same time attachment and detachment, the familiarity and the strangeness of the place. It is precisely the traveller's experience at the inn in 'Over the Hills', 'where all were kind, / All were strangers'. Estrangement and union, solitude and community are part of the same complex of feeling.

It is the same ambivalence about society and the England he values as in 'Tears'. Why he had lost connection and under what circumstances he had managed to regain it we do not know; but in a way characteristic of Thomas's poetic method, he hints at a context of events from which tentative but not exhaustive explanations might be inferred. The 'somehow' and the 'somewhere', by their evocation of a mythical (timeless and placeless) exile and return, demand recognition of an aspect of our humanity not entirely explicable in either historical or psychological terms; but they establish the 'normality' of exile among the assumptions of the poem, and the mystery itself is modified a little by faint intimations of a war-time occasion for the poem's emotions – features are sufficiently visible in the twilight of meaning to invite speculative identifications. 'Nationality', suddenly detaching itself from the local emphasis of 'this way' and 'home', gives first warning of the larger context. 'One nationality / We had' would have for the envisaged reader of 1915 a tone and significance not immediately perceptible to us, but for any reader familiar with Thomas the implication of war and the cadences of epitaph in the last two stanzas are inescapable. There is, of course, the elm, and there is the atmosphere of endings.

> The thrush on the oak top in the lane
> Sang his last song, or last but one;
> And as he ended, on the elm

> Another had but just begun
> His last; they knew no more than I
> The day was done.

The last two lines are charged with Thomas's personal sense of the end of an era as much as with premonition of his own death; the two fates are not felt to be separable.

In the last stanza the labourer returns home and the day ends in silence;

> And, through the silence, from his shed
> The sound of sawing rounded all
> That silence said.

It speaks both of fullness and emptiness. In pondering what it does say we may recall the perfect but desolate stillness of the orchard scene in 'It Rains'; but the 'silence' in 'Tears' comes closer, and perhaps also the 'Sunday silentness' in 'The Manor Farm', where there is also one sound that in breaking the silence draws attention to it as a positive presence. There the ineffectual annoyance of the solitary fly underlines the scene's imperviousness to disturbance; here the sawing gives shape to, filling out and drawing a line round, the message contained in the silence. In the logic of the central analogy, the end of song and the end of day coinciding, it tells of the 'death' of England, and we are driven by this logic to associate the image of sawing with a threat to the English oak and elm – an implication that glimmers at 'the edge of consciousness' (Leavis's phrase) with the half-reality of a fear not yet owned as a conviction. Yet the (unsymbolic) 'charm' of the moment also contradicts this impression: the labourer returns 'half with weariness, half with ease' – a natural completion of the day's work; in the ending there is also a contentment, a fulfilment. The silence speaks at the same time of death and of a kind of ripeness; out of death is distilled an essence of England.

But silence has something more to tell about the solitary imagination (and social life). As I said in the course of discussing 'Tears', only in the silence and solitude of imagination could Thomas feel the sense of community he was unable to enjoy in his daily life. As the silence is somehow deepened by interruption, so conversely the human 'sound of sawing' stands out clearly against its background of silence; the moment has an echoing quality – human life speaking out of the silence of things come to an end with the thin clarity of a memory. He responds to a loneliness in the sound, which nevertheless admonishes him with the recollection of all the sounds of day in which, having only just returned from 'somewhere far', he has *not* participated. But in this mood remembering shades into commemoration, epitome into epitaph. Thomas wrote no war poems, only muted elegies for a vanishing England, but the war was undoubtedly decisive in his development: it needed the threat of catastrophe to bring him to this urgent awareness of his social and national identity. There is no single reason for Thomas's sudden outburst of creativity in the first months of the war. The old sentimental explanation – that the cause of England awakened the simple patriot in him – certainly will not do; on the other hand due weight should be given to the fact that the poems themselves sometimes imply, by the analogy of birdsong, a relation between this release into poetry and the death of what it celebrates. 'Home' is an example: in the third stanza the last song before nightfall, sung by one thrush and then another, is also the poet's. It *was* their last song, the day *was* ending, the silence gathering, and yet, he says, 'they knew no more than I / The day was done'. This might mean that they did know – how could they not? – but sang *as if* they did not; it is more likely to mean that the songs had, without their knowing it, the kind of perfection that signifies finality, the purity of summary and valediction.

II *'Dark . . . without end'* ('Old Man')

Thomas's feelings about the passing of England and about war as the culmination of a historical process of decline are a particular expression of his general sensitivity to the transience of all things. The theme of loss has three circles of meaning: the smallest is the personal; outside that is historical and social loss, and the widest circle, containing the other two, is the metaphysical. 'The Sun Used to Shine' has all three circles of meaning. The innermost circle constitutes the overt occasion of the poem, commemoration of the 'easy hours' of an idyllic month in Thomas's friendship with Frost; the friendship remains but the chances of being together and the charmed life of deep mutual sympathy and understanding have passed irretrievably. The second circle is reached as 'rumours of the war remote', unheeded when 'the sun used to shine' on their friendship, become less remote with the approach of night: 'The war / Came back to mind with the moonrise / Which soldiers in the east afar / Beheld then'. The outer circle is the dark counterpart to the world of light, the underworld of 'sunless Hades fields' (the battle-fields of France are merely absorbed into this larger reality); there 'Everything / To faintness like those rumours fades'. It is an almost imperceptible touch of irony – depending largely on the placement of 'everything' and the cue to the voice to linger contemplatively over its implications – but one on which the poem turns, that as they treated the world outside the magic circle of friendship so will they be treated, and as they ignored the soldiers so life will ignore them.

'The Combe' has the national and the metaphysical levels of meaning. It can be read both as an emblem of divided England – the bloodthirsty England of the hounds and the imperilled England of the badger – and, in the wooded combe itself that excludes most of the light and 'the singing birds', as an image of primordial darkness; at this level of meaning the two Englands are instead two views of the dark side of existence. 'The Combe was ever dark, ancient and dark', but becomes 'far more [or in a different sense] ancient and dark' after the killing of the badger; those are the two views. In the first view it is sombre, forbidding, almost impenetrable but not hostile; it is hospitable to one songbird, 'the missel-thrush that loves juniper', and if 'the sun of Winter, / The moon of Summer . . . are quite shut out', this also means that some of the time light filters through. 'No one scrambles over the sliding chalk . . . / Down the half precipices of its sides', it is true, but 'with roots / And rabbit holes for steps' ('steps' envisages human entry) it would not be impossible. It is an ancient source of being whose 'mouth is stopped with bramble, thorn and briar' – an ancientness that is both prehistoric and eternal, an '*ever* dark' principle of being. In this meaning the metaphysical and the psychological meet; for a reality that is dark, has its 'mouth' stopped with undergrowth, yet occasionally gives utterance in the voice of its one songster the missel-thrush, could also suggest the unconscious mind as a half-choked creative source. (The 'ancient and dark', as a simultaneous metaphysical and a personal reality, was indeed a positive creative source for Thomas.) The second view of this ancient darkness is associated with the killing of the badger. Nature is bloodthirsty, and man, hound and badger, as its creatures, share a primordial strain of savagery. The words 'ancient and dark', used to evoke both a non-human mystery and the strain of inhuman savagery, indicate, of course, a close relationship between the two; yet it seems clear that they are separate, or that they express separate views of the dark world.

Edna Longley gives a different interpretation, one which emphasizes the connection, rather than the distinction, between the combe and the brutality of the hunters. 'By killing the badger,' she writes, 'man has both violated his bond with Nature and revived an older more savage link between them (the Combe was already "dark")' (p. 181). Where for her the phrase '*far more* ancient and dark' means simply what it says – older and darker but basically the same, I find a grim play on the words and the implication that this is both a deeper and in some respects a different darkness. I would not disagree, however, that the point of the poem is the triumph of brutality and evil, though I see it as the triumph of a power of darkness not always and not necessarily evil. I stress the positive associations of the combe, as signifying a source of being and a creative source for Thomas, because it is possible to feel that his sensitivity to the impermanence of life is excessive, producing a distortion of vision, and to see his preoccupation with time and eternity and non-being as an impoverishment of subject-matter. Like a number of modern writers – from de la Mare at one end of the modern poetic spectrum to Eliot at the other end – Thomas was exceptionally vulnerable to feeling the 'unreality' of existence. Mortality and temporality (the fact that 'everything . . . fades', that any scene, like the tiny wood of 'beech and yew and perishing juniper' in 'The Combe', is a mixture of life and death), the non-human world and the ultimate silence and nothingness, loomed large in his consciousness, liable at any time to empty all meaning and value out of human life. While recognizing this in Thomas, I would agree with Coombes that he never totally surrenders to the invasion of meaninglessness, and never succumbs to the seductions of easy cynicism or the 'life-is-futile' brand of pessimism.

This is even true of 'The Hollow Wood' and 'Two Houses', poems that give uncharacteristically emphatic expression to the negative significance of their images: 'the pale hollow wood' where nightmarish 'birds swim like fish – / Fish that laugh and shriek' and 'Lichen, ivy and moss' give a grisly appearance of life to 'trees / That stand half-flayed and dying'; in the second poem, the dark ghost house, an irruption of 'the hollow past' that 'Half yields the dead that never/More than half hidden lie' and seems to make a mockery of its present successor, a farmhouse idyllically situated 'Between a sunny bank and the sun'. (The motif of hollowness is related in significance to the emptiness of life and meaning pictured in the abandoned chalk-pit, 'vacant of a life but just withdrawn'.) 'The Sun Used to Shine' gives us 'the yellow flavorous coat / Of an apple wasps had undermined' as an image for the hollowness at the core of reality; it would seem that description of the monstrous life and death-in-life in 'the pale hollow wood' is meant to undermine the golden life enjoyed by the goldfinch out in the sun, and that the 'dusty thought' of death is introduced to undermine the sunny perfection of the farmhouse scene. Yet this is not the effect. In fact 'The Hollow Wood' starts with and returns to the goldfinch, that effortlessly 'flits and twits / *Above* the hollow wood' with a feather-light unconcern, apparently impervious to the malign influences below. On the other hand, in 'Two Houses' the dark house and its gothic horrors do have the last word. The description of them takes up the second half of the poem; the smiling farmhouse –

> Far out of reach
> Of the road's dust
> And the dusty thought
> Of passers-by . . .

– enjoys a privileged but precarious sequestration. Nevertheless, though its sunny existence is threatened by the 'dust' of time, death, weariness and envy (implications of the image generated in the lines quoted), the note of aristocratic disdain in the phrasing offers resistance to the threat. The goldfinch has an insouciance and the farmhouse a serenity that may not defeat mortality but do effectively challenge it.

Whether or not this reading of 'The Hollow Wood' and 'Two Houses' proves acceptable, the general suggestion that Thomas's habit of presenting life as divided between contraries, clearly exemplified in these two poems, has an expansive rather than a reductive intention, is not likely to seem implausible to most readers. In the poems whose imagery supports my description of their common theme as a preoccupation with the dark side of being, poems that contrast and confront light and dark, life and death, the total effect is usually affirmative. The plot of 'There's Nothing Like the Sun' – a long build-up followed by a quick let-down – would at first glance seem to refute that statement. Despite the strategy of its plot, however, there is nothing Hardyesque about the feeling of the poem. It is true that the hyperbole of affirmation, beginning with the opening line and maintained for another eighteen lines, ends with death's rude one-line rejoinder: 'There's nothing like the sun till we are dead'. While this is a mere truism – the sun is unique, life is unique, and that is even a reason for celebration – there is no denying that the energy of the title phrase is the energy of the idiom used to express a genially dogmatic enthusiasm ('there's nothing like a good cup of tea . . .'), and consequently the effect of the last line is, at least in part, to bring the speaker's confidence seriously into question. Yet Thomas has already anticipated the deflation of the ending in the fourth line, with that mock-pedantic, scrupulous qualification of his general assertion, 'To all things that it touches except snow', and the poet's delicately amused detachment from his own absolutism removes some of the shock from the last line; we are left then with a poem that knows the limits of celebration, knows that all statements can be disputed, that all things have their opposites (sun and snow, life and death) – but celebrates none the less.

Both 'Liberty' and 'Out in the Dark' are more sombre poems. 'Liberty' begins:

> The last light has gone out of the world, except
> This moonlight . . .
>
> It is as if everything else had slept
> Many an age, unforgotten and lost –
> The men that were, the things done, long ago,
> All I have thought; and but the moon and I
> Live yet and here stand idle over a grave
> Where all is buried.

Yet it moves towards a ruefully affirmative conclusion:

> And yet I still am half in love with pain,
> With what is imperfect, with both tears and mirth,
> With things that have an end, with life and earth,
> And this moon that leaves me dark within the door.

The last line declares a different relationship to the moon. They are no longer partners in illusory freedom; the moon alone is free and the poet, taking his place in the dark with 'things that have an end', embraces, or resigns himself to, the mixed, 'imperfect' life of earth. Paradoxically, however, acknowledgement of limits is here the key to freedom. Relegated to obscurity by the moon, the poet is released from self-consciousness to awareness and half-love of what is beyond self, to the point of accepting the virtual extinction of self by the power of otherness. 'Out in the Dark' is Thomas's last published poem. Its concluding stanza is unsparingly bleak:

> How weak and little is the light,
> All the universe of sight,
> Love and delight,
> Before the might,
> If you love it not, of night.

The single rhyme in each stanza, relentlessly, monotonously repeated, blankets the poem in sameness – as the darkness itself subdues life to the one power of night; the world of light suffers defeat and has to be abandoned. But the terror of the universe also awakens a fellowship in fear; the penultimate stanza at the same time imparts an awesome grandeur to what is not loved:

> And I and star and wind and deer
> Are in the dark together, – near
> Yet far, – and fear
> Drums on my ear
> In that sage company drear.

Night is not simply the opponent of light; it provides a kind of 'company', which is 'drear' but – a reluctant concession – 'sage'. This is not a poem of religious belief, but the quality of awareness and response displayed might fairly be called religious.

The 'religious' note is stronger in 'Lights Out'. The emphasis is less on the terror than on the mystery of sleep's kingdom, in its prefigurement of death: it is 'the unfathomable deep / Forest where all must lose / Their way', 'the unknown / I must enter'. As sleep, so death compels its subjects; the poet's perception of sleep–death and his response to the inevitable are, for one without belief in a life beyond death, appropriately mixed. The day's journey that brought them 'to the forest brink', he says, 'Deceived the travellers' – here is a note of quiet disillusionment; and in his ambiguous praise of what is beyond love, despair and ambition – a 'sleep that is sweeter / Than tasks most noble' – wistful regret for the life left behind blends indistinguishably with a sense of relief and acquiescence. But these are no more than variant tones of one voice, unprotesting acknowledgement of necessity, and in the last three lines it speaks in the language of religious commitment:

> Its silence I hear and obey
> That I may lose my way
> And myself.

The poem is about sleep, only hinting at death; fear is not a positive presence as it is in 'Out in the Dark'; the 'silence' of 'the unknown' is not the unloved night that inexorably hunts down its prey, the rhyming antithesis of 'love and delight'. 'He that loseth his life for my sake shall find it' (Matthew 10, 39); Thomas does not, and cannot, say that, but seeking to express the willing surrender of self and self-possession he consciously echoes part of what Jesus says (the whole passage in Matthew concerns hearing and obeying).

The imagery of light and dark often co-exists, as in 'Lights Out', with the image of the dark impenetrable forest. It is a recurrent symbol in Thomas's poetry. The significance of symbol, as Coombes warns us (p. 220), can only be translated clumsily and approximately into general terms. The context for the forest symbol provided by each poem gives greater salience to certain areas of association than to others; adding to the difficulties of critical exposition, it does this without entirely excluding from consciousness the other associations; the symbol has a foreground and a background, active and potential meaning. Having issued his warning, Coombes does, however, attempt a general explanation, as one must. He gives a variety of descriptions to suit its various appearances in the poems: it is 'the dark region of human experience, which cannot be illuminated by thought or reason, a pathless region'; it is 'the gulf of nothingness or eternity that waits behind the temporal and the tangible', 'a darkness, an immensity, existing behind the appearances and sounds of life'; or it is 'simply sleep, or death' (pp. 220–1). The polarization of existence into light and dark aspects has its parallel here. In 'The Other' the world, or existence, is divided into 'forest' and 'road and inn, the sum / Of what's not forest'; a similar division is implied in 'Lights Out' (as also in 'Green Roads' and 'The Path'), where 'road and track', the ways 'straight / Or winding' of journeying man, are the antithesis of 'The unfathomable deep / Forest where all must lose / Their way'. In using the words *impenetrable* forest, I have in mind such lines as 'And evermore mighty multitudes ride / About, nor enter in' ('The Dark Forest'), and the language of demarcation: the 'borders' in 'Lights Out', the 'forest verge' in 'The Sun Used to Shine', and 'The old man, the child, the goose feathers at the edge of the forest' in 'The Green Roads'. It is, as Coombes says, a dark, pathless region, inaccessible to the reasoning mind, but this is not to say that the thought of it is raised merely to be repudiated or dismissed as meaningless. It is, rather, as 'unfathomable' suggests, a mystery, and the image evokes both fear and fascination. 'Dark is the forest and deep', the opening words of 'The Dark Forest', have the same haunting splendour as 'The Combe was ever dark, ancient and dark'. The division between forest and non-forest insists on opposition but does not align the poet absolutely with one side – the human, social, conscious world outside the forest. 'The unfathomable deep / Forest' implies something more than 'impenetrable'; the pausing, retarded movement from 'unfathomable' to 'deep', and the fractionally longer pause encouraged by the line-ending, seem to enact first a gradual surrender to an irresistible enticement and then entry into the forest depths. The words have no trace of reluctance or defensiveness in them; here, as elsewhere, the symbol opens out into the unknown.

The very fine poem 'The Owl', by dramatizing the overcoming of defensiveness, provides the most satisfying demonstration of this expansion of consciousness.

> Downhill I came, hungry, and yet not starved;
> Cold, yet had heat within me that was proof
> Against the North wind; tired, yet so that rest
> Had seemed the sweetest thing under a roof.
>
> Then at the inn I had food, fire, and rest,
> Knowing how hungry, cold, and tired was I.
> All of the night was quite barred out except
> An owl's cry, a most melancholy cry

Shaken out long and clear upon the hill,
No merry note, nor cause of merriment,
But one telling me plain what I escaped
And others could not, that night, as in I went.

And salted was my food, and my repose,
Salted and sobered, too, by the bird's voice
Speaking for all who lay under the stars,
Soldiers and poor, unable to rejoice.

The poem's thought starts from the contrast between the poet's sense of his own comfort and security and the suffering of those 'soldiers and poor', who are without shelter for the night: they are exposed to the elements, and he is not. But the drama of the poem centres on 'the night' and the 'owl's cry', and the action, beginning literally with the poet's arrival at the inn, is in essence a movement of feeling, a change in response, between the first sentence and the last, to what is signified by those and associated images. Night and the owl's cry, stars and the north wind together make us vividly and pressingly aware, not only of physical hardship, but of a world outside the range of human feeling, the chilling otherness of an indifferent, alien universe, of evil and suffering as part of the texture of creation; night represents everything – a metaphysical all – that daylight consciousness tries to exclude, the whole dark side of reality. At first the poet's response is self-protective, his one thought to *bar out* 'all of the night', but the baleful cry of night's predator, seemingly the voice of all cruelty and misery, breaches the inn's defences and floods the poet's mind with night's presence. The disparity between the solidity of the bars in which the poet puts his trust and the impalpable terrors of the night intimates man's ultimate defencelessness.

The first two sentences, then, set the scene, communicating gratitude for and a sense of order in basic things with a plain, grave, almost archaic voice. The third sentence, disclosing the ineffectiveness of the inn's defences, adds to the gravity a painful note as the words enact the poet's admission and confrontation of hard facts, 'telling' himself and us ungarnished, unpalatable truths. 'No merry note' recalls the rough sarcasm of Shakespeare's 'Winter Song' in *Love's Labours Lost* – 'Tu-whit, tu-who: a merry note / While greasy Joan doth keel the pot' – and at the same time, by removing the ironic disguise ('*no* merry note'), gives us the meaning 'plain'. And that meaning goes beyond Shakespeare's: the word 'melancholy' adds to the owl's role of predator that of victim; it is no less vulnerable to cold and hunger than other creatures of the night. The gap between 'melancholy cry' and the third stanza gives an anticipatory expressiveness to 'shaken': the cry lengthens and shudders in literal imitation of the owl's voice; but it combines with mimicry the suggestion that it has been *wrung out* of the bird by some violent external force, and thus epitomizes the double role, active and passive, played by the owl as a symbol of suffering. The poet has moved from self-protection and the attempted exclusion of the night world of pain and privation to a painful awareness of its victims.

The last stanza gives us the final, meditated assessment of the experience. It has the tone and pace of sombre wisdom, informed by a feeling of pain assimilated and subdued to a kind of stunned wonder at its existence and deep compassion for those who suffer. The most surprising, indeed shocking word in the poem is 'salted'. It seems to say that awareness of others' suffering has sharpened his enjoyment of the comforts they lack, as salt spices and flavours dull food. After the sensitive and far from complacent sampling of pain in the second and third stanzas, the experience of shock is only partly due to the fact that he admits, or seems to admit, to such feelings; it jars so much against the whole movement of feeling in the poem that we also find it difficult to believe that it says what it does say. The modified repetition, 'salted and sobered, too', reassures us without entirely quelling our misgivings; 'sobered', setting the poet's privileged possession of comfort and security in a context which includes privation, has the right moral implications, we feel, but more importantly, the repetition of 'salted' sends us back to its first use. We had expected a word that conveyed a sympathy with suffering and were shocked because we thought we had found the opposite. The unexpected use of the word and our reluctance to grant its meaning, reinforced by the pairing of 'salted and sobered', startles other implications into life: the harshness in the sharpness of salt, the salt that stings in salt tears, perhaps even the salt in the wound that sharpens pain. The word almost groans under the awarenesses it comprehends. The contrast of 'sweetest' in the first stanza with the disturbing complexities of 'salted' in the last measures the distance the poet has travelled. The tension of contrary feelings locked and buried in the word is partly relaxed by the expanded repetition, and then opens out into the full compassion of the last two lines. The 'bird's voice' has been speaking *of* evil and suffering, pointing to its existence. For a moment we may not notice that it has grown from emblem to spokesman; now it speaks *for* them, on their behalf, and thus blends with the voice of the poet. The poet who at first tried to block out consciousness of the night, and who when forced to admit its terrors did so in guilt-ridden, self-castigating tones, now identifies himself with the world of suffering which he had feared. The owl, in effect, speaks a prayer, the prayer with which the poet chooses to conclude his poem.

The speaker's response to evil and suffering has transformed itself during the course of the poem. The last stanza also introduces a new perception of the non-human. The owl speaks for 'all who lay under the stars' – an image here of human destitution and homelessness in a non-human universe, but it is not an image, like the north wind or the night or the owl's cry, to sharpen a sense of the enmity between them; for the more usual associations of the image, the glamour and grandeur of living in connection with the elemental world, are also inherent in the simple dignity and sweep of the words. The non-human universe does not lose its terror, but it is accepted as the larger field of human action, the grander tragic setting of all life. More clearly than any other poem of Thomas's 'The Owl' shows his imagination responding positively to the theme of darkness. Raised to the pitch of tragedy, his preoccupation with the forces of non-life and anti-life has been transformed into a means of growth in scope of awareness and feeling – namely, into a vital source of creative thought.

The combe, it will be remembered, 'was ever dark, ancient and dark', and the poem meditates on the implications of both epithets. Ancientness, I suggested, is part of the meaning of darkness; the combe represents at the same time a dark principle of being and an ancient source of being. The poem hovers between a positive view of this source, as a non-human otherness, and a negative view of it, as the primordial strain of inhuman savagery in life. Ancientness, a prehistoric or eternal source of being, is the central concern of several poems. The ambivalence shown in 'The Combe' is also characteristic, though it does not take precisely this form. In the negative view of this ancient source, darkness is sometimes explicitly associated with it, but the imputation of savagery is a feature almost unique to this poem.

'Old Man' starts with the herb's elusive scent and concludes with a vision of nothingness, 'an avenue, dark, nameless, without end'; yet, although the literal search for origins fails, the exploratory movement of the poem is a gradual stretching and enlargement of the imagination which, in travelling to the very boundaries of human understanding, arrives at the threshold of mystery; the source of the poet's memory is untraceable, but although it is 'nameless' it is not without meaning, untranslatable meaning. The fount of memory points to the ultimate source of being, and the poem glimpses a negative eternity in which life and non-life dissolve into each other. The same wresting of creative meaning out of a vision not unlike Donne's, of 'absence, darkness, death; things which are not', distinguishes other treatments of the theme. 'The Mountain Chapel' paints an energetic picture of the wind on the uninhabited mountain – 'The eternal noise / Of wind' that speaks mockingly to the homely chapel, its congregation, the sun and 'garden of wild flowers', with which it shares this piece of the world, of transience, death and the non-human void:

> Man lies in earth
> For ever; but I am the same
> Now, and shall be, even as I was
> Before he came:
> Till there is nothing I shall be.

'And yet somewhere,' the poet fancies,

> Near or far off, there's some man could
> Live happy here,
> Or one of the gods perhaps, were they
> Not of inhuman stature dire,
> As poets say
> Who have not seen them clearly . . .

This leaves all in doubt, and yet – there is always an 'and yet' – the poise and lightness of touch at this point, and the liveliness of tone and versification throughout the poem, counterpoint the bleak message, and permit us to imagine – if not here then somewhere – an accommodation of the human and the non-human, a condition beyond the opposition of sun and wind.

Donne's 'absence', or lack, which is a feature of the landscape in 'The Mountain Chapel' – 'The loss of the brook's voice / Falls like a shadow' – is the theme of 'The Mill-Water', imaged in the derelict mill's loss of its human function. 'Gone is the wheel' and 'the music of the mill-wheel's busy roar', making audible, most strongly at night, the constant undersound of the waterfall:

> Only the idle foam
> Of water falling
> Changelessly calling,
> Where once men had a work-place and a home.

It is the eternal sound of all that 'mocks' human purpose and meaning, the shadow trailed by all human action:

> Solitude, company, –
> When it is night, –
> Grief or delight
> By it must haunted or concluded be.

But we are listening to more than mockery; we are hearing the voice of ultimate reality. What 'The Mountain Chapel' says of the wind – 'When gods were young / This wind was old' – this poem says of the mill-water's sound:

Sometimes a thought is drowned
By it, sometimes
Out of it climbs;
All thoughts begin or end upon this sound . . .

Beginning and end, it is the source of meaning. It is a force neither for good nor evil, an eternal potential. The effect is one of grand neutrality rather than desolation.

'Solitude, company', both, 'begin or end upon this sound'. But it was through solitude that Thomas became an intimate of the non-human background to all human activity:

Often the silentness
Has but this one
Companion;
Wherever one creeps in the other is.

Thomas the social being enjoyed the idyll of companionship with Frost, commemorated in 'The Sun Used to Shine'; but it is the solitary who at the same time attends to the counter-reality indicated by 'dark betonies / . . . At the forest verge' and 'crocuses / Pale purple as if they had their birth / In sunless Hades fields', and in recollection sees that time fading into the impermanence of all things. 'All things forget the forest / Excepting perhaps me', he writes in 'The Green Roads'. Even though his moral imagination constantly engages with the world of others, it begins and ends in isolation, a place of depression, or exile, or self-absorption, or merely separateness; there is a tension between his temperament and his values, but solitude is his element. But his values are not simply social: in 'Tears', for example, the experience of separateness is the imaginative medium in which he is able to feel the general life – a social solitude, as it were, the achievement of which he claims for his poetry, perhaps for all poetry, in 'Aspens'. Although in conversation and in his letters he deplored and ridiculed his 'selfconsidering brain' (Farjeon, p. 13), his poems show a more complex mixture of feelings. Thomas's positive and negative views of the non-human and the dark side of being, indeed, correspond to the contradictory evaluations of his own solitariness.

We only need to read 'Wind and Mist' to be reminded of the connection between Thomas's loneliness and his awareness of a world unshaped by human meaning and purpose, a world of cloud and mist – 'mist / Like chaos surging back' – and wind:

There were whole days and nights when the wind and I
Between us shared the world, and the wind ruled
And I obeyed it and forgot the mist.

His susceptibility to such experiences and to a strong sense of life's vanity could submerge him in terrible depression: 'Never looked grey mind on a greyer [dawn]'. A poetry that specializes in such moods drastically limits its range. Thomas was aware of the dangers, both poetic and spiritual. Excessive preoccupation with non-being, the dark forces of the universe, and human insignificance ('How weak and little is the light / . . . Love and delight, / Before the might, / If you love it not, of night') could lead in times of nervous exhaustion to a collapse of the will and the 'love of death' named – but resisted – in 'Rain'. Whenever this feeling is present in a poem, however, it is treated critically; a counterbalancing social impulse affirms the humanity nearly lost. In 'Rain', for example, love and love of death are in tension with each other. In 'The Mill-Pond', courting danger by dangling his feet in the fast waters of the mill-stream and ignoring the threat of a coming storm, the poet is saved from himself by a girl's voice warning him to 'take care'; she startles him out of a kind of trance and breaks the spell of the scene luring him to self-destruction. The situation is repeated in 'The Brook'. Here the self-critical implications are so quiet that to be aware of them requires attunement to the faintest modulations of an even, uninsistent voice; yet this quiet voice, while it conveys the poet's undisturbed contentment with the pleasure of 'sight and sound', at the same time, as it were unwittingly, confides a yearning for absolute seclusion. He and 'A grey flycatcher' sat 'silent on a fence', as if they had not moved since the horseman buried in the nearby tumulus, 'The horseman and the horse with silver shoes, / Galloped the downs last' – so motionless and silent that when he adds 'And then the child's voice raised the dead' we know that 'the dead' includes the poet. Once again the voice of a companion – hitherto unnoticed or neglected – draws him back into the human fold.

His solitariness is not always viewed so critically; it is sometimes responsible for a more rewarding intimacy with the non-human world. In 'Out in the Dark' the speaker confesses 'fear' of the night but also a feeling of communion with it – fellowship if not love. In some poems the mystery of the forest is juxtaposed with the song of birds, a light allusion to Thomas's poetry.

> In the thicket bordering the forest,
> All day long a thrush twiddles his song.

This is the middle stanza of 'The Green Roads'. 'All things forget the forest / Excepting perhaps me', a later statement, does not give the whole story; the thrush–poet also manages to ignore the forest. Poetry may be only play and time-passing – some of the connotations of the mimetic 'twiddles' – but it is nevertheless a counter-force to whatever secret menace is represented by the forest; the suggestion of nonchalant or foolhardy courage may partly derive from an echo in my mind of 'fiddling while Rome burns'. Thomas never forgets the forest, but neither can he avoid hearing (in the last words of the poem) 'all day long the thrush repeat his song'. 'Under the Woods' begins with the same association:

> When these old woods were young
> The thrushes' ancestors
> As sweetly sung
> In the old years.

Like 'The Combe' the poem explores the feeling of ancient time; the first line may even recall de la Mare's 'Very old are the woods' from 'All That's Past', a poem that similarly makes ancientness seem like another order of existence. (Except for a reference to silence the resemblance ends there; the differences – in language, rhythm, voice – are more striking and would make an interesting subject for comparison.) The method is, as in 'Old Man', to press memory to its limits, taking it back to a strangely still time when the old becomes the ageless ('Most silent beech and yew'); the thatched cottage then lacked garden, apples, mistletoe, and children, and the keeper who 'was old' and 'had not / Much lead or gold', who hardly disturbed the silence of the trees, has a legendary air. He is beyond 'most memories', taking his place with the trees at the threshold of the immemorial. A dead stoat, described in the last stanza, 'with no scent at all, / And barely seen / On this shed wall', is an enigmatic sign with no memory of life in it, the one relic of him and the silence to which he now belongs. In fact, only the thrushes are as ancient as the woods, ancient without being old. Sharing the first stanza with 'these old woods' and 'the old years', their continuous life, perpetually renewed in the repeated song, stands as counterpoise and counterpart to the ambiguous image of the unknown in the last stanza. The life of poetry half partners, half challenges the forest. The role of the thrushes' song in both 'Under the Woods' and 'The Green Roads' makes plausible, in my view, an interpretation of 'The Combe' that finds a connection between the 'mouth' of the combe, 'stopped with bramble, thorn and briar', and the singing of 'the missel-thrush that loves juniper', the one bird to penetrate its dark tangled undergrowth; a connection between an 'ancient and dark' source of being and a source of poetic inspiration for Thomas.

8 Language and movement

I

In *Walter Pater* Thomas defines style as the representation of a man's 'singularity'.[1] In the foregoing discussion of the preoccupations, attitudes and values of his poetry, analysis of technique has of course been an integral part of my exposition. But without a full, concentrated examination of its linguistic and formal qualities this study of Thomas's 'singularity' will be incomplete. The word means more than what is commonly meant by technique: suggesting both difference and wholeness, it reveals far more about the nature of poetic excellence and originality than those shallow terms of the classroom, 'innovation' and 'experiment'. Thomas's verse is as finely wrought and as individual as that of any poet who began publishing in the 'innovative', 'experimental' second decade, during which period the foundations were laid for the renewal of English and American poetry. What he said in praise of Keats's Odes is also true of his own poems, that in them 'the poet made for himself a form in which the essence of all his thought, feeling, and observation could be stored without overflowing and disorder'.[2]

A poet's singularity is this 'essence' of perception: a compression of the mind's fullness rather than an expression of the man. Thomas's verse, though bearing everywhere the stamp of its author's peculiar temperament, is never disablingly personal, and what he goes on to say about the Odes, the most personal of Keats's poems, is, I think, equally applicable to his own work: 'of its source in his daily life there was no more shown than made his poems quick instead of dead'.

Few readers come to Thomas's poetry without knowing something of his life and personality. They will be familiar with at least the bare, mythic outlines of his story: the fifteen years' toil in the slave mines of literary journalism followed by two brief years of poetry, given, as it were, in exchange for his life. They will know of the solitariness, the crippling self-consciousness and the bouts of depression, and will find further confirmation of the general picture they have formed both in the photographs they have seen of him, looking sullen, strained, shy, or heavy-lidded with melancholy, and in the subject-matter of a few poems (and, if they ignore all contrary indications, in the tone and feeling of several others). They will, in short, find what they expect to find. 'This poetry is devoted almost wholly to expressing the characteristic unhappiness of his life': that comment, from a review of *The Childhood and As It Was . . . World Without End* by Leavis, gives the standard view.[3] It is not untrue, but even as a summary of the life it represents but a fraction of the whole truth. The biographies based on Helen Thomas's and Eleanor Farjeon's moving but partial accounts tell us too little; if only Frost had substantiated his criticism of Helen's book[4] with a memoir of his own, we should have had, between them, a rounder portrait. The letters, to Bottomley, Frost, Edward Garnett and others, show us more of the man; but how he appeared, and what he revealed of himself, even to his family and his closest friends, was never the whole person. We enter further into his inner life through his books and his poetry than by any other means. Whereas the legend throws into high relief one aspect of Thomas's personality and leaves the rest in romantic shadow, the poetry gives us, in a special sense, the complex whole. The legend is a distortion of the life; a more radical objection is that it is an intrusive irrelevance when it is allowed to colour our response to the poetry, for the personality diffused in the poetry is there only incidentally ('no more . . . than made his poems quick instead of dead'). The poetry goes furthest in showing us not the real man but, what others could not know, the potential man, or rather, the real man of partial vision, victim of his temperament, absorbed into the potential man who has poised possession of his full experience.

If it were possible to read through the poems without preconception, preferably in order of composition, I think our strongest impression would be not of uniformity of theme and mood but of variety of substance, style and form. After 'Up in the Wind', his first poem, which as Edna Longley remarks is closer in structure to Frost's 'unmistakable blend of dialogue/monologue, narrative and description'[5] than any subsequent poem, he went his own way, and only 'Wind and Mist' and 'The Chalk Pit' at all resemble the long blank verse poems of *North of Boston*. Indeed, to escape the danger of unconscious imitation he deliberately made sparing use of Frost's characteristic mode: 'since the first take off they haven't been Frosty very much or so I imagine,' he assured John Freeman early in March 1915, after three months of incessant poetic activity, 'and I have tried as often as possible to avoid the facilities offered by blank verse and I try not to be long'.[6]

A glance at the early poems will confirm this modest disclaimer, and the intention, swiftly realized in those first few weeks, was amply fulfilled during an amazingly prolific two years in a diversity of forms and voices. It is hardly necessary to point to the multiplicity of forms, received and invented, that Thomas mastered with such apparent ease;

apart from the blank verse and couplet poems there are hardly any repetitions. Most of the poems rhyme in some fashion, for, as he told Frost, the rhymes 'dictated themselves'. Out of 142 poems only sixteen are in blank verse, and half of those were composed in the first six weeks between 3 December 1914 and 17 January 1915; during this time, however, he also wrote twice as many rhymed poems. As for these, by far the larger portion of his total work, they exhibit every shade of rhyme and permutation of rhyming pattern. There are true rhymes, that range from the single rhyme of 'Two Pewits' and the fluent, energetic couplets of 'The Signpost', 'Lob', 'The Brook' and several other poems, through a variety of stanzaic forms, simple and elaborate, to the many irregularly rhyming poems. He soon also developed a facility with para-rhymes; 'The Combe', his fourteenth poem, dated 30 December 1914, was his first attempt at a poem rhymed entirely in this way. 'The Combe', 'October', and 'Rain' between them might seem to exhaust the possible variations of para-rhyming: half-rhymes, 'off-beat' rhymes, assonance, and correspondences for which I know no technical terms; the partial consonance, for example, of 'roots . . . birds . . . hounds . . . beasts' in 'The Combe' and 'solitude . . . loved . . . dead . . . reeds . . . disappoint' in 'Rain' is sufficiently insistent to contribute noticeably to the sound-texture of those poems. 'Rain' is further knit together by an irregularly recurring internal rhyme and half-rhyme chiming with the title word.

Taking courage from Frost's example, Thomas performed with versatility in the accentual–syllabic metres and with more freedom than his mentor, but sometimes with such freedom we have to suppose that his ear was attuned to the rhythms of stress metre. It is a plausible conjecture, since it happens mostly when the voice and the mood as well as the rhythm echo the folk rather than the literary tradition. 'November' ('November Sky'), for instance, in which the lines stretch from four to twelve syllables, starts like a weather rhyme, switching between three-stress and four-stress lines, and goes with a recognizable swing; there is no way of measuring the audible metrical equivalence of lines such as these –

> Few care for the mixture of earth and water,
> Twig, leaf, flint, thorn –

other than by the number of accents. (The second of those lines prompts the reflection that Thomas may have arrived, by an easier route than the one taken by Hopkins, at the central principle of sprung rhythm, as it is illustrated in a letter to Bridges (21 August 1877): 'Why, if it is forceful in prose to say 'lashed: rod', am I obliged to weaken this in verse, which ought to be stronger, not weaker, into 'láshed birch-ród'?)[7]

Flexible rhyming and versification are matched by a greater variety of 'voices', corresponding closely to the variety of forms, than the critical stereotype of Thomas's poetry commonly allows. At one end of the spectrum is his personal development of Frost's loosely organized conversational poem. It has less narrative, and is less overtly dramatic, and its structure is organic rather than architectonic – a seemingly unpremeditated, undirected movement of thought that 'comes together' as it were by chance; the tone is intimate and quietly ruminative, the verse charting the contours of his own and others' voices; it may be in blank verse or couplets or even, like 'The Sun Used to Shine', in stanza form. Not infrequently – ' "Home" ' is an example – the relaxed pace and intimately thoughtful voice will adapt itself to a more literary language and syntax. At the other end of the spectrum are the short stanzaic poems. There are songs, either elegantly urbane or borrowing a robust energy from folk music, and there are spare, plain lyrics such as 'Under the Woods'; comparison of two other lyrics, 'Interval' and 'Roads', the one compressed and terse, the other open and fluid, will show how differently quatrains of two or three stress lines can be made to sound in Thomas's hands. Between these extremes there are as many tones as there are forms. I will just mention here the bare but cumulatively intense rhetoric of 'Rain', the paradoxical, almost Metaphysical ratiocination of 'Parting', the riddling word-play of 'The Word', and the grander cadences of 'Liberty' and 'The Glory'.

There are major poets who, as Pound said of Yeats, can play only one or two 'chunes' and ring all the changes on them, and there are others, like Herbert, who have an immense repertoire. Thomas belongs with the second group. He admired the author of *The Temple* and *The Priest in the Temple*, an edition of which he introduced for Dent's Everyman Library; he had an ear as fine as Herbert's and was very nearly as musically inventive. Taking only one aspect of his verse, his contrivance of something graceful out of awkwardness and angularity, we discover examples that show not only suppleness but a diversity of effects. His ear for the natural rhythms of the language was such that he outdid Frost again, surpassing him both in the risks taken and in the varieties of music created. For both Frost and Thomas this was the chief stumbling-block to immediate appreciation by their contemporaries, but it has had the most far-reaching consequences on verse since, especially in the last thirty or forty years. Hardy, who has been given chief credit for this development, rarely commands the finesse with which Thomas unfailingly practises this particular skill. To sample this, only compare the spikey, clipped rhythms of 'But These Things Also' with the gusty bursts of blurted speech in the opening lines of 'The Barn', or the sturdy rough-hewn shape of the verse in the first stanza of 'Women He Liked' ('Bob's Lane'). With less striking instances than these, our ears – being now more attuned to the music of awkwardness, the 'sound of sense', than to euphony – are liable not to hear at all what so offended and baffled the ears of his friends. They will perhaps have little difficulty in registering the nervously abrupt rhythms in 'These Things that Poets Said', which express pain ridden and curbed by a willed rationality (it would be a mistake to read the first two stanzas without internal pauses and with smooth enjambements). But will they as easily perceive subdued nervousness in the *flow* of the first ten lines of 'Sedge-Warblers'? This is an effect of the syntax, which by its piling up of clauses systematically delays the rounded resolution of the sentence, creating a movement that seems repeatedly about to stop, then to catch its breath and start again.

There are other contrasts in Thomas's work. He is a naturalist in several senses, but most obviously in the sense that his poems are a minutely accurate record of his responses to the natural world. He is known in particular as a poet of nature who has a distinctively tentative, oblique approach to the significance of his experience. It may come as a surprise, then, to notice that several of his poems are not, in fact, descriptive, but poems of statement, and that the approach in them is not oblique but direct. Most readers also feel that Thomas's verse has a certain recognizable timbre, that his voice transmits, so to speak, within a narrow wave-band. Certainly the voice has its limits, and yet its range is none the less remarkable. To express this once more by listing opposites: against the melancholy, wistful cadences, which embody his sense of loss and homelessness, of a hollowness at the heart of experience, we must set the energy and bite of other poems, especially those showing the influence of the folk tradition; and against the tentative exploratory movement of many poems, the evidence, provided in different ways by 'November' ('November Sky'), 'The Manor Farm', 'The Owl', 'The Gallows', of a counterbalancing firmness, resilience and grit. The blend of these different strains of feeling in several poems is best described as displaying, in Alun Lewis's phrase for the directing courage of poetry, 'robustness in the core of sadness'.[8] The combination of qualities in single poems and the effect of this range of feeling in the total work is invigorating and liberating.

Thomas's reputation as a poet of exquisite observation and fine nuances, but a restricted range of feeling, has made it necessary to emphasize the actual scope of his achievement. But now I must return to the theme of singularity. Coleridge remarked in a letter of some lines of Wordsworth: 'I should have recognized them anywhere; and had I met these lines running wild in the deserts of Arabia, I should have instantly screamed out "Wordsworth!"' Thomas's verse is no less distinctive, and in all its variety is recognizably the creation of one mind. This is not to say that there is one representative poem; Leavis's choice of 'Old Man' to illustrate Thomas's sensibility and poetic method, inadvertently suggesting that this was such a poem, has indeed helped to establish a slanted view of his work. But his poetry as a whole displays a certain combination of characteristics, and every poem exhibits what in Thomas's opinion Pater's prose lacked, a 'personal accent' (p. 101) – meaning, not a confessional tone, but a quality that, as he said of Keats's poems, makes them 'quick instead of dead'. He criticized Swinburne's poems for being 'seldom personal' and therefore 'not real as Donne's or Byron's or Browning's are', noting particularly that they showed 'little variety of tone',[9] and deprecated the 'detachment' of Pater's style because 'it retained no sign of an original impulse in it': by losing or severing connection with its living source language is made to seem 'as hard and inhuman a material as marble' (p. 101). Six months after starting to write poetry Thomas hoped 'that at last I have stepped into the nearest approach I ever made yet to self-expression'.[10] The history of his struggle to find a 'natural' style makes it plain that his hopes were not, as we might suppose from this, to become a self-conscious personality in his writing but to be fully human. His meaning is best annotated by a statement made in an early letter to Eleanor Farjeon, the closest he came to a declaration of poetic intention: 'If I am consciously doing anything I am trying to get rid of the last rags of rhetoric and formality which left my prose so often with a dead rhythm only' (p. 110). For by self-expression he meant the utterance of a previously unexpressed self, a process of self-discovery, of getting at the quick – the living, particular, essential reality – of his experience. We must set his words to Eleanor Farjeon beside the reference in 'And You, Helen' to a lost self, the disappearance of which and its usurpation by an unkind self has embittered relations with his wife.

In the previous year, reviewing *North of Boston*, he had praised Frost for having accomplished precisely what he was now aiming to do himself: 'These poems are revolutionary because they lack the exaggeration of rhetoric . . . In fact, the medium is common speech and common decasyllables.' The revolution was simply this: 'It speaks, *and* it is poetry' (my italics).[11] But although revolutionary, the idea was not new to Thomas, as the sentence to Eleanor Farjeon reveals. His criticism of Swinburne's and Pater's styles quoted above, the burden of which was that they lacked all reference to the common idiom of living ('personal' or 'human') experience, were written in 1912, two years before his meeting with Frost. A former admirer and imitator, he was now repelled by the 'exquisite unnaturalness' of Pater's 'picture writing' (p. 220): the young author of *Diaphaneité* took 'great pains with the expression' but 'he did not write as he spoke . . . The language is colourless, and from beginning to end each word has a mere dictionary value, and not one conferred by the context and the writer's personality. The essay has no gesture, no advancing motion, and is painful to read aloud' (p. 97). His criticism did not imply, however, the naïve belief that prose should try to duplicate the spoken language; he was only certain that there must be a relationship between them. Later in his study of Pater, discussing Coleridge's praise of Southey's style – 'It is as if he had been speaking to you all the while' – he makes a necessary distinction: 'But he does not say that Southey's writing was the same as his speech; for a mere copy of speech might have a different effect from the spoken word, in the absence of the individual voice and its accompaniment of looks and gestures' (pp. 205–6). Literature makes not a copy but 'an equivalent of speech. It has to make words of such a spirit, and arrange them in such a manner, that they will do all that a speaker can do by innumerable gestures and their innumerable shades, by tone and pitch of voice, by speed, by pauses . . .' (p. 210). These convictions about prose style worked out in the course of re-examining Pater's writings are essentially the same as the theory of poetic language he ascribed to Frost three years later in a letter to Gordon Bottomley. He writes that T. Sturge Moore was mistaken in 'supposing that Frost wanted poetry to be colloquial. All he insists on is what he believes he finds in all poets – absolute fidelity to the postures which the voice assumes in the most expressive intimate speech. So long as these tones and postures are there he has not the least objection to any vocabulary whatever or any inversion or variation from the customary grammatical forms of talk.'[12] The slight change in terminology – 'postures' of the voice and '*intimate* speech' – suggests not only that he is sure that written words must reproduce the *combined* effect of speech and accompanying gesture, tone and variation of pace, but also that, with Frost's example before him, he has now discovered how to make them do it. 'Intimate' perhaps introduces an adjustment of emphasis; certainly it denotes a tone which Thomas's verse has far more precisely and variously than his prose; more than any other quality of his verse it justifies his claim to have come closer to 'self-expression' in his poetry than in his previous writings. Critics have disagreed about the extent of Frost's influence. The question is not cardinal since no one doubts the independent achievement of Thomas; some readers – and only Americans* will be

* But not all Americans: see Louis Coxe, *Enabling Acts*.

surprised at this – rank it higher than Frost's. For the record, however, a comparison of what Thomas has to say about language and imagination in his books on Jefferies (1909), Maeterlinck (1911), Swinburne (1912), Pater (1913) and Keats (written in 1913, published in 1916) with what he wrote in a letter to Frost ('you will find me mistaking your ideas for mine . . . [but] my *Pater* would show you I had got onto the scent already')[13] and with the no doubt unduly self-effacing remark of Frost's that he merely referred Thomas to some paragraphs in *In Pursuit of Spring* and 'told him to write it in verse form in exactly the same cadence'[14] – a comparison of these passages alone would furnish sufficient material for a balanced assessment. Evidently he had already worked out the ideas for himself, both in relation to prose, and, as the little book on Keats most clearly reveals, to poetry too; but though Frost was not the first to suggest that he try verse, Frost's poetry, as Edna Longley says, 'accelerated all his imaginative processes by its practical demonstration of what was possible' (p. 399).

What it chiefly demonstrated for Thomas is not in doubt: it showed him the possibility of writing verse that 'speaks *and* is poetry' (my italics). The possibility was made reality in his very first poem, 'Up in the Wind', and the idiomatic intonations and rhythms of speech pervade the language of every poem he wrote. Their presence in his poetry has so often been remarked and described by critics – nor have I ignored it in previous chapters – that the fact itself needs no illustration. Certain facts *about* his poetic voice, however, will bear being repeated, and will perhaps, in the light of Thomas's own critical ideas, come into sharper focus. The significance of Thomas's criticism here is that it implies standards of diction, movement and tone that clearly played a part in the formation of his poetic style. The coherence of his critical position and the consistency with which he applies his standards are notable. When he points to the 'lack of a natural expressive rhythm' (p. 104) in Pater's writing, or, specifically, the 'lack of an emotional rhythm in separate phrases, and of progress in the whole' (p. 103), he is applying to rhythm his general charge against the style, that it has lost the momentum of an 'original impulse', and against one essay in particular, that it has 'no gesture, no advancing motion' (p. 97). The same standards govern his characterizations of Keats's style when it is adjectival and static; they are expressed in terms of a contrast between still life and action. *Isabella*, the story notwithstanding, is 'a very still poem', the self-contained stanza enabling Keats to display his 'choiceness of detail' and to 'make tragedy a luxury'; it is filled with 'inactive pity' and 'complacent melancholy' (pp. 49–50). When he says of 'The Eve of St. Agnes' that 'it is impossible to suppose that poetry of this immobile, sumptuous, antiquarian kind can go beyond it' (p. 52) the implied preference for an opposite kind – animated, plain, direct, fresh, colloquial – does not lessen his ability to appreciate the peculiar richness of this poem. The connection made in his criticism of Pater, between the lack of natural movement in 'separate phrases' and in the larger whole is also made in his judgment of *Hyperion*: 'The failure of the style, congested, much divided up, abrupt in its transitions, to give a sense of progress' (p. 66) corresponds to 'the lack of concrete active qualities' in the rendering of detail (p. 68). A common criterion of excellence may be inferred from these specific judgments: a good style is an imitation – or, since Thomas looks for 'signs of an original impulse' in the finished work, let us say a transmission – of livingness; further, the vitality of a style derives from the inflections of a speaking voice – its 'personal accent' – and an energy, a progressive movement, transmitted through rhythm and syntax.

If I seem to be labouring the point that Thomas had a specific conception of style, let me say that my purpose is not merely to assert the fact, but, taking my cue from Thomas's own criticism, to transfer the emphasis, in my account of it, from the speaking voice to what necessarily precedes it – the 'impulse' from life that transmits the energy of active thought and feeling to the verse, the need and drive that shape the poem. The word for this conception of poetic language is 'organic'. Coleridge said more than once that poetry brings 'the whole soul of man into activity', and this more than any other brief statement epitomizes Thomas's poetic ideal. He opposes 'organic ideas' to Keats's 'habit of dealing with separate beauties' (p. 41) in *Endymion*, and the metaphor is assumed in most of his statements about the creative use of language. The 'signs of original impulse' are of primary importance, then, because they signify that the poem has been given a life like its author's – not a copy of it but animated by it or paralleling it. The theme here is not organic form, the self-contained organic life of the poem, but the relation of the work to its creator or to life – the pulse or impulse of life from the poet that gives the poem its own life, a life like nature's. Because in Thomas's view it is a dead art that fails to maintain – as Pater, according to a reviewer quoted by Thomas, failed to maintain – the connection with 'other forms of life of which it is an expression' (p. 91), he looked in literature for a 'personal accent', an 'emotional rhythm', for *some* impression of the speaking voice. Hence the word 'gesture' in his accusation that Pater's essay has 'no gesture, no advancing motion'; for it reminds us that the writer must create the equivalent of an individual voice with its *accompanying bodily expression*, namely an imitation of the whole active life of a man uttering himself. Hence too his condemnation of a style that lacks momentum, that fails 'to give a sense of progress'.

The style of Thomas's poetry never, in any of its variations, resembles that 'immobile, sumptuous, antiquarian' kind the supreme example of which is 'The Eve of St. Agnes'. Although the attraction of still moments and the desire to immobilize time are motifs as insistent in Thomas's as in Keats's work, the verse that explores them is itself never at rest, his sentences never fixed in adjectival entrancement: they are shaped more by a propulsive verbal energy than by the stillness contemplated. What is true of the verse in poems about stillness is certainly true of the poems written in other moods. A simple way of illustrating Thomas's 'personal accent' is to refer the reader to the opening lines of several poems. The challenging voice in the first three lines of 'Beauty', though not unique ('What Will They Do?' has a similar acerbity), is not to be heard frequently in Thomas's work; but it is what he meant by 'personal':

> What does it mean? Tired, angry, and ill at ease,
> No man, woman, or child alive could please
> Me now.

It has an emotional rhythm, gesture, an advancing motion: it expresses pain and impatience, urgency and self-mockery. Each sentence – not only the short question – drives straight through to the verb; the adjectival list at the beginning of the second sentence is a delaying gesture of resentment that only gives greater impetus to the next line once released, and the pitch of the voice rises to a main stress on 'alive' and a dismissive savagery of emphasis on the rhyme word as it shoots into the next line and rams home into the immediate full stop. It has a single movement and exactly demonstrates Frost's definition of a sentence as 'a sound in itself on which other sounds called words may be strung'.[15] These and the succeeding lines of 'Beauty' unexpectedly recall Donne; it is a chance association since there is no natural affinity between the two poets, but the accidental resemblance to the attack of Donne's openings and the rapid changes of tone characteristic of his poems serves to make a point that otherwise might be missed: in their usually quiet way these poems, by flouting conventional expectations of poetic language, were no less revolutionary than the earliest of Donne's *Songs and Sonnets*, in the same sense as, according to Thomas, Frost's *North of Boston* was 'one of the most revolutionary books of modern times, but one of the quietest and least aggressive'.

The last half of that statement unmistakably describes the voice most commonly associated with Thomas – subdued, temperate, eschewing 'the exaggeration of rhetoric'. 'Birds' Nests' is often cited in illustration of it:

> The summer nests uncovered by autumn-wind,
> Some torn, others dislodged, all dark,
> Everyone sees them: low or high in tree,
> Or hedge, or single bush, they hang like a mark.

That is the first stanza. It is modestly reflective and factual, as though careful to say nothing that is not empirically true; the style is plain and unliterary. But it is not in fact colloquial: 'in tree' is not idiomatic speech and the order of syntax almost exactly reverses the natural order. Yet it sounds natural, and this, I think, is because the sentence seems to unfold the actual sequence of spontaneous thought, unconstrained by the rules of English usage. The same is true of 'Women He Liked' ('Bob's Lane') in its first stanza, though in Chapter 5 I actually speak of its 'idiomatic syntax'.

> Women he liked, did shovel-bearded Bob,
> Old Farmer Hayward of the Heath, but he
> Loved horses. He himself was like a cob,
> And leather-coloured. Also he loved a tree.

The idiom would be, 'He liked women, did Bob'; the first inversion, 'Women he liked', is, however, entirely in the spirit of the colloquial inversion and the duplication only reinforces the gusto of the idiom, as, with greater dislocation of the grammatical forms, often happens in Hopkins's verse. The line deviates from speech in order to imitate and intensify the effect of speech, transposing for the reading eye and the inner ear the sound of the voice (with its 'accompanying looks and gestures'). 'The living part of a poem is the intonation entangled somehow in the syntax idiom and meaning of a sentence'; that is Frost, once again making the best sense of what is happening in this sentence. A moment's reconsideration of the expressiveness of that first line and of the relish enacted for us by the momentary separation of 'he' from 'loved' would also, I am sure, bear out the truth of his next assertion: 'It is only there for those who have heard it previously in conversation.'[16] Turning our attention to the rest of the stanza, in particular the transitions of thought between the three sentences, we find that the sense-connections are not grammatically explicit but implicit in the intonation, an intonation signalled by the different lengths and structures of the sentences, the pauses between them and the manner of their juxtaposition, which mime rapid associations and jumps of thought. The intonation, it is plain, gives us immediately what the careful, elaborate subordinations of syntax could not give.

II

'Absolute fidelity to the postures which the voice assumes in the most expressive intimate speech' is not the same as a reproduction of that speech; it entails selection – a whittling down to essentials, 'the most expressive' elements – and a dramatic staging of what is left. In this sense the transposition of oral speech into written speech is always a dramatic act. This is the implication of my remark that the first line of 'Women He Liked' ('Bob's Lane') is an imitation, in heightened form, of the effect of speech. But it is dramatic in a more obvious sense: the voice we hear is an assumed voice. One critical convention makes an invariable separation between 'the poet' and 'the speaker in the poem'. There are indeed mild hazards involved in identifying them, but English must be kept up, and the risks of being misunderstood or of misconceiving the poem are so slight that a critic is well advised to live dangerously and follow normal usage. If he does he can then reserve 'speaker' for poems in which a kind of stylistic flourish advertises a deliberate act of impersonation, whether for reasons of personal concealment, as in some of Hardy's poems, or to give accentuated expression to certain attitudes, as in 'Women He Liked' ('Bob's Lane'). We have a strong sense in this poem of being addressed – held in conversation by a specific person with specific qualities.

He closely resembles the character he is describing, and the voice we hear apes the robust temper of 'shovel-bearded Bob' in conveying a hearty admiration of it. When in 1912 Thomas said that he wanted his writing to be 'as near akin as possible to the talk of a Surrey peasant', the ideal expressed was for a vigorous, earthy prose style. But this is the voice that speaks also in 'Women He Liked' ('Bob's Lane'); more often than not, when a poem is impersonative the tones are those of some such 'Surrey peasant' as George Sturt's Bettesworth. 'For the life in them he loved most living things': this relish of life shared by the speaker is what the voice mimes, and what is suggested too, developing a grimmer theme, by the voice in 'The Gallows'. This poem celebrates the roguish vitality of the thieving, murdering crow and of the magpie that 'could both talk and do' (striking here an interestingly Chaucerian note); it even implies a sense of kinship with the creatures that have fallen to the keeper's gun – 'There was a weasel lived in the sun / With all *his family*' (my italics) – and a love of all life without distinction, its pleasure and its pain (death is to be, as the refrain has it, 'Without pleasure, without pain'). There is no protest, however, only a sardonic awareness of death – 'He could both talk and do – / But what did that avail?' – and the sardonic joke that the animals hung by the keeper on

the tree shall 'swing and have endless leisure'. The tone of the opening
lines of 'An Old Song' has a similarly sardonic ring, even as Thomas
uncomplainingly, almost heartily, acknowledges his bondage to the
trade of journalism; in this instance the verse swings to the folksong
rhythms of 'The Lincolnshire Poacher':

> I was not apprenticed nor ever dwelt in famous Lincolnshire,
> I've served one master ill and well much more than seven year.

Thomas in his poetry reports the talk of several folk characters, farm
worker or vagabond, expressing such attitudes in similar tones of voice.
His encounter with the wandering jack-of-all-trades discovered gazing
covetously at the mistletoe high up in a poplar tree, recorded in 'Man
and Dog', furnishes an example:

> He fell once from a poplar tall as these:
> The Flying Man they called him in hospital.
> 'If I flew now, to another world I'd fall.'

The gruff humour of this remark is allied to the jokes, if that is what they
are, in 'An Old Song' and 'The Gallows'. The attraction of such talk for
a man of Thomas's temperament is not hard to understand: it has an
extrovert strength which he uses to offset the influence on his style of an
inordinate introversion.

This is obvious when he abandons literal impersonation of a Surrey
peasant and the folk voice is absorbed into his own. Consider his reply
to the ploughman in 'As the Team's Head Brass':

> 'Have you been out?' 'No.' 'And don't want to, perhaps?'
> 'If I could only come back again, I should.
> I could spare an arm. I shouldn't want to lose
> A leg. If I should lose my head, why, so,
> I should want nothing more.'

This is not gruff but urbane, almost elegant. Yet there is no doubt that
its wry, offhand humour, armoured against the rhetoric of self-pity, has
developed out of the tough impersonality of traditional speech. The folk
tradition is equally responsible for the rustic turn of phrase and
curmudgeonly gesture of a line in 'The Manor Farm' – 'But earth would
have its sleep out, spite of the sun' – and generally for the proverbial
element in Thomas's verse. 'Lob' is a celebration of the folk mind and an
anthology of its contents, but in a poem so fashioned to the needs of the
introverted poet, and as far from the folk mind, as 'October', a line like
'And gorse that has no time not to be gay' finds its place with 'And now
I might / As happy be as earth is beautiful'. There is a country saying,
'When gorse does not bloom, kissing will stop'; he was perhaps

recollecting some version of this saying when he devised his own. Set beside such lines as these in 'October' and 'The Manor Farm', it becomes clear that the tough self-mockery of the neurotic speaker's language in 'Wind and Mist' and the voice of maturity in 'The Signpost' have the same ancestry. Each has a personal tone braced by an earthiness and resilience that he has learned from the conversation of archaic countrymen, heard in person or found in balladry and folklore and books like Sturt's. In 'The Signpost', relentless truth-telling ('At twenty you wished you had never been born'), a sardonic tone and jaunty rhythms ('A mouthful of earth to remedy all / Regrets and wishes shall freely be given') blend joy and sorrow indistinguishably into the one flavour of acceptance.

My point is that many of Thomas's poems are in some degree dramatic. A number are wholly or partly impersonative; most, but not all, of those mimic the tones of the immemorial English countryman who also appears as a rascally stoical character in other poems. The folk impersonations bear a family resemblance. The voice assumed in the first stanza of 'The Barn' (later it shades into the poet's own) has something in common with the voice we hear in 'Women He Liked' ('Bob's Lane'): each has the abrupt energy, the unselfconscious impulsive openness that distinguishes it from, say, the musing tone and winding, tentative movement of his more introspective pieces. But the two voices are also individual: they each display a different kind of vigour. The speaker in 'The Barn', for example, is bluff, practical, downright:

> They should never have built a barn there at all –
> Drip, drip, drip! – under that elm tree.
> Though then it was young. Now it is old
> But good, not like the barn and me.

The shape and sequence of the sentences follow the rapid, erratic motions of impulsive thinking, dramatizing the mental process itself; the same is true, in fact, of 'Birds' Nests' and 'Women He Liked' ('Bob's Lane'), though the mimicry of the first is less obtrusive and the second adds a touch of histrionic exaggeration. But 'The Barn' is dramatic in yet another sense. The speaker is responding in the present, as though to something before his eyes – 'a barn *there* . . . under *that* elm tree'. It has an immediacy that is frequent in Thomas; it is perhaps a more significant component of his style than the impersonations.

> There they stand, on their ends, the fifty faggots
> That once were underwood of hazel and ash
> In Jenny Pinks's Copse.

These are the opening lines of 'Fifty Faggots'. They make a directing gesture: following the pointing finger the eye takes in the unnamed bundle, then the mind gives it a name, 'fifty faggots', and at last fills in the detail of what, when and where.

The sentence ends with a local name. Many passages in Thomas's prose betray his fascination with the regional names of flowers and place-names that are distinctive of their locality, and in the chapter on Hardy in *A Literary Pilgrim in England* he pays special attention to the use of place-names in his work. The man who could praise a poet because he wrote 'no poetry that could suffer by names and dates' (p. 144) already had an ear attuned to the possibilities of verse soon to be revealed by Frost; he was to close a review of *North of Boston* in the *New Weekly* (8 August 1914) with a quotation from Frost's previous volume, *A Boy's Will*, the last six lines of 'Mowing', and the comment, 'he can make fact "the sweetest dream"'. If, as he says of Hardy's 'rustic names', 'the general effect is to aid reality by suggestions of gross and humble simplicity' and 'to make sure of keeping the poem to earth by keeping it to Dorset', (p. 145) they also have more particular functions, which Thomas identifies in his descriptions of individual lines. Indulgently conceding, in a review for *Poetry and Drama* (December 1913) of Oxford and Cambridge poets, that their intentions were praiseworthy, he nevertheless assures them and his readers that 'intensely personal and intensely local poetry can go much further yet'. The linking of the personal and the local comes close to explaining the effect of those first lines of 'Fifty Faggots'. The point is the freshness and intensity. The individual voice and the dramatic reality of the occasion are largely responsible for that; but not a little is contributed by 'Jenny Pinks's Copse'. It is the source of the faggots and the climax of the statement; it is the culmination of the growing specificity of the sentence. It is pretty, feminine, rustic, and, as he says of Hardy's place-names, carries 'the sense of past times and generations' (p. 148): the voice and the name together focus an elegiac feeling – give an *intimate* reality to that feeling – for an order of life threatened with the fate that has already overtaken this local embodiment of the idea of England. As he admonishes the well-intentioned University poets, 'the important thing is not that a thing should be small but that it should be intense and capable of symbolic significance'.

III

My italicization of 'intimate' is intended to draw attention to an emphasis that Thomas himself placed on the word when defending

Frost to Gordon Bottomley: 'postures which the voice assumes' not merely in speech but 'in the most expressive intimate speech'. The literary battles of the second decade were fought under the banners of idealism and realism; Arthur Waugh, a representative figure of the period, writing in the *Quarterly Review* of October 1918, revealed *his* bias when he distinguished confidently between 'crude realism' and 'the idealizing spirit of poetry'. When Eliot declared that an acute sense of fact is indispensable to the poet, and when, in the course of some 'Reflections on Contemporary Verse' published in *The Egoist* (September and October 1917), he pronounced that 'Donne sees the thing as it is' and 'the important thing is not how we feel about [a situation], but how it is', he was defining his early critical position by reference to the current debate between these two parties. He also informed his readers in the first of these articles that modern poetry was trying to 'escape the rhetorical, the abstract, the moralizing, to recover (for that is its purpose) the accents of direct speech'. In terms of this broad classification Thomas and Eliot – enemies of rhetoric and wooers of the spoken word – are comrades in the realists' camp. Seen in retrospect, however, the differences between them are more striking than the similarities. Intimacy in the manner of speech adopted and in relation to the substance of their poems makes natural allies of Hardy, Frost and Thomas, and distinguishes their language from the 'direct speech' of Eliot – or for that matter the verse of *Lustra* and *Mauberley*. Behind Eliot were the poets of the nineties; he has acknowledged a specific debt to John Davidson, but there were also poems by Symons and Dowson, and through Symons he first had access to the French poets from whom Symons had learned. 'From these men,' Eliot said, 'I got the idea that one could write poetry in an English such as one would speak oneself. A colloquial idiom. There was a spoken rhythm in some of their poems.'[17] But the kind of idiom he could speak himself – colloquial hardly seems the word for it – was the elegant, urbane, lightly ironic talk of the boulevards; there was something of the 'exquisite' in Eliot's and Pound's early poetic manners. By comparison with Hardy or Frost or Thomas – and no judgment is implied by the comparison – Eliot's style, in all its suppleness of tone, is literary.

Early readers of both Hardy and Frost were puzzled by what they denounced as prosaic. Thomas was reproached with the same offence. He told Eleanor Farjeon that Vivian Locke Ellis, a minor poet of the period, did not like his poems – 'he says their rhythm isn't obvious enough' (p. 133); later in the same month, May 1915, writing to Gordon Bottomley, he recalled a passage in a recent letter from him 'about using words in the spirit of the prose writer & not freed from everyday syntax' (p. 247). It is quite possible that the batch of poems in Bottomley's hands included 'The Path', written towards the end of March; if so, it was almost certainly one of the poems he had in mind when he made this criticism. Its first eight lines comprise a passage of sufficient length to show what might be meant by 'the spirit of the prose writer':

> Running along a bank, a parapet
> That saves from the precipitous wood below
> The level road, there is a path. It serves
> Children for looking down the long smooth steep,
> Between the legs of beech and yew, to where
> A fallen tree checks the sight: while men and women
> Content themselves with the road and what they see
> Over the bank, and what the children tell.

Although a prosodist would have no difficulty in scanning this as a species of (fairly free) blank verse, it is not until about the last seven lines of the poem, when the verse begins to sing a little, that the metre asserts itself. In the opening lines, and for most of the poem, one is conscious of hearing only the natural stresses which accentuate the sense-connections between words that shape the sentence. One's attention is drawn, as in prose, to sentences rather than lines; but they are sentences in which 'the accent of sense' is picked out by the versification. The distinction of this kind of verse is that, instead of building up a musical system of expression, it takes the everyday syntax of prose and makes it more expressive, or rather, as expressive as 'the most expressive intimate speech' out of which it has developed. The ear attuned to melodic verse is likely to be insensitive to this kind of eloquence. Notice, for example, how in the second sentence the line-divisions enforce exactly the right modulation of pitch when the voice reaches 'Children' and later 'men and women'; and again in that sentence – which, if it had to rely only on the grammatical structure of prose to guide the sense, would ramble and tumble over itself – how, by careful 'pointing' of voice inflection, the words are made to refer to and balance each other. More obviously, the placing of 'where' momentarily halts the voice in anticipation of the completion of the sense, and both line-ending and sentence-ending imitate in time the spatial check to the viewing eye of the fallen tree. 'Vowels have length there is no denying,' says Frost. 'But the accent of sense supersedes all other accent overrides and sweeps it away'.[18] That is an overstatement. Thomas uses the length of the vowels in 'long smooth steep' as any poet would, to make the reader feel the smoothness and steepness of the slope; but he also uses the shape of the syntax, as when the insertion of the phrase 'Between the legs of beech and yew' between two clauses enacts the narrowing and channelling of the children's vision by the tree trunks. Flatness is the danger risked by this sort of poetry, yet even the flat tone of the story-opening, scene-setting first sentence is expressive. The levelness of the first line is a dramatic device – the combined effect of a continuous tense, the ensuing monotone, the pause after 'bank' that kills any forward movement, and the repetition of inflection that indicates the appositional relation of 'bank' and 'parapet'; it becomes a saving firmness and foothold as soon as the voice begins its slither from 'saves' to 'below'; there the movement is halted and the voice is held for a moment by the sense and the line-ending, before it is restored to the safety, on the next line, of 'The level road', by coming so soon in that line to the conclusion of a subordinate clause.

An interest in recovering the vigour and vividness of speech and the clarity and honesty of good prose is a well-known feature of modern poetry. Eliot sought these qualities in sixteenth- and seventeenth-century verse, in Browning, in the French symbolist poets and the English poets of the nineties, but also in Henry James. Both Hardy's and Thomas's early training as writers of prose must have been deciding factors in the formation of their poetic styles. Yet Hardy owed something to the seventeenth-century poets and Browning, and to the folk tradition. If we are to seek further than Frost's example and Thomas's own prose for the origins of the prosaic poem we must look at least as far as the first generation of Romantic poets. Wordsworth – his theory rather more than his practice of poetic language – was an influence upon Hardy as he was upon Frost. But Wordsworth learned how to write 'Tintern Abbey' from Coleridge; and Coleridge's 'conversation poem', which was an individual transformation of eighteenth century descriptive–meditative verse, made possible Thomas's development of his own brand of conversational poetry a century later. It is a question not of direct influence but of a change in literary consciousness; it passed first to the prose writers, stayed with them for the duration of the Victorian era, and was, as it were, handed back to verse by the novelist-turned-poet Hardy, when at the end of the century he published *Wessex Poems*. There are other more direct influences on Thomas's poetry, but his introspective poems, in their quiet reflectiveness, their intimacy of tone, and above all in the organic correspondence of their form to the shape of feeling and thought contained by it, are closer in spirit to 'Frost at Midnight' and 'This Lime-Tree Bower My Prison' than to the poetry of any other predecessor.

Thomas referred Frost to his *Walter Pater* for evidence that he had independently reached conclusions about speech and literature in harmony with Frost's own. There was more to his criticism of Pater than a personal distaste for a style that held aloof from the idioms and rhythms of the spoken word: his judgment was implicitly supported by an organic theory of literature. Equally, his complaint that Pater was merely a 'word-fancier' (p. 216), whose attention to single words was at the expense of coherent, fluent thinking, was founded upon a considered view of the necessary relation that exists between language as a historical growth and the individual user of it. 'The words have only an isolated value', he objects; but when he develops that, as 'they are anything but living and social words', there are depths in the last phrase that need examining (p. 213). A little later he writes:

Pater was, in fact, forced against his judgement to use words as bricks, as tin soldiers, instead of flesh and blood and genius. Inability to survey the whole history of every word must force the perfectly self-conscious writer into this position. Only when a word has become necessary to him can a man use it safely . . . No man can decree the value of one word, unless it is his own invention; the value which it will have in his hands has been decreed by his own past, by the past of his race . . . [Pater's] words . . . have not been lived with sufficiently.

(p. 215)

A word is necessary to a man, we deduce, when it is an unconscious part of him, and it is that when his mind is at one with the historical genius of the language (this, I take it, is the meaning of 'genius' here). In 'Words' Thomas represents the poet as one who gives himself to the language as to a suprapersonal order to which he learns to belong:

> But though older far
> Than oldest yew, –
> As our hills are, old, –
> Worn new
> Again and again.

This picture is confirmed by a statement in a review quoted by R. George Thomas in his edition of the letters to Bottomley. 'The eye that sees the things today, and the ear that hears, the mind that contemplates or dreams, is itself an instrument of antiquity equal to whatever it is called upon to apprehend. We are not merely twentieth-century Londoners or Kentishmen or Welshmen' (p. 167). 'Choose me, / You English words', he asks in the poem, not fancifully, but seriously aspiring to be a part, and an instrument, of that suprapersonal reality. His criticism of Swinburne's *Atalanta in Calydon* follows naturally from this view of the poet's proper relation to the language: 'The words in it have no rich inheritance from old usage of speech or poetry, even when they are poetic, or archaic or Biblical' (p. 22). To live with words,

as Pater failed to do, is to belong through them to the fullness and
continuity of human experience, the experience of the race as
apprehended and embodied in one of its languages.

Practice corresponded to theory. Critics have pointed to the plain
Anglo-Saxon base of Thomas's poetic vocabulary, but have not realized
the significance of the fact. His language – and I mean not just the words
but the phrasing and grammatical constructions – frequently has, with
this plainness, a more special quality, which is not easy to isolate and
identify. The words and forms have a kind of plainness that I have called
'almost archaic'. When reading, for example, the first stanza of 'The
Owl', one has the impression that this is basic, essential, 'timeless'
English, while having no illusions that in the study of language
timelessness is a useful concept to work with:

> Downhill I came, hungry, and yet not starved;
> Cold, yet had heat within me that was proof
> Against the North wind; tired, yet so that rest
> Had seemed the sweetest thing under a roof.

The lines seem unusually strong and active, I think, because they keep to
the basic parts of speech, stripped of inessential words; consequently
'so' is made to do more than would normally be required of it. It is not
quite the 'raw poetry' he admired in Synge and recommended to
Bottomley, but it is like it in being 'wonderfully lean and bare' (pp.
190–1). He had recently reviewed *Poems and Translations* (1909), and
would have been in sympathy with the words of Synge's preface: 'when
men lose their poetic feeling for ordinary life, and cannot write poetry of
ordinary things, their exalted poetry is likely to lose its strength of
exaltation', and 'it is the timber of poetry that wears most surely'. I
would not say, either, that the language of 'The Owl' is stark, but it
comes as close to the 'stark, bare, rocky directness of statement . . .
without a shadow of a lie' which for Lawrence in the war years was 'the
essence of poetry'[19] as it comes to being 'raw poetry'. I have little doubt
either that, whether or not he shared Hopkins's opinion of Dryden, he
would have approved of his reasons for admiring him: 'his style and his
rhythms lay the strongest stress of all our literature on the naked thew
and sinew of the English language'.[20] It may be that Thomas's style in
'The Owl' strikes me as archaic because it shuns the diffuseness and
unnecessary attention to grammatical niceties of modern educated
speech; by contrast the vernacular of, for example, Tyndale – all that
part of the King James Bible which is free of the elevation supplied by
the later translators – a direct, muscular, plain yet richly concrete
language, seems to represent the core of 'real' English. Many other
examples of this quality in the language of Thomas's poetry could be

cited. Often it is a literal equivalent of the subject-matter, as, for example, the stark landscape of 'The Sheiling':

> It stands alone
> Up in a land of stone
> All worn like ancient stairs,
> A land of rocks and trees
> Nourished on wind and stone.

It is in keeping, too, with the bare contrasts of life and death in 'The Gallows' and of human life and the non-human in 'The Mountain Chapel'. It fits both the spare form and the 'metaphysics' of 'The Wasp Trap', where it becomes literally a language of being:

> This moonlight makes
> The lovely lovelier
> Than ever before lakes
> And meadows were.
>
> And yet they are not,
> Though this their hour is, more
> Lovely than things that were not
> Lovely before.

But it is not Thomas's invariable style. This is succinctly demonstrated by the last three lines of 'Sedge-warblers', where the homely simplicity of the first line and the pithy wisdom of the last are each set off, in Shakespearean fashion, by the polysyllabic wisdom of the intervening middle line:

> This was the best of May, the small brown birds
> Wisely reiterating endlessly
> What no man learnt yet, in or out of school.

IV

I have quoted Thomas's statements, with regard both to his own aims and to Frost's, that, in maintaining its link with the vernacular, literature must devise not a copy but an equivalent of speech; the tone and gesture of the speaking voice may combine with 'any vocabulary whatever or any inversion or variation from the customary grammatical forms of talk'.[21] Many readers sympathetic to the conversational Thomas have felt uncomfortable with the occasional inversions and poeticisms; it seems to them that he was not ruthless enough in ridding himself of certain superannuated poetical mannerisms. Before I begin to consider the justice of this let me quote another statement from *Walter Pater*: 'There would be no poetry if men could speak all that they think and all that they feel' (p. 209). Once it is understood that this is no defence of poetical ornament or arbitrary variations from natural syntax, it can be seen to provide the right cautionary text for those whose response to poetry is governed merely by the prejudices of contemporary taste.

Take the opening of 'I Never Saw that Land Before'. It starts with verse that is shaped by nothing but the 'accent of sense': two clauses, each a single utterance, a single curve of the voice, given a line apiece –

> I never saw that land before
> And now can never see it again.

But it continues:

> Yet, as if by acquaintance hoar
> Endeared, by gladness and by pain,
> Great was the affection that I bore
>
> To the valley and the river small . . .

Immediately the sentence takes on literary words, inversions, poetic ellipses and a poetic formality of syntax. I once thought these a disfigurement of the poem, and though I no longer think so I would not disagree that the effect is awkward; it is an awkwardness, however, that – as sometimes in Hardy – answers to a strangeness in the feeling expressed. The poetic artifice of these lines, moreover, draws out a significance latent in the intonation of the first two lines, a vocalized gesture towards a mythic largeness of expression, that by itself, left to the devices of the speaking voice unaided by deliberate music, would otherwise have gone unheard. Strangeness (foreignness and mystery) is the explicit theme of ' "Home" ', where once more it finds its reflection more obviously in the style:

> Fair was the morning, fair our tempers, and
> We had seen nothing fairer than that land,
> Though strange, and the untrodden snow that made
> Wild of the tame, casting out all that was
> Not wild and rustic and old; and we were glad.
> Fair too was afternoon, and first to pass
> Were we that league of snow, next the north wind.

The landscape has a hint of eeriness and the lines have a corresponding undertone of unease; the exalted mood patently expects the antithesis soon to be introduced by the warning phrase 'and yet' – and yet they were strangely 'homesick' for the 'cold roofs' of the barracks they had left behind. The strangeness is clearly responsible for the (characteristic) blend of, on the one hand, freedom in the versification and colloquial simplicity of utterance, with, on the other, an elevation of style, composed of poeticism ('league'), inversions, a ceremonious quality in the diction and construction of lines three to five ('that made . . . old'), and not least the repetition of 'fair'. Words like 'fair' or 'dear' or 'sweet', homely but rich in familiar suggestion ('Fair blows the wind for France', 'Sweet Spring, full of sweet days and roses' come to mind), are likely to be avoided by modern poets because their power of suggestion is too readily available, or because what they suggest is no longer exact. Thomas uses them all, tellingly and with unselfconscious ease, as though unaware of the dangers; yet he certainly was, for he accused Pater of making a cult of the word 'strange', which in his prose does 'not define the objects mentioned so much as the purpose of the writer' (p. 85). Without reducing its breadth of reference he seems here to have restored to 'fair' the hard bounding line of definition it once had: its application in turn to weather, mood and physical appearance is separately and precisely fitting, and yet it also has the power to dissolve the different senses into one common meaning, large and many-faceted but not vague. The exploitation of this word and the poetic artifices mentioned is for the purpose of creating, again, a mythic atmosphere, at once captivating and sinister. The ordinary occasion has an extraordinary significance; the language is faithful to both levels of the experience.

The interweaving of the ordinary and the extraordinary in Thomas's style is one of his triumphs. Consider how, in 'Wind and Mist', he moves from the humdrum opening exchange – ' "It is / A pleasant day, sir." "A very pleasant day." / "And what a view here!" ' – to this:

'The fields beyond that league close in together
And merge, even as our days into the past,
Into one wood that has a shining pane
Of water.'

In 'Liberty' – I refer the reader in this instance to the *Collected Poems* for confirmation of my account – the verse passes repeatedly back and forth between the neutral voice in which concrete particulars are faithfully recorded and the conundrums of abstract thought are patiently revolved, and the sometimes plangent, sometimes dreamy voice of desire.

'Adlestrop' has both levels, too, and both kinds of language. It is an extreme case, however, in that the 'ordinary' language of the first stanza is as awkwardly prosaic as that of any verse to be found in Thomas, and stands therefore in stark contrast to the rhythm and Romantic diction of these lines in the third stanza: 'No whit less still and lonely fair / Than the high cloudlets in the sky'. Here are the opening lines:

Yes. I remember Adlestrop –
The name, because one afternoon
Of heat the express-train drew up there
Unwontedly. It was late June.

No description of it fits so well as his own description of Hardy's verse:
'a certain awkwardness is almost as constant in his work as truth'. In the
same article ('Poetry and Drama', June 1913) – *The Dynasts* and the
first three volumes of shorter poems are under review – he writes with
affectionate amusement: 'It is possible sometimes to wonder if he is
poking fun at verse by making it so unwontedly substantial, then adding
a considerable quantity of rhyme, alliteration, and assonance, as frills'.
The criticism at the end could apply only to Hardy, but the first part,
playfully, offers a possible response to the sort of poetry that these lines
of Thomas aim to be. Behind the phrase 'unwontedly substantial' lies
the whole debate about idealism and realism, as it clearly lies behind his
praise of Keats for being, 'though a lover of the moon, a most sublunary
poet, earthly, substantial, precise' (p. 39); this judgment, moreover,
leaves no doubt as to what his poetic allegiances are. 'Unwontedly
substantial' would seem to mean, if we consider its aptness to the
diversity of Hardy's poems, an unconventionally prosaic attention to
particularities of both fact and thought – precisely the combination in
'Liberty'. The touch of condescension in Thomas's remarks betrays not
a distrust of substantiality, but, on the contrary, a prejudice in its
favour, qualified by a recognition that in Hardy's gaucherie there is
sometimes more of 'rustic' naïveté than awkward honesty. Thomas's
review of D. H. Lawrence's *Love Poems and Others* (*Bookman*, April
1913) reveals the same mixture of admiration and reservation;
admiration for its truthful substantiality ('he writes of matters which
cannot be subdued to conventional rhythm and rhyme'), reservations
arising out of Lawrence's cavalier attitude to his medium ('at times he
seems bent on insulting rhyme'). 'But,' he concludes, 'whether the verse
is relevant or not, Mr. Lawrence writes in a concentration so absolute
that the poetry is less questionable than the verse'. The opening lines of
'Adlestrop' may be as unconventional, as awkward, as prosaic as
anything in Hardy or Lawrence, but the verse in them is not irrelevant.
Lineation, movement, rhyme and internal rhyme are there to guide the
voice, making the speech rhythms expressive, picking out the sense-
connections. Yet even in this stanza not all is in the speaking voice: 'one
afternoon / Of heat' has an uncolloquial evocativeness, deepened by the
line-division's discovery of a languor in the phrase which the voice is
invited to enact. Though the end-rhyme is hardly perceptible, the
internal half-rhyme of 'name' and 'train' is more so and prepares for its

166

reiteration in 'came' and 'name' of the next stanza; this starts a movement in the poem from the ordinary to the extraordinary levels of experience and expression. The bare jottings of memory begin to cohere, the stumbling rhythms of seemingly aimless thought become firmer, and the speaking voice modulates easily into the entranced voice of stanza three, which then encompasses the expansive, all-inclusive gesture of the closing lines.

9 The semantics of form

I The semantics of form

'I am trying to get rid of the last rags of rhetoric and formality', Thomas told Eleanor Farjeon (p. 110). But this entailed not an abandonment of verbal artifice but a conversion of it to the purpose of conveying the immediacy of experience, spontaneity of thought and the inflections of intimate speech. Nor did he abandon 'formality', in another sense of the word. In this his road diverged from Frost's: he relied less on blank verse and took on more of the past's legacy of formal artifice than Frost was inclined to do. But, again, his aim was the naturalization of form. As in the diction and rhythms of Thomas's poetry there is a fusion of the poetic and the colloquial, so the structures of his poems, even the most elaborate of them, are moulded to their contents – the shape of the stanza is identical with the shape of the thought and feeling.

The semantics of form, especially where it is a matter of fixed rhyme patterns and regular variations of line length, is harder to expound convincingly than any other aspect of poetry; for that reason it is rarely attempted. Since form and content modify each other, the difficulty is to find a critical language that avoids implying a crudely determinative relationship between them. There is the danger of ascribing the wrong kind of significance to it in the urge to prove that it has some. It is better to say too little than too much. Let the first example, therefore, be one of Thomas's simpler formal inventions. Here are the first two stanzas of 'Green Roads':

> The green roads that end in the forest
> Are strewn with white goose feathers this June,
>
> Like marks left behind by someone gone to the forest
> To show his track. But he has never come back.

The pattern is this: the first line always ends on the word 'forest', and the second has a wandering internal rhyme. Edna Longley describes the effect of this arrangement in her notes to the poem: 'Thomas's reiteration of "the forest" becomes increasingly ominous, while the wandering internal rhyme in the second line of each couplet unfailingly trips us up with a sense of mystery or unease ("But he has never come back")' (p. 359). I think it is possible, without smothering the effect in interpretation, to say a little more about it. As glosses on 'ominous', it might be noted that 'forest' stands at the end of alternate lines like a wall preventing penetration into the mysteries of the forest, and, not having the changing consonants of true rhyme, the word begins to strike the ear with a dead or deadening sound. Not only in the stanzas quoted but throughout the poem the lines vary slightly in length; this inequality, and the unpredictable placing of the internal rhyme so that it comes randomly and often abruptly, are in large part responsible for the cumulative sense of unease. I would even propose that the pairing of the outer and the wandering inner rhyme-words suggests some undisclosed tie between the green roads outside and what is inside the forest.

This two-line stanza is a 'singular' invention; its simplicity and originality throw into relief the expressiveness of the structure. It may *seem* broadly determinative of the meaning, and consequently easier to discuss in terms of meaning than the many tighter, finely adjusted stanza forms which are more representative of Thomas's performance in stanzaic verse. There the problem of definition is more acute. In 'Digging' and 'The Mill-Water', for example, we sense a correspondence between the formal pattern, repeated from stanza to stanza, and the feeling-content, but no formulation can be constructed that will fit every repetition of it. Much of the reader's pleasure, indeed, is in response to the variations of the tune within the given limits. 'Digging' has four stanzas; I quote the first:

> Today I think
> Only with scents, – scents dead leaves yield,
> And bracken, and wild carrot's seed,
> And the square mustard field.

The short first line usually (with the exception of the third stanza) has this thrust, expressing sudden arousal of sensuous appreciation, that propels it straight into the next line; the second and third lines of all but the last stanza are packed like this one with the dense impedimenta of listed items, clogging consonants and extra or clustered stresses; in all but the last stanza, too, the middle lines subside gently from a four-foot norm into a closing line of three feet, bound by rhyme to the second line and by half-rhyme to the third. To sound a note of conclusion, certain small but significant changes are introduced in the final stanza:

> It is enough
> To smell, to crumble the dark earth,
> While the robin sings over again
> Sad songs of Autumn mirth.

The middle lines are less dense, and Thomas has engineered an evenly weighted line of four accents to end with; this is an adjustment appropriate to the change of perspective, as in the last two lines the viewer steps back and disentangles himself from the rich sensuous immediacy with the aid of a Keatsian recollection (it is not a quotation but it seems like a summary allusion to the last stanza of 'To Autumn'). The energies and feelings reflected in the form are approximately these: a rising eagerness, absorption in elemental sensation, subsidence and composure. Although the pattern is as precisely expressive as this in the four line stanza of 'the Mill-Water', it does not surrender its secret so readily as 'Digging'. We can say this much without hesitation: the general mood is elegiac; each stanza repeats an arrangement of that mood; each line marks a separate stage or aspect of it.

> Only the sound remains
> Of the old mill;
> Gone is the wheel;
> On the prone roof and walls the nettle reigns.

Each stanza has internal variants of tempo and syntax; only the last slightly alters the shape – to produce, as in 'Digging', a note of conclusion. The first trimeter line keeps a simple decorum and a sober measured pace throughout; it has a soft reflectiveness that promises to expand (since it does not meet its rhyme till the end of the stanza), but instead is checked by the two short lines following (here made more abrupt by semi-colons), rhyming on a short vowel or a sharp end-consonant; then the interrupted pensiveness – interrupted by a colder cross-current of feeling – is allowed to resume, and takes its ease in a full pentameter. The impressionistic language that I use to convey the general effect of this structure does no more than hint at a possible interpretation of it; I doubt if one can get any closer to a translation of its significance.

II Structural tensions

It defies close interpretation precisely because the relationship between inner and outer form is so completely organic. It is only an apparent contradiction of this statement to say that in many poems, amongst them some of Thomas's most individual, a certain tension between the verse-form and the structure of sense – natural syntax and the emphases of the speaking voice – is deliberately exposed. If I were invited to name an archetypal Thomas poem I should first resist the invitation and then, with the least risk of misrepresentation, choose my example from among poems of this type. The reason for my choice will appear more fully as the argument of this chapter evolves; at this stage it will suffice to say that the structural tension is one manifestation of a tension showing itself generally in the thought and technique of Thomas's poetry, between the demands of freedom and the dictates of constraint, or, put another way, between a tendency to a separate life in the parts and the attempt to subordinate their individualism to the rule of the poem as a whole. Without particular examples, of course, such terms hardly serve to differentiate Thomas's work from that of any other English poet. They will mean more, therefore, only as I develop my theme and proceed to illustrate it.

One of Thomas's finest poems is 'The Sun Used to Shine', commemorating his friendship with Frost. It opens with a conspicuous example of the structural tension I have been trying to describe:

> The sun used to shine while we two walked
> Slowly together, paused and started
> Again, and sometimes mused, sometimes talked
> As either pleased, and cheerfully parted
>
> Each night.

And so it continues – more often than not with one quatrain spilling over into the next. As the stanza's boundaries are repeatedly broken, so the rhythm, miming the pauses and sudden starts of the two friends in their perambulations, seems almost to ignore the form. Yet it requires little ingenuity to demonstrate – an oral rendering would easily make the point – that the flow of the sentence reflects the perfect ease of communion between the friends, as it were a shared reverie, and that at the same time the fractional hiatus between lines, observed and used, captures the impulsive, unreservedly spontaneous quality of their movements, feelings and thoughts. The life in the voice is at variance with the life, the particular arrangement of thought and feeling, potential in the shape of the stanza. Something similar happens in 'Roads'. But first the stanza form as a self-contained unit and a standard pattern of thought is allowed to establish itself:

> I love roads:
> The goddesses that dwell
> Far along invisible
> Are my favourite gods.
>
> Roads go on
> While we forget, and are
> Forgotten like a star
> That shoots and is gone.

(This is stress metre. In these opening stanzas the line varies between two and three accents, though for most of the poem the three-stress line dominates: so much so that I wonder whether that dominance invites us occasionally to find a third accent in apparently two-stress lines. The verse is so strenuous and emphatic that, for example, one is tempted to give equal stress to each word in line one of the first stanza, as it would be natural to do in line one of the next stanza.) 'Standard pattern of thought' does not imply that what the poem can say, the kind of substance, mood or energy it can project, is limited and pre-determined by the form – not even by a stanza as constraining as this one. The form allows a supple manipulation of rhythm and admits a diversity of contents – as different, for example, as the feelings conveyed by these two stanzas: the first expressing a romantic, rapturous self-commitment to an endlessly receding goal, the second an awed sense of life's continuity and a vicarious defiance of transience. The form can express many things even though it sets them in the same mould of thought or feeling: the circling motion of the rhyme scheme (*abba*) always confirms and brings to completion, or to its antithesis, the mood of the first line. Not until half-way through does the poem begin to challenge the stanzaic norm; this is at the ninth stanza, which begins by naming 'Helen of the roads', a Welsh goddess, then stanza after stanza, in one long winding sentence, proceeds to unfold her spiritual presence in all the sights familiar to the dedicated traveller. The lines are crowded with accumulating riches, and for a space of five stanzas the repeated action of confirming and completing a single motif is submerged by, or subsumed within, a movement of addition – one treasure added to the next in a headlong rush. I quote the last part of this sequence:

> And it is her laughter
>
> At morn and night I hear
> When the thrush cock sings
> Bright irrelevant things,
> And when the chanticleer
>
> Calls back to their own night
> Troops that make loneliness
> With their light footsteps' press
> As Helen's own are light.

There the flow of freedom abruptly ends and is immediately confronted by its negation, by the totally unexpected (the contrary to the endless expectation of the traveller):

> Now all roads lead to France
> And heavy is the tread
> Of the living; but the dead
> Returning lightly dance.

I have argued that these two poems, and others like them, reveal a tension between a formal and a natural order. With these instances before us, however, it may seem that we have no such thing, but only a local eccentricity of design tailored to fit a specific content. By this account, the winding, erratic movement of the five stanzas in 'Roads' is expressive of the roving life acclaimed therein, and in 'The Sun Used to Shine' a particular kind of living, an unpremeditated ease of living in the present, is enacted by the verse. Certainly this is so, but the function of the tension is not narrowly mimetic. The contrast between the opening and the closing stanza of 'The Sun Used to Shine' reveals a more general conflict. The opening lines have the air of not noticing the stanzaic structure and yet consenting to use it for purposes of their own. Only in the closing stanza does the elegiac mood of the poem at last correspond to the self-contained certainties and symmetrical resolutions of the form. 'Everything / To faintness like those rumours fades' – so the last sentence begins, continuing for four more lines with comparisons, and ending

> like memory's sand

> When the tide covers it late or soon,
> And other men through other flowers
> In those fields under the same moon
> Go talking and have easy hours.

The difference between the opening and the closing stanza is the difference between directly experiencing or re-experiencing 'easy hours', and talking about them, which is to say, between rendering the actual process and particularities of thought–feeling and the interpretative ordering of it. The first stanza – indeed, much of the poem – dramatizes the resistance that felt life offers to the levelling, generalizing effect of the stanza form. When, in 'Roads', the poem begins to release itself from the restrictions of its form, it gives free rein to the excitement which is implicit in the first stanza but held back by the tautness of the lines and the rhyming; our delight is that life itself has, so to speak, broken through the concept of life embodied in the form. I have insisted that a certain range of expression is intrinsic to the circular shape of the stanza so that I shall not be misunderstood when I say that we encounter the line 'Now all roads lead to France' – saying 'freedom, at least bodily freedom, is ended' – with a sense of recognition, as though we have been waiting for its message. For, though the determinations of the stanza's interpretative pattern are here identified with physical constraint, that was not the message of the opening stanzas. The temporary, partial escape from structure, beginning half-way through the poem, here dramatizes a larger truth – more precisely, two halves of a truth: that any mental form is a simplification and confinement of life's possibilities, but that, conversely, there is no final escape from ideas, from the necessity of structuring life.

Sometimes virtual freedom from formal constraint seems to be the norm, as it does in 'November' ('November Sky') and 'The Gypsy'. These are two of the nineteen poems written in rhyming couplets; all of them are as unlike the eighteenth-century poem in heroic couplets as any poem nominally of the same form could be, but the hexameter lines of 'The Gypsy', chosen to permit maximum freedom, loosely tie together a more vigorously irregular verse than occurs even in 'The Signpost' or 'Lob', the freest of Thomas's performances with pentameter couplets. The freedom of versification in 'The Gypsy' corresponds to something in the subject-matter – the pagan vitality in the vagabond life of the gipsies, reflected in the 'rascally Bacchanal dance' played on the mouth-organ by the Romany. The poem celebrates the zest of living and presents life lived energetically for its own sake instead of, or not primarily for, its meaning. One of the gipsy women bargains with the poet:

> 'My gentleman,' said one, 'you've got a lucky face.'
> 'And you've a luckier,' I thought, 'if such a grace
> And impudence in rags are lucky.' 'Give a penny
> For the poor baby's sake.' 'Indeed I have not any
> Unless you can give change for a sovereign, my dear.'
> 'Then just half a pipeful of tobacco can you spare?'
> I gave it. With that much victory she laughed content.

The language and rhythms here, and in most of the poem, concede so little to the conventions of metre and rhyme that whatever tension between verse and speech remains would seem to be negligible – would, indeed, be insignificant without the sequel of these lines:

> I should have given more, but off and away she went
> With her baby and her pink sham flowers to rejoin
> The rest before I could translate to its proper coin
> Gratitude for her grace.

There is a clear contrast between the beginning and the end of this sentence. The momentary elegance of 'proper coin' and the high civility of that last clause transmute toppling rhythms and runover lines into an image of defiant anarchy brought to order. We feel a tension, as we do in 'Roads', but at the same time or afterwards we experience release from tension: the freedom is not so much curbed as consummated, 'brought to order' but in a courteous form of words, a cadence and a balance of phrasing and sound (alliteration and the chime of 'translate' and 'grace' joining the head of the clause to the tail) that contain all the riches scattered over the preceding lines in generous disorder. The 'message' of 'Roads', I suggested, is that form is both a confinement and a necessity. Form at this point in 'The Gypsy' seems for a moment not an artifice at all but, miraculously, a natural occurrence, a fleeting felicity.

Let us look again at 'Adlestrop' – the opening lines. They are, I said, awkwardly prosaic; they also contrive a music out of awkwardness. The rhymes seem almost accidental, and yet, as with the phrase 'afternoon / Of heat', the line-division is used subtly, and when the rhyme is completed in a bare sentence that arrives like an afterthought to tie up a loose thread – 'It was late June' – the casualness of the observation says something: that the harmony of this moment came as unexpectedly as the rhyme. The internal half-rhymes even sketch the ghost of an alternative form in competition with the ostensible form, as though the sense flowed naturally into a pentameter couplet but was rechannelled into a quatrain. We have to feel that the simple structure is a loose fit to the sense before we can find any significance in the disparity. In the second stanza the shape of the sense adapts itself more closely to the form:

> The steam hissed. Someone cleared his throat.
> No one left and no one came
> On the bare platform. What I saw
> Was Adlestrop – only the name . . .

The juxtaposition of the stanzas shows more starkly the idiosyncrasy of the first. In his essay on Hardy's poetry Thomas loosely associates awkwardness with truth, truth being there synonymous with substantiality, that is, fidelity to the particularities of sensation, feeling and thought. We might substitute 'tension' for 'awkwardness', and conjecture that the tension between formal and natural controls in so many of Thomas's poems displays his concern for fidelity to the facts of experience. The association of awkwardness with truth suggests, in particular, a way of explaining the pose of stumbling maladroitness in 'Adlestrop'. For it *is* a pose, a dramatization of authenticity: it purports to guarantee the trustworthiness of memory by giving the facts unvarnished and without the rhetoric of feeling, and thus to gain credence for the sequel, a revelation of wholeness linked to a particular time and place, and win assent to the surge of feeling that flows out of the phrase 'only the name' into the third and fourth stanzas.

III Poetic realism

Whether we choose to formulate the structural tension as one between idea and fact or as between formal and natural order or as between order and disorder, Thomas's desire to keep close to the facts of experience clearly plays a crucial part in it. The temperateness of expression characteristic of his poetry, a continence that invariably qualifies his affirmative statements, is best understood as a stylistic manifestation of this desire. The measured emotion of 'And I am *nearly* as happy as possible' ('It Rains') and 'I still am *half* in love with pain' ('Liberty'), the reticence of 'I liked it' offsetting the resonance of the Tennysonian 'dark house' and its sequel, in 'The Long Small Room', the studious moderation of 'I *like* to see the nests / Still in their places' ('Birds' Nests') – all are uses of literal truthfulness to ballast strong feeling with understatement. The polemic for factuality or realism explicit or implicit in the poems needs to be examined more thoroughly. An *Annual of New Poetry*, published in 1917, included eighteen poems by Thomas under the pseudonym of Edward Eastaway. The T. L. S. reviewer commented: 'like most of his contemporaries, he has too little control over his eyes . . . they make the world for him too like a chaos of scattered and disconnected impressions'. He goes on to compare 'Mr. Eastaway' who 'makes his poems wholly out of natural fact', with Wordsworth, in whose work 'the voice of Nature' is always 'a voice that has a human message'. Is 'the new method', he asks, 'an unconscious survival of a materialism and naturalism which the tremendous life of the last three years has made an absurdity? If spirit is more, much more, than it was three years ago, how can Nature be kept outside the charm of its compelling unity?' The review appeared in late March, in time for Thomas to see it. In September T. S. Eliot, reviewing contemporary English and American verse for *The Egoist*, ascribed to the typical American poet 'an ingenious if sometimes perverse visual imagination in complete detachment from any other faculty'. Imagism is the target here, but his criticism is essentially the same as the complaint against Thomas's poems; it was a complaint made generally about the 'new poetry'. Eliot's implied criterion is the integrated mind concentrating its full powers on the object. Although the T. L. S. reviewer wrote in the language of unembarrassed moral exhortation commonly employed by literary journalists of the period, and Eliot practised the drier ('technical'), morally more reticent style favoured by the new generation of critics, it will be noticed that, speaking very approximately, they are in agreement about standards of judgment. Thomas shared with Frost a belief in the poetic value of fact, a value that we might not now be inclined to question, but if what the reviewer implied had been true – that Thomas's poetry is merely visual impressionism and the 'natural fact' out of which his poems are made has no interior life – then, by the (surely plausible) standards of unity and full humanity invoked by both critics, his judgment would have been justified. It is, of course, a commonplace of criticism about Thomas now that the 'outer scene' of his poetry has human implications. The T. L. S. reviewer failed to recognize them only because he expected the signs of their presence to be of the obvious, detachable kind for which 'human message' is a not inappropriate label. But the 'truth' that Thomas looked for in poetry and found in Hardy, the truth that is manifested also in his own poems, is what he noted in Keats's mature work, 'an exceptional fidelity' 'to the facts of outward and inward feeling' equally.

'November' ('November Sky') stands at the beginning of Thomas's work – it was his second poem – as 'Mowing' does at the beginning of Frost's, each being in part a manifesto for poetic realism.

> Anything more than the truth would have seemed too weak
> To the earnest love that laid the swale in rows . . .
> The fact is the sweetest dream that labor knows.

That is Frost. Thomas does not take quite the same position. He takes the sentimental idealism of one, perhaps a younger self, who 'imagines a refuge there / Above the mud [of November, with possibly a glancing allusion to the trenches in France], in the pure bright / Of the cloudless heavenly light', and sets it against his later estimation of the true relations of earth and sky:

> Another loves earth and November more dearly
> Because without them, he sees clearly,
> The sky would be nothing more to his eye
> Than he, in any case, is to the sky.

For neither poet is in fact neutral: 'naturalism' in Zola's sense, with its scientific pretensions, is precisely the wrong word to describe their brand of realism: fact is pursued because it is the necessary ground of love – as Frost said elsewhere, 'Earth's the right place for love'. Seeing what and how things are is at the same time seeing with a loving eye.

In 'November' ('November Sky') fidelity to the facts is also facing the facts, an attitude to them evident in the epigrammatic snap of the second couplet quoted above. It means facing the facts when in 'The Mountain Chapel' he remarks that the gods are reputed to be of 'inhuman stature dire, / As poets say / Who have not seen them clearly', with the implication that in saying so they are adorning the truth. Neither poem, of course, is advocating a mere realism of the eye: to see is to perceive with the whole mind, a mind more often than not tempered by a sceptical intelligence. The facts faced are generally unwelcome facts, and such words as 'clearly' and 'plain' herald the arrival and stoical reception of bleak news, the truth and nothing but the truth. The owl's cry is 'No merry note ... But one telling me plain what I escaped / And others could not'. 'When first I came here I had hope', another poem begins, but his departure twelve years later brings with it the 'plain' recognition of a momentous truth, that 'hope has gone for ever': 'For infinite / The change, late unperceived, this year, / The twelfth, suddenly, shows me plain'. 'March', his third poem, written the day after 'November' ('November Sky'), teases out the exact state of the truth, and demonstrates, without saying anything about it, all that clear seeing means. The faith of the opening statement – 'Now I know that Spring will come again / Perhaps tomorrow' – emerges out of a meticulous scrutinizing of the evidence and balancing of portents:

> The sunset piled
> Mountains on mountains of snow and ice in the west:
> Somewhere among their folds the wind was lost,
> And yet 'twas cold, and though I knew that Spring
> Would come again, I knew it had not come,
> That it was lost, too, in those mountains cold.

In 'Mowing' (though not in later poems of Frost) the real and the ideal are identified. Thomas's extended realism – fidelity to the facts of observation and the facts of feeling and thought – retains the distinction. In 'November' ('November Sky') the real and the ideal are opposites but are not actively in opposition: each is necessary, each implies the other and is valued equally. In the essay on Hardy mentioned earlier, Thomas criticized some of Hardy's poems for their 'superstition', a term which we may adapt. The realism of 'The Mountain Chapel' is a poetic insurance against the superstition of poets who, not seeing clearly the nature of the gods, make bogies out of them. It does not, however, exclude idealism; there are, as he said of Keats, objective and subjective facts; it is indeed the bigotry of 'materialism' (the T. L. S. reviewer's misinterpretation of Thomas's preoccupation with sense–experience) to suppose otherwise.

If 'November' ('November Sky') is the manifesto of poetic realism and 'March' its illustrative sequel, 'But These Things Also' is Thomas's most intransigent assertion of it. The entire posture of the poem is one of contradiction: it begins with a 'but' and is a refutation of sentimentally partial descriptions of spring in the name of truth-telling. 'But these things also are Spring's' is the first line, and the list includes

> The shell of a little snail bleached
> In the grass; chip of flint, and mite
> Of chalk; and the small birds' dung
> In splashes of purest white.

The realism is ascetically strict – nothing is added to the truth. These relics of winter are as minute and as unremarkable as could be; the clipped monosyllables give the aural equivalent of their meanness. And yet the clear-cut sounds, by miming the keenness of the observing eye, at the same time convey sharp appreciation for the clean, bright distinctness of the normally unregarded objects named here. There is the same blend of objectivity and subjectivity as in 'November': dead things are acknowledged and then made lively to the eye; pleasure transforms fact. In that transformation we have the most telling answer to the T. L. S. reviewer's charge that Thomas's eyes create 'a chaos of scattered and disconnected impressions'. On the contrary – and this is the most important point to make about his realism – in the process of enlivening the dead scene they enlarge and unify it. The realism of 'November' is neither neutral nor partial. Where the sentimentalist divides the 'mud' from the 'heavenly light', the true lover of earth combines them in a single reality; his love of the month as it is, of 'even the mud whose dyes / Renounce all brightness to the skies', derives its intensity from his consciousness of what it is not. 'But These Things Also' similarly advocates and exemplifies wholeness of view; not merely, however, by giving the complement to a one-sided view of spring, but by making the two aspects of spring resemble each other. The superlative, 'purest white', is charged with all the poet's yearning for its opposite:

> All the white things a man mistakes
> For earliest violets
> Who seeks through Winter's ruins
> Something to pay Winter's debts.

Bleached shell, flint, chalk, birds' dung are not harbingers of spring, but the emotional significance of 'earliest violets' (a matching superlative) has been transferred to the tiny delicacy of these bleak reminders of winter; debts for a moment dissemble riches.

IV Semantic tensions

The poem ends: 'And Spring's here, Winter's not gone'. The last line of 'Swedes' (a condensed version of two lines in Coleridge's 'Work Without Hope') is almost identical: 'This is a dream of Winter, sweet as Spring'. And compare this with the seasonal reversal depicted in 'October': 'The late year has grown fresh again and new / As Spring, and to the touch is not more cool / Than it is warm to the gaze'. They have in common a *unitary vision* and the method of suggesting it by a tremulous balancing of opposites. It might be said that Thomas's aim is the same as Arnold's, 'to see life steadily and to see it whole', but accurate and subtle self-awareness has revealed the inaccessibility to him of a view as firm and lasting as this injunction seems to expect, and emotional honesty dictates a way of rendering it that is truer to the facts of feeling. His view is not steady and substantial but a fleeting, scarcely communicable glimpse, and his characteristic method of imparting it, by a juxtaposition of opposites, answers to its elusive, fragile, paradoxical nature. The simultaneity rendered by omission of connectives in 'And Spring's here, Winter's not gone' may be said to border on paradox; the care taken to avoid identifying the dream with spring itself in the conclusion of 'Swedes', while hinting at the same paradox, emphasizes more the poignant fragility of the vision. What is at stake for Thomas is most clearly revealed in 'Under the Woods', which seeks through paradox to enter into a more mysterious totality, a condition like eternity in which youth and age, life and death, cease to be distinguishable:

> When these old woods were young
> The thrushes' ancestors
> As sweetly sung
> In the old years.

The scentless dead stoat that yet survives all memories of the old keeper who shot him is the poem's final emblem of this larger reality.

The method has been noted in the course of a slightly different argument by Vernon Scannell, specifically in 'Interval'. The poem presents a twilight interlude briefly separating a 'wild day' from 'A wilder night', a moment poised between calm and menace, 'gleam' and 'gloom'. Scannell comments that it 'shows clearly the way in which Thomas used opposites to create associative tensions which move gradually towards the final reconciliation of "This roaring peace", the calm which is actually a suspended violence'.[1] 'Reconciliation' is, surely, a misleading name for 'suspended violence' and the oxymoron expressing it. 'Roaring peace' is, if anything, further from a reconciliation of the conflicting forces in the poem than 'stormy rest', the milder phrase that anticipates it. It widens the distance between the antithetical conditions spanned, but not reconciled, by both phrases, and increases rather than lessens the tension between the two halves of a totality contained with difficulty in one view. And this, it seems, is deliberate.

> The beeches keep
> A stormy rest,
> Breathing deep
> Of wind from the west.

The poet is like the trees in being alive to the tension, partaking equally of storm and rest; while seeking to encompass both, he does not allow himself to forget the obstacles in the way of a whole, unitary vision.

This vision is insusceptible to reasoned demonstration, and therefore there had to be an element of paradox or tension in the language expressing it; but it is not always as conspicuous as in 'Interval'. In the image of the farmhouse, 'So velvet-hushed and cool under the warm tiles', in 'Two Houses', we are more conscious of successful mediation than potential conflict between the opposite conditions. Frequently Thomas uses the ambiguous transition from day to night or the pause between two kinds of weather as a prelude to one of his idyllic 'moments of everlastingness'. The ground is thus prepared for the still-life picture of an immemorial England in 'Haymaking', and for the introduction, in 'May the Twenty-third', of Jack Noman, whose gait and figure, 'Jaunty and old, crooked and tall', a carefree blend of incongruities defying time, duplicates the auspicious early-morning association of rain and sun and embodies the subsequent perfection of the day. In 'Man and Dog' another wandering man encountered by the poet is described as 'straight but lame', and the unity of being attributed to this half-mythical folk character whenever he appears is regularly symbolized by such adjectival oppositions. The aptness to all moods and occasions of the folk melody celebrated in 'An Old Song' ('I was not apprenticed . . .') also signifies unity of being. This is conveyed stylistically in the repeated pairing of alternatives. Examples of such pairings, or merely lists, are numerous. One remembers 'The sun and the frost, the land and the sea, / Summer, Autumn, Winter, Spring' ('The Signpost'); and 'The lovely visible earth and sky and sea / Where what the curlew needs not, the farmer tills' ('For These'); and the sun in 'There's Nothing Like the Sun', which is kind 'To stones and men and beasts and birds and flies'. Their common purpose, varying only in the degree of strain manifested, is to embody a wholeness of view. Whether emphasizing the impediments to such a vision or not, Thomas's aim in all his poems is to provide in some measure a poetic counterpart of its possession. For him the poetic bird is not the aspiring lark or the melodious nightingale but the sedge-warbler; nimble, more tireless than the lark, its charmless song is offered as symbol of a wisdom coveted by the poet; its power, as the previous examples would lead us to expect, is that it is a 'song to match the heat / Of the strong sun, nor less the water's cool', the poles of its existence.

Contraries, complementarities, alternatives and inclusive lists are frequent in Thomas and have a cumulative force, but in the reading of any one poem they are no more than pinpricks on the reader's total attention; they are rarely startling, and it is possible to have known the poetry well for a considerable time before the frequency of their appearance is consciously noted. If my own experience is representative, a structural device occurring in only a handful of poems having the same end in view of contriving a unitary vision, is on the contrary immediately so arresting, continuing to tease and fascinate, that it is more likely to strike the new reader as peculiarly expressive of Thomas's poetic individuality than the pervasively antithetical cast of his mind. It eludes easy categorization but I have come to think of it as manipulation of perspectives. They may be temporal or spatial perspectives. In 'Old Man' there is an anticipatory change of tense as the poet turns his attention to the child ('I love it, as some day the child will love it'), but the real change of temporal perspective comes later:

> And I can only wonder how much hereafter
> She will remember, with that bitter scent,
> Of garden rows, and ancient damson trees
> Topping a hedge, a bent path to a door,
> A low thick bush beside the door, and me
> Forbidding her to pick.

Speculatively adopting his daughter's future viewpoint, the poet goes forward in order to look back, disengaging himself from and then re-entering the present. The octet of the sonnet 'February Afternoon' reverses this procedure. In this instance the poet goes back in order to look forward. He compares familiar sounds and sights of the present – 'the roar of parleying starlings', birds following the plough – with their predecessors, which men heard and saw 'a thousand years ago even as now'; a strange mirror-effect occurs when, taking this further, he imagines that

> one, like me, dreamed how
> A thousand years might dust lie on his brow
> Yet thus would birds do between hedge and shaw.

'Liberty', which presents (self-critically) a solipsistic view, 'the moon and I' enjoying a cosy illusion of absolute freedom, makes a distancing shift of spatial perspective in the last line, 'And this moon that leaves me dark within the door', by dint of which the self-contemplating poet suddenly becomes the object of impassive contemplation. 'The Long Small Room' manipulates both spatial and temporal perspectives. The room was probably not one that Thomas had lived in, but the poem hints at dark events in the past that connect the man to the place. It begins, reticently, in the first person; 'I liked it', making a show of ingenuous candour, actually reveals little and conceals whatever secrets the room is presumed to hold; it is none the less the only direct statement of feeling. Widening the gap between himself and the unspecified experience, the poet then steps outside his own mind into the putative consciousness of 'the moon, the mouse and the sparrow' peeping in through the casement-window on the tragic life of the room. The last step in dissociation is taken when he assimilates his retrospective view to the incomprehension and helplessness of these blankly dispassionate observers:

> When I look back I am like moon, sparrow, and mouse
> That witnessed what they could never understand
> Or alter or prevent in the dark house.

These four episodes exhibit a common pattern, and, whether the shifts of consciousness are from the present to vantage points in past or future time or from the poet's mind into another's, they have, I think, a similar purpose. Something of what that is will have emerged from my brief descriptions of them in the previous paragraph. Let me approach a general formulation by way of 'Old Man'. To anticipate what his daughter, looking back, will remember of the scene before him is to imagine a prototype of what he cannot trace in his own memory, and is a means of vicariously locating the intensity of feeling and sensation induced by the 'bitter scent' of the herb; it makes a feint at explaining what cannot be explained. In its passage from contemplation of the herb and its alternative names, through considerations of the child, the garden scene, and the enigmatic 'meaning' of the herb's 'bitter scent', to the infinite vista of the last line, 'Only an avenue, dark, nameless, without end', it guides us towards a totality that is beyond the mind's grasp, inexpressible, which may be nothing at all or a nothing that is also ambiguously something. Like the part played by opposites in the design of Thomas's poems (and the pair of names here, 'Old Man' or 'Lad's Love', linking age and youth, furnishes an instance), the shift of temporal perspective – the assumption of another's future viewpoint to 'explain' the present by conjuring a hypothetical past – contributes to the adumbration of a possible whole view beyond the scope of the poet's single consciousness.

Yet 'Old Man' is *about* uncertainty; subsequent reflection upon the statement that introduces the child into the poem, 'The herb itself I like not, but for *certain* / I love it, as the child will love it', suggests an irony additional to the paradox of love co-existing with dislike. The manipulation of perspectives has the dual purpose of at once implying and withholding the larger objective reality. And some such tension distinguishes each example. The movement in 'February Afternoon' is from the personal to the total human view; but though the message is bitter – explicitly so in the Hardyesque ending, which interprets the unchanging as the law of divine indifference – the effect of finding a mirror image of oneself in the past is to mitigate the bitterness, rather as, in Hardy's 'The Subalterns', the attribution of sentience to the agents of Necessity alleviates the poet's sense of helplessness in being subjected to it. The uncertainty here is in whether this extended, impersonal view is satisfying or not: is it liberating or constricting to acknowledge that the law of handy-dandy is eternal – 'men strike and bear the stroke / Of war as ever, audacious or resigned'? Similar questions are left unanswered in other poems. The burden of oppressive memories connected with 'the long small room' is lightened by a shared retrospective view, but do fellowship in helplessness and the lapse of time make one any the less subject to that condition? And is freedom from the illusion of freedom to be regarded without irony as 'liberty'? Such questions in the reader's mind are prompted by the ambivalence of the poet towards the enlargement of vision reflected in his play with temporal and spatial perspectives. Let 'The Sun Used to Shine' stand as my principal illustration of this ambivalence; for the form it takes, a tension between particular and general, personal and impersonal meanings, will serve to make the connection between the structural tension discussed earlier (in relation to this poem), and the peculiarly indeterminate, veiled relation – tension is not quite the word – between the literal and the metaphorical levels of meaning in Thomas's poetry.

The transition between temporal viewpoints, reflected in ambiguities of tense, is particularly subtle in this poem. The opening stanzas are a commemoration of the recent past, an idyllic time of friendship (the unnamed friend was Frost), which, while it lasted, made all but its own state of mind seem unreal. Still using the past tense, he mentions the war:

> The war
> Came back to mind with the moonrise
> Which soldiers in the east afar
> Beheld then –

a war which is still in progress, however, as he writes. Thus without formal grammatical indications the past glides into the present, and in the process the domain of the unreal is extended: the language takes on a legendary resonance ('the east afar / Beheld'); then he abandons equivocation and, glancing at a more remote, historical past, confesses that 'Nevertheless, our eyes / Could as well imagine the Crusades / Or Caesar's battles' as the battlefields of France. The poem then switches – in mid-stanza and mid-line – to the present tense, but it is a present that includes the past and the future: 'Everything / To faintness like those rumours [rumours of the war] fades'. In his development of this statement Thomas does all he can to blur the distinction between times: 'Like the brook's water glittering / Under the moonlight' – glittering then, now and always – 'like *those* walks / *Now* . . .' More comparisons follow that refer unambiguously to the past, but the last comparison, though it continues in the present tense, also carries an elusive suggestion of the future:

> like memory's sand
>
> When the tide covers it late or soon,
> And other men through other flowers
> In those fields under the same moon
> Go talking and have easy hours.

The solipsism which made everything outside the private world of the two shared subjectivities seem unreal – war had faded into 'rumours of the war remote' – has in its turn been exposed as a state of unreality: everything fades, and what was real for us will die and give way to the 'realities' of other men and other fields. But all takes place under 'the same moon' – the same inconstant moon, unchanging–changing, implacable queen of this realm of unreality; the poem begins in the sun and ends under the moon's reign. The poet's earlier closed perception of reality has been opened to the most inclusive vision possible – past, present and future seen as an eternal continuous present. But the poem does not try to persuade us that this wider awareness is preferable to, or more real than, the closed circle of thought and feeling that contained his happiness with Frost. The state of mind relived in the first part of the poem is similar to the solipsism anatomized and judged with severe impartiality in 'Liberty', but is presented here very differently: viewed not as a morbid state but as a generous contentment, it is lovingly re-created and recalled with a wistful regret for its passing. Where, then, does reality lie – with the subjective or the objective, the particular or the general, view? The general vision unites discrete times and places, emphasizing the common experience of the friends and their successors-in-happiness in the same scenes as well as the humanity they have in common with their opposites 'under the same moon' elsewhere, the soldiers who have no 'easy hours' to enjoy but whose fate is soon to be Thomas's; with this emphasis and with the symmetries and elegiac ceremony of the last stanza the general vision brings a kind of serenity. Yet the treacherous blandness of 'the same moon' ensures that our sense of the 'easy hours' contains at least a measure of uneasiness. The opening-up of vistas is also, in part, a closing-down of hope. The semantic tension is related to the structural tension discussed earlier in the chapter; it is unresolved, and the question about general and particular realities is not for answering. At the roots of the unease and uncertainty generated by Thomas's manipulation of perspectives in this poem and in the other poems mentioned is the contradiction between their recognition that subjective consciousness is inescapable, and the aspiration to transcend that condition.

V   A tremulous poise

Thomas's realism found a place for idealism; the balance or tension of opposites and the mirror effect of shifting viewpoints are verbal and structural devices for intimating – rather than asserting – a suprapersonal inclusive awareness. In this connection Pater is represented by Thomas as having a symptomatic significance. 'He felt himself one of a disillusioned, exhausted age which had lost the large sense of proportion in all things, "the all embracing prospect of life as a whole", which the Middle Ages had from the top of a cathedral' (p. 185). Although elsewhere in *Walter Pater* Thomas has ironic things to say about the pose of disillusion, and here he is plainly sceptical of an idealized mediaeval world view, he concurs in Pater's interpretation of the age. He rejects Pater's inference from the latter-day 'isolation of the individual among the terrible inharmonious multitudes' that 'art should become an end in itself, unrelated, unassociated' (p. 185), but he had no reason to doubt – indeed, his own experience confirmed – the reality of that isolation. His view of the consequences for art, however – a view expressed several times in the book, and one in conformity with the direction of his subsequent poetic efforts – is diametrically opposed. 'For it is evident,' he writes, 'that his passion for the concrete and his "living in and through the eye" were not the same thing as a profound, proportionate and vital sense of reality' (p. 150). Thomas was himself accused by the T. L. S. reviewer of an excessive reliance on his eyes, but the implication of Thomas's criticism is that the sensationalism and spectatorial outlook of Pater, by themselves, constitute a capitulation to, not an imaginative compensation for, the disconnection and disorientation of modern man. The key word is 'proportionate'. 'A large sense of proportion in all things', Thomas's equivalent for Pater's 'all embracing prospect of life as a whole', is what he would expect to find in great works of art and what he strives for, with appropriate modifications, in his poetry. The modifications, however, indicate an important difference. He cannot be complacent about the loss of a whole ordered view of life, but neither does he believe that it can be restored by fiat, and his consciousness of the difficulty, even the quixotry, of undertaking such a task is reflected in the characteristic tentativeness and delicacy of his attempts to give it imaginative embodiment, expressing as they do the precariousness of his vision. 'Proportion', which when applied to poetry suggests intellectual confidence and clarity of form, does not identify what we actually find in Thomas's poems, which is, in fact, not a firm balance and inter-relationship of parts but a tremulous poise, a provisional, momentary adjustment of simultaneous discrepant awarenesses.

I have remarked upon this poise incidentally in previous chapters. I noted in 'The Wasp Trap', for example (though not in precisely these terms), the strange fusion of entrancement and clear seeing, surrender to and exposure of illusion. 'That jar / For wasps meant' is at the same time deadly and in the moonlight brighter than any star: the poet refuses to separate the fact from the appearance, and the prayer – 'long may it swing / From the dead apple-bough, / So glistening' – expresses an ambivalence so perfect that it is even seriously misleading to speak of a double view; it is a sentiment, as I said, 'poised with horrible tremulousness between "dead" and "glistening"'.

In a number of poems involvement and detachment are so adjusted as to achieve what might be called – giving greater prominence to the adjective – an *urbane* poise, a social manner that could not be predicted for a poet of Thomas's disposition and affiliations. The urbanity, if that is the right term, is, to be sure, more intimate than that of the Elizabethan poets, and gentler and more vulnerable than its Caroline exemplars; its light elegance endows the poem not so much with a hard finish, though the manner is polished, as with a shimmer of uncertainty. Thus, in 'These Things that Poets Said' (quoted in Chapter 2), the aplomb with which Thomas juggles the concepts of love and poetry, saying and knowing, falters – the whole air of impersonal rationality wavers – as it encounters vibrations from another voice, wistful, tender, wry, quizzical. Moreover, neither voice has the final word – together they give way to and open out into another order of feeling, cryptically indicated in the last line: 'I, loving not, am different'. The crisp neatness of 'Song' is similarly deceptive:

> At poet's tears,
> Sweeter than any smile but hers,
> She laughs; I sigh;
> And yet I could not live if she should die.

The second stanza here quoted (the first in all printings prior to R. George Thomas's edition of the *Collected Poems*) is, rather, a tangle of logic – a criss-cross of tears, smiles, laughter, sighing – to which the comparison of sweetnesses brings not clarity of distinction but further disorder: the aim is not finality but an inconclusive openness.

The structure and manner of these two poems, a pattern of logical argument overlaying feeling, are not repeated in 'And You, Helen', and yet in quality of feeling it resembles them. It has a softer urbanity; or, since that smacks of paradox, I had better say that its urbanity shades into something else. Trying to define this, I spoke of 'an achieved inner *proportion*'; even though the balance of affectionate banter and an implicitly painful content is a delicate one, with the translation from affection to irony, resonant suggestion ('all you have lost / Upon the travelling waters tossed') to clipped reticence ('or given to me'), so deft as to be barely perceptible, I would, despite the reservations expressed earlier, in this instance keep the word. The poise of the poem is, after all, not unlike that equilibrium between lightness and seriousness, an urbane 'balance and proportion of tones', which, according to Eliot, 'makes Marvell a classic'.[2] Thomas's proportion is, of course, not Classical; its reticence is too personal, and for that reason it would be more accurate to say that the poem has a spiritual, rather than an urbane, poise. Simultaneous awarenesses of what has been, what is and what might be in his relationship with his wife fuse and become a shimmering vision of 'life as a whole'.

In Chapter 2 I remarked that the *Sehnsucht* expressed in 'Ambition' and 'A Lofty Sky' is presented with full intensity and irony combined – in these poems, as in 'These Things that Poets Said' and 'Song', the poet treads a fine line between self-expression and self-dramatization. Something similar is true of 'The Unknown Bird'; however, the tender ingenuousness with which the poet confesses his yearning for the dream-like, disembodied life conjured up by the bird's 'three lovely notes' may at first so hold the attention that the faint accompanying undertone of misgiving may go unheard. But it is clear that a certain self-detachment, judicious rather than ironic, is implied by the poet's preoccupation with the degree of reality to be claimed for a song heard four or five years ago by him alone ('though many listened'), and which belonged to no bird that naturalists could identify. This preoccupation is revealed in his meticulous care for accuracy in recording the circumstances, no less meticulous than his concern for accuracy of observation in poems that could well be called naturalistic. The tone, we soon recognize, is tender but not self-indulgent. The unknown is weighed in the balance with the known, uncertainty of fact ('All the proof is – I told men / What I had heard') with subjective truth:

> But I cannot tell
> If truly never anything but fair
> The days were when he sang, as now they seem.
> This surely I know, that I who listened then,
> Happy sometimes, sometimes suffering
> A heavy body and a heavy heart,
> Now straightway, if I think of it, become
> Light as that bird wandering beyond my shore.

In an interview with Michael Schmidt, Charles Tomlinson has praised Thomas for 'an easy elegance';[3] it is certainly a quality his poetry has, but, as far as I am aware, no one else has thought it significant enough to mention. It is worth remarking, however, because it occurs not only where I have noted it, as an expression of urbane poise in such poems as 'Song' and 'These Things that Poets Said', but in many poems where one would not expect to find it. I have been illustrating the structural and semantic tensions in Thomas's poetry – the outcome of a conflict between an aspiration to a whole ordered view of his experience and an actual tentativeness, uncertainty or inconclusiveness in his expression of it. We are made aware of these tensions by some structural surprise, a device such as the manipulation of perspectives, that unsettles our provisional anticipation of the unfolding sense; frequently an elegance in the phrasing or the shaping of a sentence is part of that surprise. The elegance, promising without actually delivering a cool, ordered vision, and so failing to reassure the reader, is the main cause of disturbance wherever it appears – an example is the third stanza of 'Roads'. Celebrating the continuing existence of the ancient green roads of England, the words make a glancing reference to Ariel's Song 'Full Fathom Five' ('Nothing of him that doth fade, / But doth suffer a sea-change . . .'):

> On this earth 'tis sure
> We men have not made
> Anything that doth fade
> So soon, so long endure.

The point of echoing Ariel is both to parallel and to contrast his claims for what could be termed a limited immortality with Shakespeare's image of metamorphosis: 'fade' limits the expansive ambitions of 'long endure'. The shape of the sentence is balanced and rational; it seems to display a scrupulous concern to claim for the roads he loves no more than is strictly true. Yet the paradoxical form of the statement opens a crack in the logic, and the assertion of 'endure' is felt to contradict rather than complement the admission of transience. The emotion animating and intensifying the paradox is at variance with the judicious temper of the antithesis.

Something similar – a pretence of scientific precision lightly affected and as lightly dropped – happens in 'There's Nothing Like the Sun':

> There's nothing like the sun as the year dies,
> Kind as it can be, this world being made so,
> To stones and men and beasts and birds and flies,
> To all things that it touches except snow,
> Whether on mountain side or street of town.

The solemn tenderness of this is already tinged with whimsy by the end of the third line. Whimsy is then changed to tender irony by the mock-solemn, finical qualification 'except snow', which blandly pretends that the statement is not a hyperbolic thanksgiving for the gift of life but a neutral observation applied to a simple definition of solar heat. The immediate cause of the irony is the simultaneous recollection that there is no month of the year but, when the sun shines, it calls forth the same extravagant expression of gratitude. But death is in the poet's mind, not only the year's decline but human mortality, and what at first seems merely playful is, in retrospect, seen to be a muffled prelude to the last line, 'There's nothing like the sun till we are dead': the snow's cold prefigures his own death, and the kind of control, the mincing precision, exhibited by that line, 'To all things that it touches except snow', is thereby made irrelevant.

Tomlinson associates the elegance in Thomas's poetry with the unpredictability of his sentences, and he quotes as an example these lines from 'October':

> The late year has grown fresh again and new
> As Spring, and to the touch is not more cool
> Than it is warm to the gaze.

He presumably means the unexpectedness and unlooked-for precision of the comparison, which yet has an elegant appearance of simplicity, between literal coolness and metaphorical warmth; but perhaps he also has in mind the momentary uncertainty we experience as we are tricked by the line-ending into misreading 'fresh again and new' as parallel adjectives, and then forced by the continuation into the next line to correct that reading (mentally inserting the suppressed 'as' and allowing the lines their proper, if now slightly hesitant, momentum). In fact, the lines epitomize the ambiguity of the whole poem. The scene seems to hold one of Thomas's timeless moments, the identity of seasonal opposites being reinforced by the fine equipoise of 'cool' and 'warm'; the poet briefly enjoys an illusion of freedom from the movement of time, a freedom imaged in the line, 'The gossamers wander at their own will'. But the idyll in this poem is only a light disguise of transience: the elm 'Lets leaves into the grass slip, one by one', and grass is the king 'That blackberry and gorse, in dew and sun, / Bow down to'. The allusion to Wordsworth's 'The river glideth at his own sweet will' defines a difference. For Thomas's wistful appreciation lacks the rapt faith in the miracle of feeling that irradiates Wordsworth's early morning prospect of London from Westminster Bridge; the line in 'October' has neither the entrancement nor the weight and assurance of the line it echoes. The Romantic poet is so completely absorbed in his vision that without a qualm he can dissolve the city into nature and attribute personality to both; but Thomas, in the very act of creating his 'moment of everlastingness', must concede its illusion. Unlike Wordsworth, Thomas retains an awareness of his sleight of hand, and eschews the grandeurs and affirmations of Romantic poetry. As the content of the moment is uncertain, so is the feeling that for Thomas comprises the personal significance of the scene. Neither 'melancholy' nor 'happiness' identifies it; both names are partly justifiable, but ultimately it is unnameable. Words are a loose fit on the body of reality, which does not finally disclose itself through the appearance of the scene or of the poet's mood. These uncertainties are focused in the lines cited by Tomlinson; the fastidiously precise, coolly analytic words purport to define the strictly indefinable, measure the immeasurable.

The appearance of elegant rationality is employed in a general strategy to expose the limits of a conceptual order. The aim of the mental acrobatics on display in 'The Word' is apparently to make genial sport with the pretensions of logical and analogical thinking. Logical distinctions between the real and the possible, what was and what might have been, collapse in the opening lines:

> There are so many things I have forgot,
> That once were much to me, or that were not,
> All lost, as is a childless woman's child
> And its child's children, in the undefiled
> Abyss of what will never be again.

The poem is a fantasia on the theme of forgetting and remembering, as an expression of the vanity of things, but its deepest theme is not memory but something that memory can neither lose nor recover, 'the empty thingless name' which 'Never can die because Spring after Spring / Some thrushes learn to say it as they sing'. It does not depend on memory for its survival, but is resurrected with the season, and has the peculiar immortality of nature. It is 'the word' of the title – single (where the 'names of the mighty men . . . Of kings and fiends and gods' are all plural), 'thingless' – without reference beyond itself – and invariable, and though 'empty' not *vain*:

> While perhaps I am thinking of the elder scent
> That is like food, or while I am content
> With the wild rose scent that is like memory,
> This name suddenly is cried out to me
> From somewhere in the bushes by a bird
> Over and over again, a pure thrush word.

If the mode of thought imitated in the poem's opening sentence is logical, the 'thinking' mentioned here in the conclusion is analogical. Logic is violated in the former; the latter discovers in 'a *pure* thrush word' an image for what eludes assimilation by analogy: the 'elder scent' is 'like food' and 'the wild rose scent' is 'like memory', but the 'thrush word' is like nothing – it is incomparable, nonpareil. It is as though reality, without the mediation of the organizing mind, has thrust itself naked at the reader. By letting the forms of conceptual thought discredit themselves these poems seek to sharpen consciousness of what is, or may be, just beyond the reach of words: intimations of the ultimate, the long enduring, a timelessness other than that of seasonal repetition, a pure thingless name. We may add to this list the sound of the water by the abandoned mill, a sound that seems to the poet in 'The Mill-Water' to be the close companion, the voice as it were, of an underlying 'silentness'. It is a comparison between things not comparable that first draws attention to something disquieting in the sound:

> Pretty to see, by day
> Its sound is naught
> Compared with thought
> And talk and noise of labour and of play.

The least predictable comparison is the more unsettling for being the first in a series of three. More silent than thought, this sound has mysteriously taken to itself the character of thought; at night it has the darker quality of nocturnal broodings: 'All thoughts begin or end upon this sound'.

10 Metaphor and symbol

Whether wholly or in part, the poems 'Roads', 'There's Nothing Like the Sun', 'October', 'The Word' and 'The Mill-Water' dramatize the disparity between the presented facts of experience and their logical or analogical interpretation. Yet all thought, including poetic thought, is an interpretation, an ordering and generalizing, of facts; the problem as Thomas sees it is to find meaning without seeming to impose it, and at the same time to remain faithful to the phenomenal reality of experience. According to the analysis I have offered, his method of dealing with the problem is to make the disruption of conceptual precision and elegance a means of implying and pointing the way towards an unbroken order of significance not completely contained in the words. If these terms begin to sound familiar it is because the power to do this, or to create the illusion of doing this, is commonly attributed to poetic symbol and the more adventurous kinds of metaphor. Thinking in poetry uses analogy more often than logic, and Thomas's poetry is no exception. The tension I have been discussing is most apparent in his handling of metaphor. By itself, however, my description of his method does not clearly distinguish it from the practice of other poets; what is peculiar to Thomas's art is the puzzling, tentative, tenuous connection between the literal and figurative dimensions of his poems.

A brief example is provided by 'In Memoriam (Easter, 1915)':

> The flowers left thick at nightfall in the wood
> This Eastertide call into mind the men,
> Now far from home, who, with their sweethearts, should
> Have gathered them and will do never again.

Though brief, it is representative of Thomas's method in the delicacy of its effects. The overt connection between the flowers and the dead soldiers is a narrative one: left ungathered, the spring flowers merely *remind* the poet of the lovers who in other years would have gathered them. The word 'Eastertide', underlining the hint in the title, sets in motion another train of thought, and the narrative connection begins its slow passage – moving, as it were, at the solemn, halting pace of the verse – from casual association to analogy and metaphorical identity. Easter and Spring – death and resurrection, the natural cycle enacted by the flowers – are fused and put into tense relationship with the 'never again' of these deaths. In the transition to metaphor portents of death are picked up in 'nightfall', and, contradicting the suggestion of natural fecundity, in 'left thick' (corpses thickly strewn on the battlefields of France): finally the fallen men are themselves the flowers. An image of pastoral is faintly echoed, and we may recall – we are perhaps meant to recall – Milton's '*Proserpin* gathering flowers / Her self a fairer Floure by gloomie *Dis* / Was gatherd'. Analysis of even these four lines could be more searching and yet fail to exhaust the metaphorical implications. But at this stage it is sufficient to remark that the emphasis is on plain description and psychological realism (this brings to mind that related fact) and that the symbolism is made to appear incidental, almost accidental, to the literal sense.

The scene described in 'Tall Nettles' could scarcely be more homely, the personal voice more unassuming:

> Tall nettles cover up, as they have done
> These many springs, the rusty harrow, the plough
> Long worn out, and the roller made of stone:
> Only the elm butt tops the nettles now.
>
> This corner of the farmyard I like most:
> As well as any bloom upon a flower
> I like the dust on the nettles, never lost
> Except to prove the sweetness of a shower.

Its plainness and modesty would seem to discourage any search for metaphorical significance; certainly it does not occur to Fred Inglis, commenting on its 'modest perfection' in *An Essential Discipline*, to mention any. Yet, as often in Thomas's poems, the simple is also enigmatic. Why, in the first stanza, these particular details? They differ from those listed in the prose passage, quoted by Edna Longley, in which apparently the same memory is put to use. What part is played by the nettles? We must conclude that they have some significance other than the factual from Thomas's care to exclude their common associations – those exploited, for example, by Hardy in his poem 'Nettles', where they are emblems of heartlessness and neglect. Nor should the feint of saying something so simple that it needs no elaboration, in the phrase 'I like', be allowed to disguise the fact that the reasons for his liking are far from obvious; his preference for a dusty, disregarded 'corner of the farmyard' requires explanation. Looking for answers to these questions, we begin to discern in the particulars of the poem an unexpected glimmer of general symbolic significance. The whole poem, being neither elegiac nor nostalgic, is a reversal of the conventional response to such a scene. The nettles have here a protective rather than an aggressive character: they conceal from the casual eye, reserve for the tenderly appreciative eye, and keep undisturbed, these signs of a past life; the settled dust of time, correspondingly, signifies not decay but freedom from disturbance. The nettles thus serve the piety of memory, in which the past attains a kind of immortality. The impression made by the related description quoted from *The Heart of England* in Mrs Longley's note (p. 340) is quite different: by contrast with the romantic appeal of the 'noble, blue waggon' and the 'antique plough', and the dilapidation of 'broken wheels' and a 'rude wooden roller', the farm implements listed in 'Tall Nettles' stand out as venerably plain, functional, solid and, though worn and discarded, durable, similarly, 'elm butt' sounds more like the indestructible core of elm than the lifeless stump of a tree. Entrusted to memory, the dead past, and the human values associated with it, have a continuing life – a condition sharpened to paradox by the notion of the dust of ages that is 'never lost'. In the context of the poetry as a whole, pervaded as it is by a sense of loss, that phrase is especially suggestive; we are reminded of 'The Word' with its record of forgotten things, 'all lost . . . in the undefiled / Abyss of what will never be again'. Dust, butt, implements, all are images of the long-lasting; the nettles, like the orchard fence in 'It Rains', are memory's insurance against intrusion upon their (relatively) unchanging state. Two principles are contraposed: the 'sweetness' of what lives and refreshes but is transitory, and the permanent life in memory of what is dead; their opposition *proves* (tests, demonstrates) and enhances the separate value of each.

In this formulation these are paradoxes, but it is characteristic of Thomas's art that they are latent paradoxes, which reveal themselves only in the speculative extension of the poem invited by its reticence. What has happened is this: thoughts about the continuous beneficent presence of past time, its agelessness counterpointing the actual passing of time and endearing to us its transient blooms, have been raised to consciousness by contemplation of this scene; they are, as it were, inherent *in* the scene – cannot be, and have not been, detached from it. The psychological principle governing the composition of such a poem is one made familiar to us by the Romantic poets. It is explained by De Quincey in his *Suspiria De Profundis*: 'I have been struck with the important truth that far more of our deepest thoughts and feelings pass to us through perplexed combinations of *concrete* objects, pass to us as *involutes* (if I may coin that word) in compound experiences incapable of being disentangled, than ever reach us *directly* and in their own abstract shapes.' Jonathan Wordsworth, who quotes this in a review,[1] comments that, though De Quincey was reflecting on personal associations with the death of his sister, yet 'as the one Romantic to be influenced by the long-unpublished *Prelude* he could as well have had in mind the scene in which a stone wall, a hawthorn bush and a single sheep . . . become involutes in the death of Wordsworth's father'. It is reasonable to assume that Thomas was referring to this kind of phenomenon when, in his review of Oxford and Cambridge poetry, he had this to say about poetic subject-matter: 'The important thing is . . . that it should be intense and capable of unconsciously symbolic significance.'

Harrow, plough, roller, elm butt, nettles, dust are, to employ De Quincey's useful term, involutes; the full scene is what Thomas means by an unconscious symbol. There are many such landscapes and places in Thomas's poetry; the long small room, in the poem of that title, is one:

> The long small room that showed willows in the west
> Narrowed up to the end the fireplace filled,
> Although not wide. I liked it. No one guessed
> What need or accident made them so build.

The density and careful precision of fact in the first sentence, the disjointedness of the next two, enacting the casual sequence of spontaneous thought, would seem to proclaim their status as an exclusively literal record. Yet, as in 'Tall Nettles', the bare confession of liking, simply by its reticence, its unspecificness, excites a curiosity that must be satisfied. In the reasons for his liking lie the meaning for him, the unconscious symbolism, of the room, and the seemingly accidental conjunction of 'I liked it' with 'No one guessed' generates a further air of mystery around the facts. The phrases act upon each other: as no one could explain why the room was given this particular shape, so the speaker is implicitly disclaiming any conscious understanding of why he liked it. The immediate effect of the juxtaposition is to suggest that the very dearth of reasons, the obscurity of meaning, is what stimulates his interest. Buried meanings, things hidden and covered up, are a magnet for Thomas's fascinated attention; 'The Long Small Room', 'Tall Nettles' and 'Birds' Nests' have this motif in common. He is drawn to this unique room and that neglected corner of the farmyard because they resonate with elusive significance. There is an evident connection between the mystery of the speaker's feelings and of the builders' motives and the shape of the room: long, small, narrowing, dark, it is, as it were, introverted – seemingly designed for holding secrets. But the secret meaning of its shape harbours a deeper reason for his liking. It is implicit in this first stanza, but we are not in a position to recognize it until the third stanza, which alludes to happenings that he and the only other witnesses, 'moon, sparrow, and mouse', 'could never understand / Or alter or prevent in the dark house'. It was literally dark and figuratively a place of sorrow, like the dark house of mourning in Tennyson's *In Memoriam* that it recalls, and that reminiscence perhaps brings with it recognition of the room's likeness to a coffin. The likeness thickens into symbol as we allow the images of fire (in the east) and willows in the west to contribute their associations to the total impression: the room then becomes a close container of life's full span, its ending and its source. The mystery is the mystery of human mortality. He likes the room for being at once itself and an image of life as a whole. All meanings that haunt and cling, the important meanings, are those that are immanent in the facts and, because they cannot be disentangled from them, must always lie half-dormant.

What has been said about immanent symbolism in 'The Long Small Room' applies equally to 'Birds' Nests'. The poem begins with a description of 'The summer nests uncovered by autumn wind' and the mixture of shame and satisfaction felt by the poet at seeing them thus exposed. Description and expression of feeling alternate rather than mingle, and not until the last stanza is there even a suspicion of symbolism in the poem. The advantage of drawing attention to this particular poem after an examination of 'The Long Small Room' is that its thought evolves in such a way as to provide the reader with an opportunity to trace the gradual establishment of a metaphorical level of meaning. The first stanza is purely descriptive, though perhaps two phrases for the revealed nests – 'all dark' and its rhyme 'they hang like a mark' – are tinged with some as yet undeclared feeling. If so it is a little more pronounced in the admission of the second stanza that, laid bare by the autumn wind, their exposure 'made the seeing no game'. It is a boy's game to find the concealed nests – that is the reference – but the phrase has an undertow of darker feeling, associated with the season, the imminence of winter, and the emptiness of the nests – 'vacant of a life but just withdrawn' (these words from 'The Chalk Pit' come to mind). ''Tis a light pang', he quickly assures us in the next stanza, although at the same time the word 'pang' exposes the emotion felt as starkly as the dark nests have been exposed in the trees stripped of their leaves. 'I like to see the nests / Still in their places now first known', he then explains – the apparent sufficiency of this simple statement inviting us to speculate further, as similar statements do in 'Tall Nettles' and 'The Long Small Room'. The fourth stanza is the last:

And most I like the winter nest deep-hid
That leaves and berries fell into:
Once a dormouse dined there on hazel nuts,
And grass and goose-grass seeds found soil and grew.

It takes no more than the tiny surprises of the dormouse and the word
'dined', and a slight change of pace and tone in the last line –
unobtrusive signs – to alert the reader to a faint shadowing of
symbolism: displaced from its human context, 'dined' has a touch of
amused tenderness in giving unexpected significance to an animal's
good fortune, at the same time as it is modest about the analogous
satisfaction of human (literal or metaphorical) appetite; and the
relatively insistent echoes, clustered stresses and long level pace of the
last line, modulating from the general tone of factual report and mildly
ruminative comment into one of hushed celebration, contrives a brief
resonant finale for the poem.

After Thomas's tributes to the *unguessable* meaning of the long small
room and his testimony of gratitude to the nettles for *covering up* what
he likes most in a farmyard, this statement of preference, in the same
words ('And most I like'), is not surprising. The reason for his
preference is less easily ascertained. But the appeal of the hidden and
latent is central both to his sensibility and to his poetic methods. The
delight of finding what was successfully concealed, in a literal sense, is
itself not hard to understand: the context makes it plain that because
this nest was 'deep-hid', unlike the others, it survived intact to give
shelter to a dormouse and to catch leaves, berries and seeds and foster
growth. However, survival, shelter and growth are the points of literal
meaning that have potentially a less distinct metaphorical dimension.
We may say that the stanza celebrates the generation of life, a
second, gratuitous, different kind of life. But there is a relationship
between this poem, 'Tall Nettles' and 'I Never Saw that Land Before',
the recognition of which supplies a decisive missing element in any
explanation of Thomas's preoccupation with the hidden. 'I Never Saw
that Land Before' introduces a previously unknown landscape – valley,
river, cattle, grass, ash trees, chickens from the farmsteads, 'all /
Elm-hidden' – with which the poet nevertheless feels an inexplicable
rapport: 'some goal / I touched then', he is certain, though he cannot find a name for it. He says no more about the landscape, but he
sees an image in it for an ideal poetry: he chooses 'the breeze / That
hinted all and nothing spoke' and filled the trees with sounds of
an untranslatable speech, as an apt symbol for a poetic language
so inseparable from its content that it 'would not even whisper [his]

soul' –

> A language not to be betrayed;
> And what was hid should still be hid
> Excepting from those like me made
> Who answer when such whispers bid.

It is not necessary to spell out the connections or make the correspondences between this and 'Birds' Nests' mechanically precise. Both poems are concerned with hiddenness as a condition of creativity; 'I Never Saw that Land Before' explicitly relates it to poetic creativity. Both imply that it is safe only if its source remains hidden. Perhaps these similarities may suggest an explanation for the sense of personal arrival in this last stanza and the concluding note of celebration. It provides one of many images in Thomas's poetry – the image of mid-winter spring in 'The Manor Farm' is comparable – of unexpected, hoped-for, potential growth the model for which was the sudden late flowering of his poetic gift. 'I Never Saw that Land Before' shows – might have been written specifically to show – how a landscape can have 'an unconsciously symbolic significance', and imagines the sort of language that might communicate it; 'Birds' Nests' gives us, in a modest instance, a source of secret life, of unpredictable growth: the parallel reveals the close link between the theme, Thomas's discovery of his poetic self, and the peculiarly veiled symbolism characteristic of his poetry. His gift had developed slowly in the dark, as it were unwatched; its emergence was unaccountable, gratuitous, and the more precious for being so. His gathered trust in the benevolence of unconscious processes influenced or, more probably, was accompanied by a related attraction to a poetic language that 'hinted all and nothing spoke'. A language that does not betray his meaning is one that, by keeping close to the fount of inspiration, the 'involutes' of his thoughts and feelings, by remaining unabstract, would seem to guarantee a continuing poetic vitality. In hiding, a thing might seem dead or non-existent – the long period of germination is, as Thomas knew, not unlike a death – but these secret hiding-places are also a source of renewal, a second life, and in them things survive, grow and bloom.

Examples of the unconscious symbol in Thomas's poetry could be multiplied. My aim, however, is not to enumerate examples but to use different illustrations to examine different facets of the same phenomenon. Thus, in turning to 'Fifty Faggots', though the faggots have essentially the same function in the poem as the birds' nests have in the poem named after them, I want to emphasize other aspects of his metaphorical technique. The 'fifty faggots' standing by the hedge were cut from the underwood of 'Jenny Pinks's Copse'.

Now

> they make a thicket fancy alone
> Can creep through with the mouse and wren. Next Spring
> A blackbird or a robin will nest there,
> Accustomed to them, thinking they will remain
> Whatever is forever to a bird.

But they won't. They will feed several fires and

> Before they are done
> The war will have ended, many other things
> Have ended, maybe, that I can no more
> Foresee or more control than robin and wren.

It is a poem about endings – whether of good or bad omen is uncertain. But time is running out for the poet and perhaps for England, at least the England of such local names as Jenny Pinks's Copse. The link between the literal subject-matter and its analogies is easy enough to see, once it has been pointed out. But the correspondences between the fate of the underwood and that of the poet or rural England are incomplete and far from exact, no more than signposts to an uncharted region that waits to be explored. The assembled details are only loosely associated. The literal glints with metaphorical suggestion, but it also has a separate life some of which is not absorbed into the analogy; the worlds of fact and meaning overlap rather than lie neatly superimposed upon one another.

Each reader must decide for himself how far he goes in the process of translating fact into meaning, but in a poem of this kind with its 'maybe', the unforseeable and the conundrum about endings, there is no warrant for certainty of interpretation. Of course, where poetry is concerned there is no such thing as certainty of interpretation. As Eliot says in his introduction to Wilson Knight's *The Wheel of Fire*, although interpretation is instinctive in us, and necessary, the meanings assigned are necessarily partial and constrictive; 'interpretation' is most useful when 'not too clearly formulated'.[2] Thomas's poetry only differs from poetry in general in the *degree* of uncertainty, and the number of obstacles and distractions planted in the path of the would-be interpreter. Some things are clear: when the copse was cut down for firewood, in the words of Edna Longley, 'an old natural cycle was terminated'; but I think she is mistaken in believing that the poet's anticipation of blackbird's or robin's return represents even a tenuous continuity. The implication is, surely, not that it 'will eventually establish a new cycle' (p. 270), but that it will be deluded. The scene has the half-life of aftermath. Yet, though I think the poem points in that direction, the meaning I have assigned to it is indeed 'too clearly formulated'. Everything in the poem contributes to a strategy – such it seems – of removing attention from the dimension of general idea or symbolism. The references are particular and local, the tone is unassuming, the rhythms are those of light spontaneous thought; the concrete objects of a minutely particular scene and the voicing of a particular response so fill the consciousness as almost to block out the universal. The serious notion of aftermath is disguised by the elegant caprice that pictures fancy creeping through the thicket with mouse and wren, and the bird's delusion of permanence, which makes its 'thinking' incipiently symbolic, is shrugged away in what might be taken for a brisk afterthought, 'Whatever is forever to a bird'; by casting doubt on a bird's ability to think such thoughts the word-play seems also to turn the notion of continuity into a casual pleasantry. Linguistically such an achievement must be considered a feat of decorum, a totally convincing twentieth-century version of 'low style', adopted to display the origin of analogical thinking in accurate realism: standing at the point where details begin hesitantly to cohere, and particulars to converge on a generality, we are witnesses to the first stirrings of meaning.

I have allowed De Quincey's description of what I have termed immanent symbolism, in combination with Jonathan Wordsworth's comment, to suggest a connection between Thomas's methods and Wordsworth's. I do not withdraw this suggestion but I would concede that almost as strong a case could be made for a poem like Keats's 'To Autumn' as the seminal influence. It is not necessary for my argument to establish exact derivations but it is relevant to show that some kind of relationship exists between Thomas's handling of symbol and the type of symbolism and method of revealing it used in a number of Romantic poems. For this purpose Keats and Wordsworth do not provide the most convenient examples, and I can urge the existence of a poetic lineage more persuasively, and with appropriate brevity, by adducing the 'conversational poems' of Coleridge, which in their 'spontaneous' organization have a more evident affinity with Thomas's compositions. The step from the seemingly haphazard emergence of meaning out of narrative and descriptive details presented chiefly for their own sake, in a poem like 'This Lime-Tree Bower My Prison', to the extreme reticence of Thomas's technique, the tentative hinting of incomplete correspond-ences between the assembled facts and possible analogous meanings, is – despite great differences of voice and manner – not a large one.

I cite this particular example of Coleridge's conversational poetry because in thought and symbolic design it is modelled, whether con-sciously or not, on Vaughan's poem 'They Are All Gone into the World of Light'; and this double link, from Thomas through a Romantic poem to the seventeenth century, enables me to outline a significant piece of poetic history. 'They are all gone into the world of light! / And I alone sit lingring here': Vaughan complains that he has been left behind, but radiant memories of his departed friends illuminate his mind with an inner view of them

> walking in an Air of glory,
> Whose light doth trample on my days:
> My days, which are at best but dull and hoary,
> Meer glimering and decays.

Coleridge, reluctantly confined to his garden by an accident, follows in imagination a walk taken by his friends in the surrounding countryside. At first he is depressed by the contrast in circumstances:

> Well, they are gone, and here must I remain,
> This lime-tree bower my prison! . . .
> . . . They, meanwhile,
> Friends, whom I never more may meet again,
> On springy heath, along the hill-top edge,
> Wander in gladness . . .

But gradually his mood changes, and his feelings quicken in sympathetic excitement as his 'friends emerge / Beneath the wide wide Heaven' and 'A delight / Comes sudden on my heart, and I am glad / As I myself were there!' He is moved, finally, here in his garden bower, to give thanks to Nature for its consolations – 'Henceforth I shall know / That Nature ne'er deserts the wise and pure' – and he concludes that

> sometimes
> 'Tis well to be bereft of promis'd good,
> That we may lift the soul, and contemplate
> With lively joy the joys we cannot share.

The poems have other points of contact – an imagery of light, for example, is diffused throughout 'This Lime-Tree Bower My Prison' – but enough has been quoted from each to indicate the character of the relationship between them. Vaughan is speaking directly of the heavenly kingdom; the light and walks of nature have been totally transformed into their spiritual equivalents. The walk taken by Coleridge's friends, down from the hill-top into the almost sunless dell and out again to a wide prospect 'Of hilly fields and meadows, and the sea', is first and foremost a literal journey and only secondarily a spiritual adventure. And yet the symbolism – though indirect, a matter of shading only – is not in doubt: the poet is freed from the prison of his melancholy to 'wander in gladness' with his friends, and their path down into darkness through 'The roaring dell, o'erwooded, narrow, deep' and past

that branchless ash,
Unsunn'd and damp, whose few poor yellow leaves
Ne'er tremble in the gale, yet tremble still,
Fann'd by the water-fall!

finally to 'emerge / Beneath the wide wide Heaven', is a mythical descent and ascent of the spirit. The gap opened by Coleridge between immediate experience and its meaning is further widened in Thomas's poetry. Though the description of, say, the 'branchless ash' is meticulously realistic in its accuracy of detail, and its analogical relation to the poet's state of mind is not formally signified, yet the relationship exists and is unambiguous, and every detail can be given a metaphorical application. The avoidance of overt metaphor merely expresses a circumspection in the manner of revealing the connection between outer and inner experience, a circumspection stemming from the philosophical and theological uncertainties of Romantic thought. In 'This Lime-Tree Bower My Prison', as in Wordsworth's 'Nutting' or, in a different fashion, 'The Thorn', recognition of correspondence between objects and feelings or ideas does not have the instantaneousness of formal metaphor: the poem starts, as it were, behind the threshold of consciousness and then enacts the coming to consciousness of its contents. The process of recognition is gradual, but the literal and the metaphorical senses do eventually match. As I have argued with reference to 'Fifty Faggots', this is not usually true of Thomas's poems. They point towards possible meanings, but either connections are not tied up neatly or there are loose ends: fact and meaning partly correspond and are partly in tension with each other. Thomas's poems are definite up to a point, and beyond that he practises an extreme but precise avoidance of definiteness. One critic has referred to this technique as the art of indefinite definiteness. I think he means the opposite, for, when reversed, the formulation is exact: these poems have a definite indefiniteness, a lucid uncertainty, peculiar to themselves.

The thesis of J. Hillis Miller's *The Disappearance of God*, which is that the nineteenth and twentieth centuries have seen the culmination of a process, begun in the late mediaeval period, of 'the gradual withdrawal of God from the world', has a bearing on this fragment of poetic history. The evidence he assembles from a study of five post-Romantic Victorian writers confirms and is confirmed by my proposition with regard to the changing nature of metaphor between the seventeenth century and the twentieth century. The part of Miller's thesis relevant here may be summarized with the help of some quotations from his Introduction.

The imagination of Edward Thomas

Our culture, at its [Hebraic and Hellenic] beginnings, experienced the divine power as immediately present in nature, in society, and in each man's heart. So Moses saw God in the burning bush, and so Parmenides and Heraclitus are philosopher-poets of total immanence . . . The Eucharist was the archetype of the divine analogy whereby created things participated in the supernatural reality they signified. Poetry in turn was, in one way or another, modeled on sacramental or scriptural language. The words of the poem incarnated the things they named, just as the words of the Mass shared in the transformation they evoked. The symbols and metaphors of poetry were no mere inventions of the poets. They were borrowed from the divine analogies of nature. Poetry was meaningful in the same way as nature itself – by a communion of the verbal symbols with the reality they named. The history of modern literature is in part the history of the splitting apart of this communion . . . The Protestant reinterpretation of the Eucharist parallels exactly a similar transformation in literature. The old symbolism of analogical participation is gradually replaced by the modern poetic symbolism of reference at a distance . . . In this evolution words have been gradually hollowed out, and have lost their substantial participation in material or spiritual reality.

(pp. 2–3)

(Though in Thomas's poem 'Women He Liked' the fact has no religious significance, the remoteness and dissociation of the train travellers from the scene dominated by the lane of elms planted in a previous age by 'Old Farmer Hayward of the Heath' symbolize the difference between a referential or spectatorial relationship to the life of nature and the identity of man and nature exemplified in Bob Hayward's active love of trees and horses. The naming of the lane after him, 'Bob's Lane', and Farmer Hayward's title, which makes him the legendary founder of Hayward's Heath, also signify his participation in the life of the place.) An attenuated sense of immanence lingered until the nineteenth century. 'Almost all the romantic poets begin with the sense that there is a hidden spiritual force in nature. The problem is to reach it, for the old ways have failed, and though it is present in nature, and in the depths of man's consciousness, it is not immediately possessed by man' (p. 3). Thereafter the power to experience a Wordsworthian presence in nature is lost. The spiritual adventures of De Quincey, Browning, Emily Brontë, Arnold and Hopkins, the five post-Romantic writers examined by Miller, are defined by him 'as so many heroic attempts to recover immanence in a world of transcendence' (p. 6). I have applied the term 'immanent' to Thomas's symbolism, although plainly it does not mean everything that it means in the context of Miller's thesis. My intention is to suggest that, in ways more tentative than those of Wordsworth and Coleridge, more conscious of the fugacity of hidden meanings in his experience of nature, Thomas nevertheless feels the possible presence of those meanings more closely than do the Victorian writers. At the same

204

time he practises a more extreme caution in approaching them than either the Victorians or the Romantics.

Frequently the final effect of a Thomas poem is one of lucid uncertainty. Questions are raised, as in 'March', and left unanswered; or the reader is prompted by the poem to ask questions of his own. Let me deal briefly with 'March'. It falls into approximately two halves. The first fifteen lines describe the poet's response to the sudden revelation of the sun on a cold day, as it were heralding spring after a day and night of storm; the last seventeen lines describe the response of the thrushes to the same phenomenon. A faint shape of metaphorical meaning, originating in an unstated analogy between the poet and the thrushes, poetry and birdsong, gradually becomes visible through the detail. Saluting the promise of spring, Thomas manages to sound at the same time confident and hesitant: 'Now I know that Spring will come again, / Perhaps tomorrow . . . And yet 'twas cold, and though I knew that Spring / Would come again, I knew it had not come'. The hesitation crystallizes into a question, but a question about the singing thrushes and only obliquely about himself: 'What did the thrushes know?' They had kept silent throughout 'rain, snow, sleet, hail', but now they sang frantically and unceasingly, 'So earnest were they to pack into that hour / Their unwilling hoard of song'. This was Thomas's third poem: the question concerns his own 'unwilling hoard of song' – the meaning of his sudden outburst of poetry. More specifically, and mysteriously, it concerns the relation of this song to silence – the long silence that preceded and the silence ahead: 'So they could keep off silence / And night, they cared not what they sang or screamed'. Here silence is a threat, but it is also a promise:

> Not till night had half its stars
> And never a cloud, was I aware of silence
> Stained with all that hour's songs, a silence
> Saying that Spring returns, perhaps tomorrow.

(R. George Thomas's text has 'Rich with all that riot of songs' in the penultimate line. His notes do not explain why he gives it priority over the familiar version, and I am reluctant to surrender the ambiguity of 'stained'.) Perhaps the silence is not only before and after, but, as in 'The Mill-Water', a backdrop to all sound. I must, however, leave further speculation to the reader; the point I wish to make does not require a full interpretation. In the previous chapter I quoted from 'November' ('November Sky') the lines that celebrate a realism (the poet's own) which 'sees clearly' the interdependence of earth and sky, fact and ideal, in an earth-lover's affections. I went on to say that 'March', written on the following day, demonstrates 'all that clear seeing means'; but the lines I quoted to support this assertion were intended to illustrate only one aspect of clear seeing, 'a meticulous scrutinizing of the evidence'. We are now in a position to recognize that the uncompleted, open-ended character of Thomas's analogical thinking is the direct outcome of his realism, a peculiarly radical truthfulness. The scrupulous care to identify what happened, or the degree of understanding reached, as no more and no less than it is, extends to an honesty about what cannot be known with any certainty. Seeing clearly is also seeing that some things are unclear: a knowledge that includes unanswered questions.

'As the Team's Head-Brass' is one of the finest examples of Thomas's symbolic technique: sensuous and narrative precision combine with unresolved questions to produce an exceptional breadth of suggestion. In this instance the questions are not explicit, but, so to speak, lurk in the margins to tease and encourage the enquiring mind. As in other poems I have examined for their latent symbolism, the factual content here is primary, but the facts are presented dramatically as well as descriptively. The poet speaks in the first person but he is there rather as a character than as a point of view: perched on a fallen elm at the edge of a field, in friendly conversation with a ploughman, their talk folded between neutral, apparently casual descriptions of the ploughing, the horse, the field of charlock, and of two lovers who in the first lines are observed going into the wood and at the end are seen coming out again.

> As the team's head-brass flashed out on the turn
> The lovers disappeared into the wood.
> I sat among the boughs of the fallen elm
> That strewed an angle of the fallow, and
> Watched the plough narrowing a yellow square
> Of charlock. Every time the horses turned
> Instead of treading me down, the ploughman leaned
> Upon the handles to say or ask a word,
> About the weather, next about the war.
> Scraping the share he faced towards the wood,
> And screwed along the furrow till the brass flashed
> Once more.

In the description of the team of horses with their head-brasses, and in the mild relaxed ploughman's talk mentioned here and recorded in the following lines, the living rural tradition is set before us without comment. The easy friendliness with the ploughman is part of a world of feeling Thomas does not want to lose. Their casual, intermittent exchange of words – 'one minute and an interval of ten' – suggests nevertheless, in its fragmentary way, a warmth of common humanity that belongs essentially to the slow world of the agrarian order. War is the subject of their conversation:

> 'Have you been out?' 'No!' 'And don't want to, perhaps?'
> 'If I could only come back again, I should.
> I could spare an arm. I shouldn't want to lose
> A leg. If I should lose my head, why, so,
> I should want nothing more . . .'

In the context of the whole poem 'come back again' reads as 'come back again to these things, this life, this kind of talk'. For the scene given us in the opening lines and the life it evokes, threatened by extinction or about to be lost to the poet, or both, suddenly appear as necessities and assume an importance larger than the individual life. Even the lovers in their sanctuary of the wood seem threatened. With grim irony the plough and the flashing head-brasses of the team bring glancing reminders of war, their antithesis; and as the ploughman scrapes the share and aims it at the wood it becomes momentarily a hostile weapon. And with the lightest of touches the wry humour of 'instead of treading me down' brings about another confrontation of peace-time and war-time activities, the ploughman guiding his slow farm horses and the cavalry charge. And so, in a familiar process, the scattering of things shown and said begins to cohere in a suggestion of general meaning. As details such as these are recorded and added to each other, however, it becomes clear that the poem's theme is not so much war as England – England in the midst of war, certainly, but also the English tradition and even England's chances for the future.

> The blizzard felled the elm whose crest
> I sat in, by a woodpecker's round hole,
> The ploughman said. 'When will they take it away?'
> 'When the war's over.' So the talk began –

The hint of a connection between the blizzard and the war is repeated a little later, when the ploughman notes that a mate of his was killed in France on the night the tree was felled. As for the tree, the coincidence of its fall with the soldier's death, the fact that the soldier poet sits *in* its boughs, and the likelihood that he too will be killed in France, suggest something of its significance: its fall forebodes the 'death' of a rural England that was still, for Thomas and many of his contemporaries, the essential England. Unlike 'Fifty Faggots' and 'The Barn', 'As the Team's Head-Brass' implies that the poet, who sits in the branches, will share England's fate. The empty woodpecker's hole, also associated with the poet, confirms this implication, for it is a place where life has flourished that is now deserted. The feeling that a life once enjoyed has recently and mysteriously been lost, of course, pervades Thomas's poetry. The poet is identified with the fallen elm not merely because he might be killed like the ploughman's mate, but because he belongs essentially with the doomed social order – before the war was, as he says, 'another world'. The empty woodpecker's hole in the tree, 'vacant of a life but just withdrawn' (like the chalk pit), symbolizes the lost vitality equally of the man and of his culture.

Mentioned together in the poem's first sentence, the ploughing team and the lovers come together again at the end. The poet having spoken wistfully of the time before the war as 'another world', the ploughman's comment and the last actions of the poem follow:

> 'Ay, and a better, though
> If we could see all all might seem good.' Then
> The lovers came out of the wood again:
> The horses started and for the last time
> I watched the clods crumble and topple over
> After the ploughshare and the stumbling team.

The two references to the lovers frame the poem, and it is reasonable to interpret their disappearance into and return from the wood as the equivalent of the kind of declaration made by Hardy in 'In Time of "the Breaking of Nations"', a poem that, as several critics have noted, Thomas may have had in mind: 'War's annals will cloud into night / Ere their story die'. Certainly the implications are both that they have come back from a place of refuge, one traditionally reserved for banished lovers, and that after a temporary eclipse or suspension of life (as when we say of a person in trouble 'he is not out of the wood yet') their private human world has been given back to society. But this is to ignore the prelude of the ploughman's words, tied by a double rhyme ('good. Then / wood again') to the last sentence. Both as tailpiece to his talk with the poet and in juxtaposition with what follows, its tentatively offered trite wisdom strikes us as touchingly forlorn; the long shadow of its pious speculation – of the, as it were, doubly conditional 'might seem' – stretches across the concluding lines of the poem. All *might* seem good, and love *might* redeem the social order: an open-ended art such as Thomas's does not confidently predict the future. In fact it makes no assertions at all, not even qualified assertions; the aura of general meaning that irradiates the particular situation is composed rather of hopes and fears and possibilities. All might seem good, and rural England too might survive catastrophic change. And so, after all the talk of war, the ploughing team does start up again, suggesting renewal; the continuity *hoped* for includes but is not contradicted by the *fear* that for the poet it *may* be 'the last time'. But if we take this phrase to refer to the ploughing (and Thomas, who actually left the poem untitled, thought of calling it 'The Last Team'), then it is the social order whose death is anticipated and the crumbling and toppling earth is, with a kind of dream logic, an image of its collapse. Once again, hope and fear contest the possibilities. It should be noted that no hope is held out for the poet himself. As the horses set off again and the lovers show themselves, both, it seems, pointing to the future, the poet, we are to assume, is left behind watching them, discarded with the stricken tree. The possibilities concern not the individual but the general fate.

The nearest one can come to translating the effect of the poem's tentativeness into discursive language, I have suggested, is to say that it leaves us with a number of questions. Will England as it has been – an England with the social cohesions and rhythms of an agrarian order, that produced men of mild grave humanity like the ploughman, that was a suitable place for the innocence and idealism of love – will this England survive? The question about love is not 'will it survive?' – of course it will – but whether it will indeed ever emerge from its wood of privacy to remake the social world. And if it does, will it retie and strengthen the bonds that now slackly and tenuously join people together? For the desultory talk between the poet and the ploughman has a wistfully faint and distant quality about it, as of a half-remembered, half-imagined wholeness of relationship adumbrated but not contained in this fragmentary, momentary companionship. And part of the strangeness that accompanies the kindness between them may be attributed to the fact that the ploughman is 'of the soil', while the poet who watches is not – he is uprooted like the elm, emptied like the woodpecker's hole. It may also be that the hope vested in the lovers involves their association with the wood, not as a place of refuge but as a living wood to set against the poet's dead tree.

Notes

Preface

1 I use the terms 'nature writer' and 'nature book', here and elsewhere, with some hesitation, since the literary genre indicated has unfortunately attracted – and the terms have therefore come to be associated with – a good deal of nostalgic and sentimental writing. But no obvious substitutes suggest themselves as brief, self-explanatory labels for this kind of subject-matter. See the opening paragraphs of Chapter 5 for a discussion of the parallel term 'nature poetry' and the question of Thomas's 'naturalism'.

1 The imaginative prose

1 William Cooke, *Edward Thomas: A Critical Biography* (London, 1970); cited as Cooke.
2 H. Coombes, *Edward Thomas* (London, 1956); cited as Coombes.
3 W. J. Keith, *The Rural Tradition* (Toronto, 1974).
4 Cf. 'Literature sends us to Nature principally for joy, joy of the senses, of the whole frame, of the contemplative mind, and of the soul, joy which if it is found complete in these several ways might be called religious' (*The South Country*, p. 142).
5 Matthew Arnold, *Essays in Criticism, Second Series* (London, 1895), p. 33.
6 He admired both writers. Conrad, to whose work he had been introduced by Edward Garnett, was one of the few novelists he ever reviewed. He preferred Hardy's poetry to his novels, but he did have reservations about it, which, interestingly, concerned precisely what he called the 'superstitious' bent of Hardy's mind (*In Pursuit of Spring*, p. 196), a more revealing name for what the critics agreed in deprecating as 'pessimism'.
7 *The Happy-Go-Lucky Morgans*, p. 221. The Wordsworth quotation is from *The Prelude*, Book XI, 144 (1850 text).
8 *In Pursuit of Spring*, p. 24.
9 *A Literary Pilgrim in England*, p. 187.
10 *The South Country*, p. 146.
11 *Ibid.*, p. 146.
12 *A Literary Pilgrim in England*, p. 153.
13 *Ibid.*, p. 54.
14 *The South Country*, p. 6.
15 *Richard Jefferies*, p. 9; my italics.
16 Raymond Williams, *The Country and the City* (London, 1973), p. 259.
17 See, for example, *The Country*, pp. 46–9.
18 *Ibid.*, p. 16.
19 *The South Country*, p. 64.
20 *The Country*, pp. 8–9.

21 *In Pursuit of Spring*, p. 101.
22 *The Literary Pilgrim in England*, p. 186.
23 *Ibid.*, p. 185.
24 *Ibid.*, p. 191.
25 *The South Country*, p. 26.
26 *In Pursuit of Spring*, p. 205.
27 *The South Country*, p. 5.
28 *In Pursuit of Spring*, pp. 240 and 241.
29 *The South Country*, p. 5.
30 *Ibid.*, p. 4.
31 *Ibid.*, p. 136.
32 *The Country*, p. 6.
33 *In Pursuit of Spring*, p. 87.
34 *Ibid.*, p. 85.
35 *Ibid.*, p. 86.
36 *Ibid.*, pp. 83–4.
37 *A Literary Pilgrim in England*, p. 113.
38 *The South Country*, pp. 109–10.
39 *In Pursuit of Spring*, p. 198.
40 *Ibid.*, p. 57.
41 *A Literary Pilgrim in England*, p. 53.
42 *Ibid.*, p. 44.
43 *The Childhood of Edward Thomas*, p. 134.
44 F. R. Leavis, *New Bearings in English Poetry* (London, 1932), p. 70.
45 *The South Country*, p. 171.
46 *The Happy-Go-Lucky Morgans*, Chapter V, 'Aurelius, The Superfluous Man'; *The South Country*, p. 6.
47 *A Literary Pilgrim in England*, p. 220.
48 *The Country*, p. 49.
49 *Daily Chronicle*, 14 January 1913. *Georgian Poetry 1911–12* 'brings out . . . many sides of the modern love of the simple and primitive, as seen in children, peasants, savages, early men, animals, and Nature in general'.
50 *The South Country*, p. 212.
51 *The Last Sheaf*, pp. 176–7.
52 *The Country*, p. 23.
53 *Ibid.*, p. 39.
54 *A Literary Pilgrim in England*, p. 89.
55 *The Country*, p. 19.
56 *Ibid.*, p. 21.
57 *A Literary Pilgrim in England*, p. 44.
58 *Ibid.*, p. 79.
59 *Ibid.*
60 *The Country*, p. 19.
61 *The Last Sheaf*, p. 84.
62 *Ibid.*, pp. 85–6.
63 *The South Country*, p. 71.
64 *The Country*, p. 6.
65 *The Last Sheaf*, p. 102.

2 The 'Desert Places'

1 R. George Thomas (ed.), *Letters from Edward Thomas to Gordon Bottomley* (London, 1968), p. 53.
2 See Introduction.
3 Edna Longley (ed.), *Poems and Last Poems*, p. 268; cited as Longley in all subsequent references to the annotations in this text.
4 Where a new title has been given to a poem in R. George Thomas's edition of *The Collected Poems*, I have printed it after the familiar title.
5 The phrase is from 'The Other', stanza nine.

3 The 'Other Man'

1 W. B. Yeats, 'The Symbolism of Poetry', in *Essays and Introductions* (London, 1961).
2 I have adopted the reading of all previous editions; I am presuming that 'weakness' in R. George Thomas's printing of the poem is a misprint.

4 The traveller's home

1 Quoted by Longley, p. 326.
2 *The South Country*, p. 35.
3 *A Literary Pilgrim in England*, p. 191.
4 I retain the reading of earlier editions. The textual situation is unclear, and, like Edna Longley, I prefer this version to R. George Thomas's '(Small church, great yew)', based on the text of the poem's first printing in *This England* (1915). (See Longley's review of *The Collected Poems* in *Poetry Wales* 15, 1 (Summer 1979), p. 112.)
5 Longley pp. 378–9.
6 Cf. *Walter Pater*: 'He is the spectator still; he sees, not life, but pictures of Life' (p. 84).
7 Cf. *Letters from Edward Thomas to Gordon Bottomley*, November 1912, in a letter to Bottomley's wife: 'I hope Gordon isn't become too classic to like Lawrence' (p. 225).
8 Longley, p. 158.
9 Cf. Keats's definition of *Negative Capability*, in a letter written in December 1817: 'That is when a man is capable of being in uncertainties, Mysteries, doubts, without any irritable reaching after fact and reason.'
10 Vernon Scannell, *Edward Thomas (Writers and their Work*, no. 163, (London, 1963)), p. 24.
11 Longley, p. 197.

5 Naturalism

1 Julian Thomas's Preface to *The Childhood of Edward Thomas*, p. 8.
2 *The South Country*, p. 136.
3 Longley, pp. 238–9.
4 Quoted by Longley, p. 200.
5 'Pent' is a favourite word of the Romantics. Wordsworth, Coleridge and Keats all use it of confinement in the city (the common source being

Milton's 'As one who long in populous city pent'). They, too, intend a contrast with the freedom of life in nature.

6 This phrase in stanza two has disappeared from R. George Thomas's version, based on the poet's presumed latest revisions. The changes in the second stanza are in some ways an improvement; nevertheless with the sacrifice of 'godsend' the poem loses something.

6 Imagination

1 I refer to two poems of Yeats, 'The Circus Animals' Desertion' and 'The Spur'.
2 Proem to *The Excursion*.
3 I presume that 'into' in R. George Thomas's text is a misprint.
4 R. George Thomas, *The Collected Poems*, p. 386.

7 World's end

1 *The South Country*, p. 136.
2 See Chapter 10 for a discussion of symbolism (immanent, veiled, tentative) in Thomas's poetry.
3 *Letters from Edward Thomas to Gordon Bottomley*, p. 53.

8 Language and movement

1 *Walter Pater*, p. 210. Subsequent quotations of Thomas's comments on Pater are all from this volume; page references are given in the text.
2 *Keats*, p. 57. Subsequent quotations of Thomas's comments on Keats are all from this volume; page references are in the text.
3 *Scrutiny, VII*, p. 442.
4 *Selected Letters of Robert Frost* (ed. Laurence Thompson), New York, 1964, p. 351.
5 Longley, p. 402.
6 John Moore, *The Life and Letters of Edward Thomas* (London, 1939), p. 326.
7 *A Hopkins Reader* (ed. John Pick, New York, 1966), p. 144.
8 Robert Graves's Foreword to Alun Lewis, *Ha! Ha! Among the Trumpets* (London, 1945), p. 11.
9 *Algernon Charles Swinburne*, pp. 22 and 84.
10 Farjeon, p. 146.
11 *Daily News*, 22 July 1914; quoted by Longley, pp. 394–5.
12 Bottomley, pp. 250–1; quoted by Longley, p. 396.
13 Unpublished letter in Dartmouth College Library; quoted by Cooke, p. 73.
14 Robert P. Eckert, *Edward Thomas: A Biography and a Bibliography* (London, 1937), p. 150.
15 *Selected Letters of Robert Frost*, p. 110; quoted by Longley, p. 400.
16 *Ibid.*, p. 107; quoted by Longley, p. 400.
17 Quoted by Maurice Lindsay in *John Davidson: A Selection of his poems* (London, 1961), pp. 9–10.
18 *Selected Letters of Robert Frost*, p. 105; Frost's lack of punctuation.

19 D. H. Lawrence, Letter to Catherine Carswell, January 1916.
20 Letter to Robert Bridges, 6 November 1887; in *Hopkins Reader*, p. 232.
21 Bottomley, p. 251.

9 The semantics of form

1 Vernon Scannell, p. 17.
2 *Selected Essays*, 3rd ed. (London, 1951), p. 302.
3 *P N Review*, 5, 1 (1977), p. 37.

10 Metaphor and symbol

1 *Times Literary Supplement*, 11 November 1977, p. 1330.
2 G. Wilson Knight, *The Wheel of Fire* (London, 1930), p. xv.

Bibliography

Collections of the poetry

Collected Poems, fifth impression (Faber & Faber, London, 1949) and all subsequent impressions. An unchronological collection, comprising *Poems* (1917), *Last Poems* (1918) and six additional poems; the standard edition until 1978.

Poems and Last Poems, ed. Edna Longley (Collins, London, 1973; Macdonald & Evans, Plymouth, 1978). A chronological arrangement of the two early volumes, therefore lacking the six poems added later. It contains an extensive commentary on each poem, biographical and critical extracts, and essays on 'Edward Thomas and Robert Frost' and 'Edward Thomas and the Georgians'.

The Collected Poems of Edward Thomas, ed. R. George Thomas (The Clarendon Press, Oxford, 1978). A chronological collection, adding one more poem to *Collected Poems* (Faber & Faber). Contains textual notes and commentary on each poem; includes *The Diary of Edward Thomas* (1 January–8 April 1917). Based on an examination of manuscripts, typescripts and notebooks, the text differs in some cases from that of previous editions. Quotations, with a few indicated exceptions, are from this edition.

A selection of the prose

The Heart of England (Dent, London, 1906)
The South Country (Dent, London, 1909)
Feminine Influence on the Poets (Secker, London, 1910)
Richard Jefferies, His Life and Work [second edition], (Hutchinson, London, [1911])
Maurice Maeterlinck (Methuen, London, 1911)
Celtic Stories (The Clarendon Press, Oxford, 1911)
Algernon Charles Swinburne, A Critical Study (Secker, London, 1912)
George Borrow, The Man and His Book (Chapman & Hall, London, 1912)
Norse Tales (The Clarendon Press, Oxford, 1912)
The Icknield Way (Constable, London, 1913)
The Country (Batsford, London, 1913)
The Happy-Go-Lucky Morgans (Duckworth, London, 1913)
Walter Pater, A Critical Study (Secker, London, 1913)
In Pursuit of Spring (Nelson, London, 1914)
Four-and-Twenty Blackbirds (Duckworth, London, 1915)
Keats (T. C. & T. E. Jack, London, 1916)
A Literary Pilgrim in England (Methuen, London, 1917)
Cloud Castle and Other Papers (Duckworth, London, 1922)
The Last Sheaf (Cape, London, 1928)
The Prose of Edward Thomas, ed. Roland Gant (The Falcon Press, London, 1948)

Bibliography

Edward Thomas and the Countryside: A Selection of his Prose and Verse, ed. Roland Gant (Faber & Faber, London, 1977)

A Language Not to be Betrayed: Selected Prose of Edward Thomas, Edna Longley (Carcanet Press, Manchester, 1981): a selection of both critical and imaginative prose

Selected Poems and Prose, ed. David Wright (Penguin, Harmondsworth, Middlesex, 1981)

Editions and anthologies cited

The Temple and a Priest to the Temple by George Herbert (Dent, London, 1908)

This England. An Anthology from her Writers. (Oxford University Press, London, 1915)

A selection of biographical material

Berridge, Anthony, ed., *The Letters of Edward Thomas to Jesse Berridge*; with a memoir by Jesse Berridge (Enitharmon Press, London, 1983)

Cooke, William, *Edward Thomas: A Critical Biography* (Faber & Faber, London, 1970)

Edward Thomas: A Portrait (Hub Publications, Bakewell, Derbyshire, 1978): an abbreviated version of the biographical section in his *Critical Biography*

Eckert, Robert P., *Edward Thomas: A Biography and a Bibliography* (Dent, London, 1937)

Farjeon, Eleanor, *Edward Thomas: The Last Four Years* (Oxford University Press, London, 1958)

Garnett, Edward, ed., 'Some Letters of Edward Thomas', *The Athenaeum*, no. 4694 (16 April 1920)

Guthrie, James, ed., 'Edward Thomas's Letters to W. H. Hudson', *The London Mercury* (August 1920)

Marsh, Jan, *Edward Thomas: A Poet for his Country* (Paul Elek, London, 1978)

Moore, John, *The Life and Letters of Edward Thomas* (Heinemann, London, 1939)

Poetry Wales, Edward Thomas centenary issue (Spring 1978): 'Letters from Edward Thomas to Robert Frost'; R. George Thomas, 'Edward Thomas and Robert Frost'; 'Letters from Edward Thomas to Harold Monro'

Thomas, Edward, *The Childhood of Edward Thomas* (Faber & Faber, London, 1938)

The Diary of Edward Thomas, (1 January – 8 April 1917), ed. R. George Thomas, *Anglo-Welsh Review* (Autumn 1971); and *The Collected Poems*, ed. R. George Thomas (The Clarendon Press, Oxford, 1978)

Thomas, Helen, *As It Was* and *World Without End* (Faber & Faber, London, 1956)

Time and Again: Memoirs and Letters, ed. Myfanwy Thomas (Carcanet Press, Manchester, 1978)

Thomas, Myfanwy, *One of These Fine Days – Memoirs* (Carcanet New Press, Manchester, 1982)

Bibliography

Thomas, R. George, ed., *Letters from Edward Thomas to Gordon Bottomley* (Oxford University Press, London, 1968)
   Edward Thomas: A Portrait (Oxford University Press, London, 1985)

Select bibliography of criticism

Ashton, Theresa, 'Edward Thomas: From Prose to Poetry', *Poetry Review*, 28 (1937)
Barker, Jonathan, ed., *The Art of Edward Thomas* (Poetry Wales Press, Bridgend, Mid Glamorgan, 1986)
Black, Michael, 'A Language Not to be Betrayed', *Use of English* (Autumn 1976 and Summer 1977)
   'Modern Without Modernism'; review of *The Collected Poems of Edward Thomas* in *English* (Spring 1980)
Burrow, John, 'Keats and Edward Thomas', *Essays in Criticism* (October 1957)
Bushnell, Athalie, 'Edward Thomas', *Poetry Review*, 38, 4 (1947)
Cooke, William, *Edward Thomas: A Critical Biography* (Faber & Faber, London, 1970)
Coombes, H., 'The Poetry of Edward Thomas', *Essays in Criticism* (April 1953)
   Edward Thomas: A Critical Study (Chatto & Windus, London, 1956; reprinted with corrections, 1973)
   'De la Mare, Hardy and Edward Thomas', *Pelican Guide to English Literature*, vol. 7 (1961); reprinted in *New Pelican Guide to English Literature*, vol. 7 (Harmondsworth, Middlesex, 1983)
Cox, C. B., and A. E. Dyson, 'The Signpost', *Modern Poetry: Studies in Practical Criticism* (Arnold, London, 1963)
Coxe, Louis, 'Edward Thomas and the Real World', *Enabling Acts: Selected Essays in Criticism* (University of Missouri Press, Columbia, 1976)
Danby, John, 'Edward Thomas', *Critical Quarterly* (Winter 1959)
Davie, Donald, 'Lessons in Honesty', *Times Literary Supplement* (23 November 1979)
Dollimore, Jonathan, 'The Poetry of Hardy and Edward Thomas', *Critical Quarterly* (Autumn 1975)
Elmslie, Macdonald, 'Spectatorial Attitudes' ['The Watchers'], *Review of English Literature* (January 1964)
Harding, D. W., 'A Note on Nostalgia', *Scrutiny* (May 1932)
Hobsbaum, Philip, 'The Road Not Taken', *Listener* (13 November 1961)
Hooker, Jeremy, 'The Writings of Edward Thomas', *Anglo-Welsh Review*, 18 no. 41 and 19 no. 43 (1969 and 1970)
   'Edward Thomas: The Sad Passion', *Poetry of Place: Essays and Reviews 1970–1981* (Carcanet Press, Manchester, 1982)
Keith, W. J., *The Poetry of Nature* (University of Toronto Press, Toronto, 1980)
   The Rural Tradition (University of Toronto Press, Toronto, 1974; The Harvester Press, Hassocks, Sussex, 1975)
Kirkham, Michael, 'The Edwardian Critical Opposition' [Edward Garnett and Edward Thomas], *University of Toronto Quarterly* (Fall, 1975)
   'Edward Thomas and Social Values', *Four Decades* (July 1977)
Lawrence, Ralph, 'Edward Thomas in Perspective', *English* (Summer, 1959)
Leavis, F. R., *New Bearings in English Poetry* (Chatto & Windus, 1932), pp. 68–73

Bibliography

Lewis, C. Day, 'The Poetry of Edward Thomas', *Essays by Divers Hands* (Transactions of the Royal Society of Literature, 28, (1956))

Longley, Edna, 'Larkin, Edward Thomas and the Tradition', *Phoenix* (Autumn and Winter 1973–4)

'Edward Thomas and the "English Line"', *New Review* (February 1975)

'A Language Not to be Betrayed: The Poetry of Edward Thomas', *Poetry Wales* (Summer 1976)

Review of *The Collected Poems of Edward Thomas* in *Poetry Wales* (Summer 1979)

Marsh, Jan, *Edward Thomas, A Poet for his Country* (Paul Elek, London, 1978)

Mathias, Roland, 'Edward Thomas', *Anglo-Welsh Review*, 10, 20 (1960)

Motion, Andrew, *The Poetry of Edward Thomas* (Oxford University Press, London, 1980)

Murry, J. Middleton, 'The Poetry of Edward Thomas', in *Aspects of Literature* (Cape, London, 1920)

Norris, Leslie, 'A Land Without a Name', *Poetry Wales* (Spring 1978)

Parker, David, 'Edward Thomas: Tasting Deep the Hour', *Critical Review*, 22 (Melbourne, 1980)

Piennaar, P., 'Edward Thomas: Poetic Premonitions in the Prose', *Theoria* (May 1975)

Quinn, Maire A., 'The Personal Past in the Poetry of Thomas Hardy and Edward Thomas', *Critical Quarterly* (Spring 1974)

'Ballad and Folk-song in the Writing of Edward Thomas', *Anglo-Welsh Review*, 62 (1978)

Robson, W. W., 'Edward Thomas's "Roads"', *Times Literary Supplement* (23 March 1962)

Scannell, Vernon, 'Content with Discontent', *London Magazine* (January 1962)

Edward Thomas [Writers and their Work] (Longmans, Green & Co., London, 1963)

Scofield, Martin, 'Edward Thomas: Syntax and Self-consciousness', *English* (Spring 1981)

Sisson, C. H., *The Avoidance of Literature: Collected Essays*, ed. Michael Schmidt (Carcanet Press, Manchester, 1978)

Smith, Stan, 'A Language Not to be Betrayed', *Literature and History* (Autumn 1976)

'A Public House and Not a Hermitage: Nature, Property and Self in the Work of Edward Thomas', *Critical Quarterly* (Spring 1977)

'Singular Men: Edward Thomas and Richard Jefferies', *Delta*, 59 (1979)

Thomas, R. George, 'Edward Thomas: Poet and Critic', *Essays and Studies*, 21 (1968)

Edward Thomas (University of Wales Press, Cardiff, 1972)

'Edward Thomas's Poetry Now', *Anglo-Welsh Review*, 62 (1978)

Underhill, Hugh, 'The "Poetical Character" of Edward Thomas', *Essays in Criticism* (July 1973)

Wain, John, *Professing Poetry* (Macmillan, London, 1977)

Ward, J. P. 'The Solitary Note: Edward Thomas and Modernism', *Poetry Wales* (Spring 1978)

Williams, Raymond, *The Country and the City* (Chatto & Windus, London, 1973) pp. 255–61

Index